TELL ME WHERE IT HURTS

TELL ME WHERE IT HURTS

A Day of Humor, Healing, and Hope in

My Life as an Animal Surgeon

DR. NICK TROUT

BROADWAY BOOKS

New York

FOR KATHY, WHITNEY, EMILY,

AND ALL WHO BATTLE CYSTIC FIBROSIS

CONTENTS

· ·

CONTENTS

AUTHOR'S NOTE

. . . .

The tales you are about to read are the truth, practically the truth, and nothing less than a half-truth, sifted from recollections of thousands of animal encounters over the course of the last twenty-five years.

The vast majority of these stories happened to me and where possible I have turned to the patient's medical record for accuracy and specifics. In many instances I have gone back and interviewed the owners, filling in the gaps, getting at overlooked and unspoken perspectives that I missed when working the clinical aspects of the case. Frequently I alter names and identifying traits, occasionally preserving a memorable and characteristic idiosyncrasy by trading it among pets and owners to maintain anonymity, except where certain individuals have insisted their identity be revealed.

There are a few anecdotes that have been narrated to me by my colleagues. I have taken copious notes, attempted to rein in my imagination (sometimes with limited success), and endeavored to preserve the essence of their messages.

Finally, in an attempt to capture the pace, the rush, and the intensity of all that is new in twenty-first-century veterinary medicine, I have squeezed everything into a single day. Please think of it as nothing more than the vehicle that takes you on this journey. I could have opted for a sleepy ride across the state of Kansas in the back of a chauffeur-driven limo. I hope you prefer a buzz across Boston on the back of a moped at rush hour!

TELL ME WHERE IT HURTS

1

· · · · · · · · · ·

2:47 A.M.

WAKE-UP CALL

This might seem strange, coming from an Englishman, but sometimes emergency surgery in the middle of the night can play out like a synopsis of a perfect season for the Boston Red Sox. The beginning may be predictably crappy, slow, and discombobulated until a rhythm develops and momentum builds leaving you stricken with that familiar glimmer of hope. When it comes to the final stretch, everyone accepts that there may be failure, there may be disappointment, but the struggle is always gritty and memorable, and occasionally, if you are really lucky, something magical will happen.

My beginning came half an hour earlier with a phone call reeling me in from a cozy dreamless void.

"Hello," I said, two disjointed syllables caught in a sticky web at the back of my throat.

"This is Dr. Keene, one of the new surgical residents. We haven't met but I've got a dog, a ten-year-old spayed female German shepherd; she's bloated and . . . like . . . well . . . I need you to come in for the surgery. Sorry."

All I heard was sound, not words I could interpret, my brain dormant on my pillow.

"Hello, are you still there?"

"Yeah, sure, I'm listening," I croaked, wiping a palm across my face. "What time is it?"

She told me and dove into her apology.

"I really hate to disturb you but, like, my backup's not answering his pager and, like, I didn't know what else to do." Her words surfed through me—a Valley Girl inflection—and sluggish gray matter dug out a memory of a recent departmental memo—"Be sure to welcome our first-year surgery resident, Dr. Sarah Keene, from the University of California, Davis."

I came awake, sat up in bed, and told my wife to go back to sleep.

"No problem, Dr. Keene. Tell me about your GDV."

As a new surgery resident, Dr. Keene may know all about GDV, an acronym that stands for gastric dilatation and volvulus, commonly referred to, with a satisfying rustic flavor, as "bloat." But more than likely, at this stage in her training, her understanding is primarily academic, words and phrases in a textbook, disease as bullets of information in shocking fluorescent pink highlights. She will be a year out from veterinary school, a year in which she will probably have diagnosed and managed several cases of GDV. She knows all about this bizarre anatomical aberration and the inevitable, rampant pathology it will incite. She even knows exactly what needs to be done. But, until now, until tonight, she has never been the one who actually picks up a scalpel and makes the cure happen. Tonight, for the first time in her professional career, she *is* the surgeon on call, and not surprisingly, she is in need of some help.

GDV is a true veterinary surgical emergency. It typically occurs in deep-chested dogs like German shepherds, Great Danes, and standard poodles but, on occasion, I've even seen it in breeds as small as dachshunds. No one is entirely sure why it happens, but oftentimes the animal eats a large meal, gets some exercise, and an hour or so later the problems begin. Fermented gas starts to accumulate in the distended stomach, and for whatever reason the entire organ twists around and flips over on its long axis. The effect is catastrophic. The twist blocks off the esophagus, so despite the poor creature's desire to throw up and rid itself of all that food and gas, nothing will budge. The stomach expands unchecked, destroying its own blood supply, driving into the chest and squashing the lungs and the blood flow back to the heart. There is no absolute timetable for how long an animal can survive in this state, but dogs can die in a matter of hours. As soon as the diagnosis is made, the clock is ticking.

"She got into a full bag of kibble around seven. Owner took her for a walk before bed. He could hear the dog trying to vomit unsuccessfully around midnight and drove her all the way up from the Cape. She looks ready to explode. Classic double-bubble on abdominal X-rays."

I had been waiting for this description, the twisted, distended stomach looking like the silhouette of a giant heavyweight's boxing glove on an X-ray. It tells me her diagnosis is correct.

"Is she stable?" I asked.

"Not really," said Dr. Keene. "Her pressures are through the floor and we're having a hell of a time just finding a decent vein, let alone placing a catheter."

My feet were swinging out of the bed and I began to fumble for clean clothes.

"Do your best. Try to pass a stomach tube. I'll be there as fast as I can."

Angell Animal Medical Center, part of the Massachusetts Society for the Prevention of Cruelty to Animals, is located in the eclectic and increasingly gentrified Boston neighborhood of Jamaica Plain. There are no world rankings of veterinary hospital size, but at 185,000 square feet I imagine Angell is one of the larger ones, with over seventy veterinarians serving nearly fifty thousand dogs, cats, and exotic pets every year.

After ten years on staff as a surgeon, I know that those nasty rumors about Boston traffic are all subterfuge because at three in the morning, an easy commute is rewarded with my pick from one of the primo parking spots close to the front door.

It is January in New England. There are a couple of inches of snow on the ground, a miniature version of the Andes has been plowed against the perimeter wall, and today's high will be only ten below. I walk across the salted asphalt like a geriatric with a bad case of hemorrhoids, poised to slip on the black ice. Despite the hour, my sleepiness is starting to burn off like fog on an imaginary sunny morning as I enter this five-story brick building and head toward the nonsterile surgical prep area. The corridors are empty, floors polished, phones silent, and pagers dead. I have entered an antiseptic ghost town and I like the way it feels. It reminds me of being a kid again, of breaking into the neighbor's backyard in order to steal the ripe apples taunting me from their tree. The mission is covert, even risky—all but guaranteeing the rewards will make it worthwhile.

Cutting through the radiology department, I catch a glimpse of my reflection in the glass window outside the MRI unit. The man I see looks unfamiliar. He has piggy eyes, a pillow-crease scar across his left cheek, and a jaunty case of bed head. Thank goodness my patients never judge me on my appearance.

My patient lies splayed across a large gurney, nervous nails clawing for purchase on the stainless steel surface. She is a big girl, obviously not lacking for love in the calorie department. Her darting chocolate eyes scream in fear of her strange situation and the changes taking place in her body, but as I enter the room and approach, her broad and bushy tail offers me a couple of friendly beats. I like German shepherds. I grew up with one as a kid, but this gesture strikes me as both uncharacteristic and, at the same time, utterly endearing. Until this moment I have been dealing with an anonymous and remote animal reduced to a list of diseases, conditions, problems, and deformities. Suddenly everything has changed. This animal has a name and a personality. This animal has become my patient. This is the moment when I begin to care.

I pat her head and run my hand across a soft velvety ear, over her chest and down to the enormous, unyielding abnormality that is her drum-tight abdomen.

"Hi, sweetheart. You hanging in there?"

For me, all my patients are "sweethearts" until proven otherwise, whether they are male or female, cute and cuddly Himalayan kittens or a slobbering and stoic 250 pounds of bullmastiff.

Holding a needle and syringe, Dr. Keene, a short, shiny-faced woman with blond hair in a ponytail, turns to me. She can be no more than twenty-five. I wonder if at forty-three I'm getting a little long in the tooth for this game. She glares through sparkly green contacts as though she thought I had been addressing her. I introduce myself, offer my hand, and assure her that I was speaking to our patient.

"This is Sage," she says, trying to apply an oxygen mask to the dog's snout. "I'm Sarah, and this is Dan." She gestures to a technician I have never met before, although this is not surprising given the hour. For most of us working in a busy animal hospital, being on call for surgical emergencies every other night, every other weekend, is simply not sustainable for more than a couple of years. Nocturnal surgical emergencies are a rite of passage, an inherent requisite in any decent residency program, a privilege to be endured and enjoyed. But now, nearly fifteen years after the completion of my training, my midnight forays into the OR are limited to the one week in every month that I am available as backup to the residents.

Dan juts a square chin in my direction and gives me a casual " 'sup." He has a pierced right eyebrow and lower lip with colorful sleeves of tattoos running down his arms in perfect contrast to the sallow vampire skin of his face. In different surroundings he might attract attention, but here, working the overnight, he can relax, setting up the EKG leads, sorting out the pulse oximeter, and adjusting the intravenous fluids with an experienced hand.

There is a small shaved square on Sage's flank where an attempt has been made to release the trapped and expanding gas in the dog's stomach by directly puncturing the organ with a large bore needle. I touch the small red bull's-eye in the center of the bald spot. The skin is impossibly taut. Clearly the attempt failed.

"No luck with a tube?" I ask, although I know the question is redundant. If they had successfully passed a stomach tube, the preferred method of decompression, there would have been no need to try to use a needle.

Dr. Keene shakes her head.

"I'm afraid not," she says. "She's in bad shape. Heart rate's two twenty with occasional VPCs. Her color looks like shit."

I'm not surprised. The shock to Sage's circulation has convinced her heart that she is running an endless sprint. This effect combined with the absorption of toxic by-products via the damaged stomach can produce runs of abnormal and ineffective heartbeats called VPCs or ventricular premature contractions. Heard over a heart monitor, VPCs make the beat of a frenetic African tribal dance sound like the chord changes of a funeral march. They can be disastrous in their own right.

Sage's tail beats a message of thanks as I relieve her of the oxygen mask and lift an upper lip to inspect her gums. Healthy, vibrant pink tissue signifying normal peripheral blood flow has been replaced by an ugly, muddy purple.

"How much intravenous fluid has she had?"

"This is her fourth liter," says Dr. Keene. "It took forever to find a vein. Isn't that right, Dan?"

Dan nods.

Sage's color looks awful. I imagine someone shoving an over-inflated beach ball under my rib cage. I know I wouldn't be faring as well.

"You're absolutely right," I say. "She looks like crap. You're certain Sage got into the kibble around seven?"

"According to the owner she did. Why?"

"Because she's acting like she's near the end, like her stomach has been distended for so long it's going to die. It's all very well trying to get her stable for surgery, but if her stomach dies, she dies. I don't think we have any more time to dick around. Start a lidocaine drip, give her some intravenous antibiotics, and knock her down. The faster we get this thing untwisted the better. I'm going to get changed into scrubs."

"Before I forget," says Dr. Keene, "the owner is waiting up front. He insisted on meeting with you before you get started."

Inwardly I groan. Don't get me wrong, good client communication lies at the heart of great veterinary care. There is enormous satisfaction in getting pet owners involved, explaining exactly what it is we are doing, why we are doing it, and making sure they are part of the decision-making process. But right now, with Sage fading fast, every minute lost is a minute closer to a patient who never wakes up from anesthesia. I just want to get going, to give this dog a measure of relief. Perhaps Sage's owner doesn't understand the gravity of the situation. I imagine myself walking into a time trap, forced to engage in idle banter with a belligerent owner about whether I really know what I am doing, how many of these things I have done before, committing to verbal assurances that I will be the one performing the operation and not my resident.

"Okay," I say, "if I'm not back in five minutes get scrubbed in, drape her off, and start setting up. If I'm not back in ten, page me to the OR, stat."

I hand comb my hair on the way to the vast waiting room, preparing myself for combat with some sort of aggressive middle-aged-lawyer type, who, despite the hour, has turned up perfectly coiffed in an immaculate pinstriped suit. But the only person I see is an old man of at least seventy, sitting in a corner, head slightly bowed with one liver-spotted hand tightly clasped in the other. He is bundled up like a snowman, frail skin swaddled in a cap, scarf, and overcoat.

"Mr. Hartman?" My mind and body rapidly decelerate as I approach.

The old man looks up, offering an apologetic expression that changes into a wince as he gets to his feet with difficulty. My nose detects the faint, menthol aroma of Bengay.

"Hi, Mr. Hartman, please don't get up on my account. I understand Dr. Keene has explained that your dog is seriously ill and in need of emergency surgery, so I thought I should introduce myself. I'm Sage's surgeon. I will be the one operating on her this morning."

Tired, frightened eyes search mine as he extends a cold hand.

"I'm so very sorry getting you out of bed," he says. "It was my daughter, you see. She's a doctor." I assume he means a doctor of humans. I am pleased to hear him refrain from saying a "real" doctor. MDs appreciate better than most that a hierarchy exists in a referral hospital—student, intern, resident, attending. She probably provoked this insight.

"She said to make sure to get a surgeon who is on staff, someone with more experience. Not a resident, she said. To be honest, it doesn't bother me. I just don't want to lose her, that's all. Sage is all I've got."

There is a tremor in his voice that he cannot fight down. He is holding it together but only just, proud, helpless, and completely vulnerable, tethered by that wonderful and inconceivably powerful bond to the animal in his life. The passion for his canine companion pours from him, washing away any residual traces of my sleep deprivation, replacing them in an instant with the awesome responsibility I have to this man and his best friend.

"You think I'm doing the right thing, don't you? I mean bringing her here, having the operation?"

"Of course," I say. "No question about it. There's a good chance that we can correct the problem. Things might get a little rough in the postoperative period, but nothing we haven't seen before, nothing we can't handle. Believe me I wouldn't be standing here ready to perform surgery if I didn't have your animal's best interests at heart."

For a moment he studies his hands, wringing them, working the thick and knotty joints and knuckles before adding, "Tell me I'm not being selfish? You see, my daughter, she means well, but she keeps reminding me that Sage is ten, after all."

I shake my head.

"Not at all, Mr. Hartman. You're doing exactly the right thing. You're taking the best possible care of the animal you love."

I can see that he is still not convinced.

"And if she were your dog? Would you put her through surgery, given her age?"

How many times have I been asked this question? It is the yardstick against which so many owners measure and weigh the difficult decisions they must make. This is the point at which the veterinarian has the unique opportunity, through a combination of experience, knowledge, and personal opinion, to totally influence a decision. It is a burden we must accept and use wisely. Fortunately, in this case, I can answer honestly and without bias.

"Absolutely. Sage seems like a great dog. Any animal prepared to beat me up with her tail, feeling as sick as she does, is definitely worth saving."

He tries his best to stifle a smile. It works but he cannot catch the tear.

"She's all I've got since my wife died. Sage helped me through the darkest hours of my life."

I swallow hard, trying not to get sucked in, unable to resist the allure of this gentle old man. He is a character out of a James Herriot novel, a cliché widower clinging to the last tangible link to the love he has lost. But the truth is these people are everywhere. Sixty-three percent of all homes in the United States have a pet. That's more than 69 million people. It may be a cat, a bird, a ferret, or a guinea pig, but the chances are high that when someone close to you dies, a pet will be there to pick up the slack. Pets devour the loneliness. They give us purpose, responsibility, a reason for getting up in the morning, and a reason to look to the future. They ground us, help us escape the grief, make us laugh, and take full advantage of our weakness by exploiting our furniture, our beds, and our refrigerator. We wouldn't have it any other way. Pets are our seat belts on the emotional roller coaster of life—they can be trusted, they keep us safe, and they sure do smooth out the ride.

"I can't tell you how much that dog means to me," says Mr. Hartman, and I see the deep pools of suffering in his eyes. I try to defend myself from his grief. I need to focus on my job.

"Believe me, Mr. Hartman," I say, pursing my lips into a smile, "it shows. I know the problem. My father had a shepherd when I was growing up. They're one-man dogs. They bond tight, like superglue, and never let go."

His smile begins to win his emotional battle. He raises a hand and gives my shoulder a gentle squeeze.

"Just do your best. I know you will."

"Doing my best is the easy part," I say. "Sage needs to do hers."

"She will," says Mr. Hartman, watching me go. "She's a strong girl. She won't let us down."

The golden iodine-stained skin yields easily to the scalpel, weeping the familiar tiny tears of blood to reveal a pure, white, fatty shellac below. I don't have to deliberate. I don't have to ask. I don't have to think. My hands are on autopilot as they gently work their way into Sage's abdomen.

I am not a natural-born surgeon. I was not blessed with what some like to call good hands. Thankfully surgery is a skill that can be learned. It is a bit like playing the piano. If we possess the desire and the diligence to practice long enough and hard enough, eventually we can make progress, eight of our ten thumbs might even disappear, and most of the time we end up hitting the right notes and playing a decent tune.

Shortly after graduation, when we make our first sortie into the operating room, we quickly appreciate that our Rachmaninoff solo at Carnegie Hall might have to wait until we have mastered "Chopsticks" on the out of tune upright at Grandma's house. Neophyte surgeons have to shout and scream at their hands, ordering them to the appropriate places, struggling to find the right touch and pressure, fumbling to select and handle the correct instrument. Only with time and practice can we begin to whisper and, occasionally, not to speak at all. The hands learn to dance, to move without effort, without hesitation, without waste. Work becomes seamless, slick, economical, and productive.

I am wearing blue scrubs, a sterile gown, and powdered size seven-and-a-half latex surgical gloves. Blue paper bootees cover my sneakers, my hair is trapped inside a disposable bouffant cap, and most of my face is hidden behind a paper mask affording me the pleasure of sniffing my own hideous morning breath for the foreseeable future. Dr. Keene peers on tiptoe through the green window of the sterile drape covering our anesthetized patient only to recoil as the bloated stomach bursts through the raw edges of my calculated slash.

Paper masks can hide only so much. With my gesture toward the distended organ, a polite "please, be my guest," she televises the emotions playing behind her eyes—a flash of excitement followed by the lingering betrayal of apprehension—so together we squeeze our gloved hands into the impossibly tight space between Sage's stomach and the abdominal wall, watching them disappear into pink tissue and the vat of red paint that is free and pooled blood.

"Get a good love handle of stomach in your right hand, and pull up on it as you push down with your left, here," I say, ensuring her grasp is appropriate and correctly positioned.

Dr. Keene begins to grunt, to strain, and I know that with every breath Sage takes, the abdominal wall is cinching down tight on her forearms, replacing her hands with cramped and useless stumps. A full minute passes and nothing has happened.

"Fuck it!" she curses, retrieving her lifeless fingers. "There's no way I can do it. You're going to have to take over."

I study her over the rim of my mask. Given their interminable workload, even the most angelic of surgery residents might occasionally cuss like a character on *The Sopranos*, but in this circumstance, I know the outburst is borne of insecurity and a fear of failing her patient. I have no doubt that she can do this. I need to reassure her that I am here as a safety net and a few first-time jitters do not constitute a fall.

"Don't beat yourself up," I say. "Your natural instinct is to be too gentle, too cautious. You're worried the stomach is going to rip." I focus on finding the right tone with no trace of condescension. "Think of it this way, if you don't correct the torsion, Sage will be dead. If the stomach rips, because it's damaged, it was going to rip anyway. At least she dies trying. You've got nothing to lose."

Dr. Keene takes a deep breath and lets it out, causing her mask to flutter. Slowly she begins to nod. Shaking the blood down to her fingers, she resumes her position, hands grappling with the enormous stomach, and once again I ensure that everything is correct. Within seconds her frustration has liberated all the greater force and vigor she requires, and with a sloppy and wonderfully satisfying whoosh of finality, this great big muscular balloon flops back into its anatomically correct position.

The green contacts beam with the satisfaction of her achievement, a triumph trumpeted by Sage herself as the dog is relieved of the kind of belch that would satiate the toilet humor of any eleven-year-old boy.

"Fantastic," I say. "Dan, if you'd be so kind as to pass the stomach tube."

I reach into the abdominal cavity and already there is more room to spare. Down by the diaphragm I can feel the esophagus as the wide-bore rubber tube slips by my fingers. Suddenly a column of liquid food and gas pours from the tube and into a collection bucket, instantly searing our nostrils with the pungent aroma of fermented dog kibble.

"Thanks," says Dr. Keene. "I mean, like, for making me keep going."

"Not a problem," I reply. "It's like I always say. Surgery is meant to be difficult, but the more you struggle, the more you learn."

Her professionally plucked eyebrows knit over her mask in an expression that says, "Okay, Grandpa, no need to get all philosophical on me."

She recovers and says, "So, now what?"

My hands begin fishing through the blood and small intestines.

"Time to check out Mr. Spleen."

I locate the large meaty boomerang of an organ located adjacent to the stomach. It is entirely purple black in color.

"What do you think?" I ask.

Dr. Keene does exactly as I had hoped, feeling for the arterial supply to the spleen and palpating for a pulse between her fingers. She takes her time moving from one vessel to the next before concluding, "Nothing. I feel no pulses. The spleen is dead."

I repeat her examination for myself and agree with her conclusion.

Unfortunately the spleen is tightly tethered to the stomach, so wherever the stomach goes, the spleen must try to follow. In the case of a GDV, the result can be damage and obstruction to the spleen's blood flow, followed by the organ's death. Fortunately, Sage can afford to lose her spleen.

"Dan, I'll take an LDS."

Dr. Keene smiles behind her mask at the mention of another three-letter acronym. It is contagious and for a second, as we wait for the instrument, I bask in the memory of those early days as a surgical resident where everything was new and every sterile instrument was like opening a present at Christmas.

LDS stands for Ligation and Divide Stapler, a surgical device that looks and handles a little bit like a gun. It has a barrel, cartridge, a grip, and a trigger, which fires metal clips that seal off a blood vessel just before a razor-sharp blade slices the vessel in two. It also comes powered by a carbon dioxide gas canister so that each "shot" makes a satisfying noise like a sound suppressor on a handgun. I don't care whether it is soft-tissue surgery or orthopedics, surgeons love toys.

In minutes, with the instrument in semiautomatic fire in her hands, I feed Dr. Keene the appropriate vessels and the dead spleen is out of Sage's body.

"Okay," I say. "Now let's go back to the stomach and see how it looks."

Her hand sweeps back a stray loop of bowel, I grab at the main body of the stomach, pulling it free of the blood and into the bright light of the surgical lamps.

Dr. Keene senses my hesitation.

"What is it?"

For a moment I say nothing, taking my time, changing the position of my hands, feeling the tissue as it slips between my fingers, noting its color and its texture. I can almost feel Mr. Hartman's hand on my shoulder.

"I don't like what I see. This area," I point to the junction of the stomach and the esophagus, "its color, that purple congestion with maybe a hint of gray. It might not be viable."

Dr. Keene is staring at me.

"So why not simply staple it off?"

She makes her question feel like a casual invitation, one I can take or leave. I wish it were that simple. Dogs and cats don't read textbooks in which line drawings, flow charts, and photographs reduce disease to black and white. Surgery is replete with everything in between, forcing surgeons to make quick, vital decisions based on experience, instinct, and faith. Mistakes are inevitable and their results are indelible. In my opinion dexterity and touch can take a surgeon only so far. Learning to make the right decisions is the art in this science.

I like to believe that my decision is objective, emotionally detached from patient and client alike. But in my peripheral vision, I can see a dog who still manages to say hello with a stomach about to burst and an old man reduced to tears at the thought of losing his closest friend. If this job came with tunnel vision our clinical judgment would be so much clearer.

"Here are Sage's three options as I see them," I say. "One, we take our chances, staple off as much stomach as we dare, and pray that nothing breaks down."

Dr. Keene nods her approval.

"Two, we seal off the end of the esophagus, seal off the end of the stomach, put a feeding tube into her small intestine, put a tube into Sage's throat and down her esophagus to suck off her own saliva because it has nowhere else to go, let the stomach decide whether it lives or dies, and come back in a few days to see if we can put her back together again."

"Wow," she says, her eyebrows performing a fine impersonation of the "golden arches." "Have you ever tried to do that?"

"No," I said. "And I hope I never will. But in theory it is possible. I just don't know if I could put an animal through all that surgery when the risk of failure is so high."

She appears relieved.

"So what's option three?"

I sigh.

"We call it a day. I scrub out and speak to Mr. Hartman right now. Explain our predicament. It might be better to let Sage die in her sleep than to have to wake her up and succumb to a slow and painful death when her stomach perforates because I made the wrong decision."

Suddenly I notice the beat of the heart monitor filling the silence and it sounds deafening.

"What do you think Mr. Hartman will want to do?"

I meet her stare. I know the answer.

"The right thing. Whatever that may be."

For a full minute neither of us speaks. My relationship with animal and owner is entirely superficial and only minutes old, yet I hold two lives in the balance—one physically and one emotionally. Who am I to make the call?

"Dan, get me a GIA, and I'm going to need at least three or four cartridges."

I read agreement and relief in Dr. Keene's eyes.

The Gastrointestinal Anastamosis Stapler chomps its way across the area of devitalized stomach, sealing and separating the good from the bad as it goes. I let Dr. Keene do most of the work. She may fire the device, but I am the one defining the line of demarcation. I am the one selecting healthy tissue from dead tissue. The responsibility for this part of the procedure is mine alone.

"Let's oversew the staple line," I say, "and then you can get on with the pexy."

"Sure," says Dr. Keene, asking Dan for some suture material. "But I've only done one before now."

Crow's feet gently land at the corners of my eyes.

"Well, you know what they say. 'See one, do one, teach one.' "

The resident loads her needle driver and picks up a Debakey forcep from her table.

She tuts, making a nice job of rolling her wrists as she passes the suture through the stomach wall. "What idiot made that one up?"

The term *pexy* means the surgical fixation of an organ. In this case a gastropexy is essential to prevent Sage's stomach from performing somersaults in the future. Rather than relying on the strength of synthetic suture material alone to hold the organ in place, a chunky flap of the outer stomach wall is created and fixed to the muscular lining of the abdominal wall for added security.

I make Dr. Keene feel for the slip, the physical separation between the inner and outer layers of the stomach, because this is the natural plane she must define, physically separate, and exploit. I watch as she traces the margins of the flap with the point of her scissors. I approve her design and let her get to work.

In my mind I am still deliberating over the merits of my gamble when I hear a curse and look down to see dark brown fluid spewing from a rent in the stomach lining where Dr. Keene has been cutting with her scissors.

"I'm so sorry," she says, fumbling with sponges, trying to mop up the contamination flooding our sterile surgical field. "I thought I was dissecting in the right place. My scissors went straight into the lumen."

It would have been so easy to snatch the instruments from her hands and take over, an arrogant misogynistic surgeon justified in shooing his resident aside. After all, the last thing my patient needed right now was a case of peritonitis because of her heavy-handed technique.

But what would Dr. Keene gain from the experience? How would she learn from her mistake?

"It's okay, Sarah. It's done. Let's fix the problem, flush half a dozen liters of sterile saline through her abdomen, change gloves, change instruments, and get out. Do you think the mucosa is viable?"

I peer down at the tiny rip she has made. It is relatively small and the tissue appears to be healthy.

"Yes," she says, but without conviction. "Look. Do you want to finish this? You'll be much faster than me."

I shake my head.

"No way," I say. "You need to get used to operating at this time of the morning. And besides, I'm useless before my first cup of coffee. I'd only screw up."

Her eyes roll up and say, "Yeah, right," but her hands are already placing some stay sutures to reduce the risk of further spillage.

Fifteen more minutes and with the click of the last staple bringing the edges of the skin incision into perfect apposition I return to the waiting room to speak to Mr. Hartman. He is still sitting where I first saw him, staring at the floor, working his hands, chewing on his lower lip as he gently rocks back and forth. Obviously he's been keeping vigil for the past hour. I make it to the bench beside him before he has time to try to get to his feet.

"Everything went well," I say, but already I can see he is searching my eyes for the caveat. I tell him exactly what we found, about how we deflated the stomach and fixed it in place to prevent it from twisting in the future. I tell him about the spleen and how Sage will be absolutely fine without it. He hangs on every word, every intonation, reading more in the expressions on my face than the words falling from my mouth. I feel like he can hear, but he is not listening because he knows I am keeping something back.

"My biggest concern is the stomach wall and whether it will live or die. There's no way to know for sure. I had to make a judgment call, a difficult one, but one that I believe is correct. The next twenty-four hours will be critical."

He lets out a deep breath, hanging his head. He has allowed himself to hope, flooded by the relief that Sage is alive and still in the fight and in doing so a levy inside him has burst. Emotional and physical exhaustion are taking their toll. He looks like he may collapse.

"You need to get home and get some rest. Do you have to drive all the way back to the Cape?"

I noticed on Sage's record an address in Orleans, Cape Cod, at least an hour and a half drive given the wintry conditions.

"My daughter offered to put me up. She lives in Wellesley."

"Great," I say. "Let's give her a wake-up call and let her know you'll be on your way. It might be better if you take a cab. Sage and I need you in good shape for visiting hours later today."

He smiles, more with his eyes than his lips, nodding his understanding that he must be patient. I make sure we have his daughter's phone number in Sage's computer record, promising to call if anything changes as we part company.

As I watch him go, my mind silences a tumult of ugly, undisclosed statistics. Mortality rates for GDV can be as high as 60 percent and factors associated with a higher chance of death include abnormal heart rhythms, extremely high pulse rates, the need to cut out part of the stomach, and the removal of the spleen. In short, Sage had checked off almost every negative prognostic factor for survival and yet I still decided to give her the benefit of my doubt. Should I have been more blunt, more cynical in my synopsis of the surgery, stacking the odds against success? Should I have used the word *die* more often, more emphatically? And even if I had, who would have been the beneficiary? Not Mr. Hartman and certainly not poor old Sage. Sometimes, early on in our careers, veterinarians tend to err on the side of caution when looking into their clinical crystal ball, seeking the safe refuge of a negative prognosis. If the animal died, the outcome was sadly inevitable. If the animal lives, the doctor has worked a miracle. I have made a huge decision—either a moment of flitting genius or enduring miscalculation—and like it or not, a stranger and his best friend are coming along for the ride. It is too late now. I may wonder if I have taken my final look at a stomach that should never have seen the light of day, but the verdict is already in. I just hope I read the decision correctly—sentenced to life, and not death by lethal injection.

· · · · · · · · · ·

7:24 A.M.

SALAD DAYS

The Critical Care Unit (CCU) exists in a state of perpetual sensory overload. Green scrubs blur to and fro, dogs bark over a mindless techno-pop rhythm of remote heart monitors and fluid pumps, and slick, freshly washed antiseptic floors sting the eyes of those who enter this heart of the hospital. A bank of oxygen cages hiss and sigh as I pass by and notice a number of animals wearing enormous plastic collars around their necks like satellite dishes, looking as if they have been clipped and shaved by a deranged groomer intent on creating characters from a Doctor Seuss book.

Sage is resting comfortably in a run (a compact yet comfortable private crib—eight feet deep and four feet wide), where she can enjoy a well-deserved postoperative cocktail of narcotics and nonsteroidal anti-inflammatories. I review the orders that Dr. Keene has written. She has done a good job and I let her know it. For right now there is nothing more to be done. I have scheduled appointments starting at eight.

From the backseat of my car I retrieve a white cotton shirt, paisley silk tie, and khaki chinos. They are scrunched together in an unruly ball, chilling nicely, unloved and abandoned in my haste to get to Sage. I have also forgotten to bring my electric razor. I wonder if my new clients will appreciate their veterinary specialist all crinkly and disheveled. Perhaps there is still time to get a decent cup of coffee from our local Dunkin' Donuts before I find out. The pager on my hip has other ideas.

"Please call 5-3-7-3, 5-3-7-3."

I recognize the nasal drone of the voice, pick up a phone on the corridor wall, and dial the number.

"Good morning," says Dr. Elliot Sweet. "I heard you were in bright and early this morning." The gentle undulation of his natural Kentucky twang is shrouded by a relentless sinusitis and a tendency to mumble, transforming his speech into an intractable warble.

"Any chance you might take a quick look at a dog of mine? I can meet you down in J ward."

Most likely Elliot has been working the overnight and wants to formulate a plan for one of his cases before he meets with the new shift at eight o'clock.

If I am quick, my java fix might still be within my grasp.

"Sure, Elliot, I'll see you down there."

At six feet four, Dr. Elliot Sweet is a rangy stickman, all wrists and ankles in a short white coat over undersized gray cotton scrubs. Any kudos from the stethoscope scarf draped around his scrawny neck is overshadowed by the bulky, well-worn notebooks crammed tight into his waist pockets. These are sacrosanct bibles—a drug formulary and a five-minute pocket textbook of small animal disease—essential, weighty, miniature tomes that strain on his bony shoulders making it look like he forgot to remove the coat hanger. Pristine Nikes glow on his size thirteen feet. An uncapped pen has already left its mark on his breast pocket and there is a troubling buff stain on the cuff of his right sleeve that I hope is ketchup. But here's the crucial detail. Elliot may wear his new uniform in a state of conscious consternation, but for all his ungainly appearance, what matters most, what shines from him with glowing, well-deserved satisfaction, is the nametag above his breast pocket, a label that proudly proclaims his status as an intern, a new veterinary graduate, fresh out of school, hungry to rid the animal kingdom of disease and pestilence and flushed with romantic notions of an exciting voyage into the uncharted professional territory of respect, reverence, and even worship.

There are only twenty-eight colleges of veterinary medicine in the United States (four in Canada, seven in the United Kingdom, and one in Ireland) and getting a place at veterinary school is an achievement in itself. Veterinarians are not the doctors who couldn't get into medical or dental school. Specific data on the chances of becoming a vet are hard to come by, but in the United Kingdom, I have found statistics that claim there are fourteen applicants for every place at veterinary school compared to five applicants for every two places at medical school. And the popularity of Animal Planet and all those reality TV vet shows only serves to provide even more tasty bait for admissions departments chumming the water with a highly desirable vocation and enjoying the feeding frenzy that ensues.

Most veterinarians graduate in their twenties with glowing, wrinkle-free skin and a full head of hair. These fresh, young faces might shine with enthusiasm, but they can leave an owner asking, "When's the real vet going to arrive?" reluctant to entrust the life of their beloved pet to a stranger who must have stolen a lab coat embroidered with the word *doctor*. They are flawed by youth and a failure to mask their underlying uncertainty, hesitation, and indecision. What else should we expect? By definition new graduates have no experience to draw upon. They have to start somewhere but given the choice we might prefer they learn on someone else's pet.

As it turns out, owners need not worry because every new class of veterinarians is blessed with a trait that trumps even the most seasoned veteran—a rapacious fervor for learning and education. In 2005, 19 percent of new veterinary graduates chose to go on to higher levels of training, and I should point out that unlike MDs, internships are not obligatory for veterinarians. Interns undergo a rigorous selection process, are paid a pittance, and can easily expect to work a ninety-hour week. If you are prepared to put yourself through this ordeal for thirteen months of your life, then by definition you have to be hungry, dedicated, and excited about the real world of veterinary medicine. New graduates may have horrendous time-management skills, but what pet owners see is a veterinarian who is unhurried, genuinely interested, and eager to please. Their willingness to seek advice and second opinions smacks of humility and their long days spent in the hospital ensure a continuity of care that cannot be matched by most senior staff.

Of course, the sailing is not always smooth. Green communication skills can lead to awkward and clumsy professional encounters. My own salad days compounded naiveté with a mysterious, untimely medical ailment. At that time in my life, I lived in perpetual fear that at precisely the wrong moment I might be ravaged by a sudden, intense flushing of the skin that always began with my ears, turning them a bright and angry red before a crimson mask of perpetual embarrassment spread across my face and washed down my entire chest, back, arms, and legs. This was shortly followed by "the swelling." Everything that had changed color—forehead, earlobes, eyelids, lips, even my palms—became puffy and distended. And then in the throes of this transformation into a cerise and puny variant of the Incredible Hulk, I would begin to itch. If you took a binge-drinking frat boy, stripped him naked, and hazed him with a gallon bucket full of ravenous fire ants poured over his entire body including his nether regions, I believe you would have a reasonable approximation of the degree of itchiness that ensued. Eventually this phase would subside, replaced by a state of weakness to the point of delirium, followed miraculously by a return to normalcy with no lasting side effects whatsoever.

The unusual, dramatic, transient nature of my metamorphosis into Lobster Boy left my analytical mind suspicious of some kind of allergic reaction. But I had been unable to pin it down until one fateful appointment with a Saint Bernard named Bailey, owned by a rather attractive brunette whom I shall call Miss Wright. As we entered the examination room, I noticed Bailey's magnificent head dipping in time to a profound lameness in his left front leg. He was a handsome but clearly nervous dog, clinging to his mother like a shy toddler in a roomful of strangers, while Miss Wright wore that all-too-familiar countenance of trepidation and consternation that I invariably spawned in clients back in those early days.

Sensing the heightening tension in our cramped quarters, I dove into Bailey's history, hoping that my thoughtful questioning might garner some respect. Unfortunately, Bailey intended to become the largest lap dog in the world, and given that his mistress wore a diminutive skirt that had already retreated a heart-stopping distance up her thighs when she sat down, it was virtually impossible to study my patient and not appear to be gawking at her spectacular legs.

"So what happened exactly?" I asked.

"It was an accident," she said, instantly on the defensive. "My boyfriend threw the dog's favorite toy out of the window and Bailey thought it was a game and jumped out after it."

"I see. And which window was this?" I said, scribbling away, reluctant to look up for fear of being labeled a pervert.

"Second-story bedroom window. Bailey fell twenty feet. He's been lame on his left front leg ever since."

I nodded sagely, making a notation in the appropriate section of the record.

"Ex-boyfriend, jealous for attention, attempted to kill pet."

I could see that Bailey's front paw lay flat to the floor at the wrist, or carpus, to use the proper terminology. Imagine leaping from a burning building and deciding, midair, that the latent acrobat inside you wanted to nail a perfect single-handstand landing. This is precisely what Bailey had done. Instead of breaking a bone, or multiple bones, the tiny yet incredibly strong ligaments that bound the rows of small bones of the carpus had been bent all the way back, overextending to the point of tearing apart, leaving Bailey, a 170-pound teddy bear, unable to support normal weight on the leg.

It was at exactly this point that an invisible person crept into the room and placed a blowtorch to the sides of my head, setting my earlobes on fire. From nowhere, with absolutely no preamble, in this confined space with a gigantic drooling dog and a woman who already believed I had both the clinical acumen and sexual yearnings of a fourteen-year-old boy, the metamorphosis from hell was about to begin. And this time it was back with a vengeance.

Within seconds I could tell my cheeks resembled those of a Victorian prostitute. I was burning up. I buried my head in my notes, debating whether to battle on or to run away, and in the silence of my uncertainty I heard the splat of a great gob of spittle (the dog's, not mine) hitting the linoleum floor, followed by a forced sigh and a swish of nylon as Miss Wright crossed her legs.

"Is there something wrong?" she asked.

I slowly, perhaps a little dramatically, raised my head, knowing I resembled a guy who had spent the last hour sunbathing inside a nuclear reactor and watched as she physically recoiled.

"Your face," said Miss Wright, her voice cracking, "you've gone completely red."

"Don't be alarmed," I said, waving a hand like a fan, "just a little hot flash. I'll be fine."

But as I spoke I realized the second phase, that hideously deforming swelling phase, was about to begin. Keeping my head down, I threw myself to the floor and engaged in the physical examination of my patient and to my great surprise, Miss Wright visibly and paradoxically relaxed. She seemed to appreciate that I was prepared to get "down and dirty" on the floor with her pet. Bailey relaxed as well. Neither of them seemed to notice that while I maintained my dialogue with the dog, trading soft words and a genuine orthopedic evaluation with liberal belly rubs, I was actually keeping my body in a perpetual state of motion, twitching and scratching my way from one pruritic patch to the next while my forehead began to inflate and my lips expanded to the size of Mick Jagger's injected with a double dose of collagen.

For a while I thought I was going to make it because Bailey's magnitude and all his beautiful fur and luxuriant feathering made it possible for me to keep relatively well hidden. But as the intensity of the itching crested like a torture ripped from the pages of Dante's *Inferno* and I began to fantasize about taking a cheese grater to my body in the manner of a bathroom loofa, I excused myself midsentence from my semirecumbent position on the floor and disappeared. Some thirty minutes later, my health completely restored, Dr. Jekyll returned to find the room empty.

What was unique about this attack was its relationship to a single variable. As a new and, by definition, impoverished graduate, eating exactly the same lunch for two consecutive days was not uncommon. But on the second day I consumed a sesame seed snack bar, the ones packed full of roasted seeds amalgamated into a dense block by molar-packing sugary syrup. It was the only disparity, offered, accepted, and consumed minutes before my appointment with Bailey.

Now I appreciate many of you reading this tale realized several pages ago that I was suffering from a classic type one anaphylactic reaction. Instead of bee stings or peanuts, I am blessed with an allergy to all things sesame. Approximately three million people suffer from peanut or tree nut allergies in this country and around one hundred Americans die annually from severe food-induced allergic reactions. Many of us with food allergies remain unsure of the cause. Testing can be difficult, often downright dangerous, and options for hypersensitization, a technique successfully employed to cure allergies to bee venom, do not exist. The treatment of choice is avoidance, necessitating that you know exactly what it is you are avoiding in the first place. And so, my thanks and belated gratitude go out to both Miss Wright and Bailey and to whoever it was who tried to kill me with that sesame seed bar in the first place.

Returning to the story, when I found the examination room empty, I decided I must contact Miss Wright to apologize and explain. She took my call at work.

"Your head looked like it was about to explode. You looked disgusting."

I thanked her for her empathy.

"The thing is," I said fervently, "I discovered that I am highly allergic to sesame seeds. What happened this afternoon might actually help save my life in the future."

Rewarded with a weary "uh-huh," I changed tack.

"I never got to discuss the treatment options for Bailey," I said. "Unfortunately, there's no way to repair the individual ligaments. Even if we could stitch them back together they would heal with a scar, and scar tissue is just not strong enough to support his weight. We need to fuse the bones together. Poor old Bailey is going to require some orthopedic surgery."

"I see," she said, too automatically, obviously not seeing at all.

I tried to regain her confidence.

"Don't worry," I said, "it won't be me performing the surgery."

"Thank God for that," she said, her relief unabashed, before adding, "it's nothing personal," as an afterthought, just to make sure that I knew that it was.

When Miss Wright returned some days later to drop off Bailey for his surgery, I made a point of admitting the dog.

"Surgery is scheduled for two," I told her.

"Fine," she said, her tone still a tad clipped. As she made to leave, she hesitated, turned, and asked, "What are you having for lunch?"

I smiled and wanted to say "A big bowl of sesame chicken with tahini and humous." Instead I risked, "Not sure. Maybe a Big Mac."

From the waiting room, I watched her go, crossing the parking lot, fumbling for her car keys, before the shocked expression on her face told me that she had just remembered what capped the famous double hamburger—the sesame seed bun!

Trusting your pet to a new graduate for worming tablets, vaccines, and antibiotics is one thing, but trusting a new graduate with a scalpel requires an even greater leap of faith. Surgical training in veterinary school is a bit like going to a shopping mall without money—you get to look, occasionally try a few things on for size, but chances are you won't walk away with something to call your own. After graduation, I remember feeling parched and restless for an authentic clinical experience in which I was the one who made a difference. Surgery had been the ultimate spectator sport and after all the years in training and waiting on the sidelines, I was eager to play on its sterile fields. It appeared to hold the possibility of instant gratification from an act of manual intervention, a clean separation of before and after, of then and now, of disease and cure, and the unique distinction of letting me experience responsibility for that change. Perhaps this is why, when I consider the first time I helped engineer something approaching a life-altering change in an animal, my mind's eye falls upon a surgery involving a Clumber spaniel called Norman.

I see an image of Norman standing in the examination room. He was a handsome, burly young man, white fur with orange freckles, a huge head, and a square rosy nose with thick leathery triangles for ears. He was four years old, in the prime of life, and despite his innate dignity and desire to please, he was utterly miserable. He did not want to move, not a single muscle, paralyzed by the fear of igniting the unendurable pain in his neck, bracing, frozen in taut and permanent spasm. When I tried to move his head even the smallest amount, in any direction, he would let out a haunting scream. And any attempt to encourage Norman to move, let alone to walk, was met with rigid front legs locked in extension and a pleading expression in his big amber eyes that begged to be left alone.

Norman had "slipped" a disk in his neck, a familiar, insipid term that really doesn't do justice to the sometimes violent nature of the disease. Disks sit between the bones of the spine as tiny shock absorbers with a tough exterior encapsulating a soft pulpy center, a bit like a stale jelly doughnut. Problems occur when the dough splits and the jam squirts out. In Norman's case the result was so painful and debilitating, we decided to recommend surgery. Of course I'm using the professional "we" here meaning that this was what the surgical resident told me to say to the owner.

During that surgery, the resident had stood across the table from me the whole time. He approved every slice and snip. He held his breath as I worked my way through the depths of Norman's neck, hovering as I swept aside various and sundry tubes and pipes (little things like jugulars, carotid arteries, esophagus, and trachea), and fortunately, he did not have to make an emergency landing for me. Then, with saintly patience and a talent for hiding his fear, the resident stood back and watched as I began drilling a tiny window into Norman's spine. The process was slow and tedious, grinding bone into dust, fighting the certainty that I was about to wrap the dog's spinal cord around the end of my drill bit like soft linguine around a fork. And then, as the last sliver of bone dissolved away, I felt an absurd satisfaction as mealy white disc squeezed free of the spinal canal like toothpaste from a tube.

By the following morning, Norman was ready for his "reveal" in an extreme canine makeover. The new Clumber I saw was trotting around and showing no restriction in the movement of his head and neck. It was not the magic of the surgeon: it was the magic of surgery. It was not simply the dramatic nature of Norman's recovery; it was the struggle, the fear, the danger, and the perseverance that made it possible. You would think that after my sleepless night and the discovery of a new dog the next morning I might remember my conversation with Norman's owners or the look on their faces when they came to the hospital to pick him up. But, the memory banks are empty. And maybe that's the point, because in the end there really is only one memory that matters—the face of a dog who could look up to make his shining amber eyes meet mine.

One of my greatest flaws as a new graduate was the desire for sensationalism. I was always hunting for an obscure, impossibly rare diagnosis, hearing the sound of hooves and thinking "zebra" and not "horse" like I was supposed to. I might have craved the unusual, fascinating, report-worthy cases, but a lot of what veterinarians do is straightforward and routine. When it is not, at the early stage of our careers, subtle flags of clinical significance may be overlooked, sometimes with dire consequences. This is to be expected. This is part of learning, of developing into a good clinician. It is an acquired art, a skill that can develop only over time; and they call it clinical intuition, a sensation that triggers little alarm bells to ring inside your head when some small piece of a clinical puzzle does not seem to fit.

I remember a particular case that tore into the parking lot while I was stranded among a poop archipelago in a sea of grass behind the hospital. The driver of the pickup truck screeched into a handicapped space, and from where I stood, politely averting my eyes as my patient squatted to pee for the umpteenth time, I noticed his rear bumper was peppered with bright stickers. Two in particular caught

31

my attention. One read, "Gun Control Is Making Sure You Don't Miss Your Target" and the other, "WANTED: Meaningful Overnight Relationship."

Although I resolved not to be judgmental about the driver, my hackles were up when I found Mr. Measley, as we will call him, and his dog, Thor, a nine-year-old boxer, waiting for me in an examination room.

"Christ, Doc, I'm in a hurry here," said Mr. Measley, looking up at me from his slouched position on a bench. His face was tanned, unnaturally so for the time of year, and a tight, black T-shirt hugged every ripple and bulge of his upper arms and chest. He winced at me, premature wrinkles crowding his eyes, as though this visit were a painful experience.

I ignored the hostility and offered my hand. I found his shake to be weak, warm, and a little sticky, his hand having recently glided through liberally gelled hair. The softness of his skin confirmed my assumption that this was a narcissistic snipe who frequented a tanning booth and the mirrored weight room of a local gym. So much for not being judgmental.

His dog, on the other hand, came toward me with that wonderful sloppy and noisy enthusiasm that boxers have. I was introduced to Thor, a name that seemed so utterly inappropriate it came as no surprise. Thor snorted and smiled, his lower jaw protruding like a toothy shovel, all the while tugging on his leash, desperate to lap me up as his little propeller of a tail spun around and around.

I could have explained that my appointments were not due to start for another fifteen minutes but thought better of it, inviting Mr. Measley to tell me what seemed to be the problem with Thor.

"What do you mean, what's wrong?" he said, flashing me his best "Duh" look. "Christ, what crap are they teaching you kids these days? I mean, really, just take a look at his tits."

Up until this point I had not noticed the fact that Thor did have profoundly pendulous breasts with dark pigmented nipples the size of my thumbs.

"I'm sorry," I said. "I had assumed that he was a bitch."

"D'ya think?" said Mr. Measley. "Was the name Thor a giveaway?"

I wondered if I had the strength in my hands to throttle his thick muscled neck, but asked, "So how old is Thor?"

"He's nine. Had him since he was a pup. Thought it might help me get some babes, you know. Cute puppy out for a walk. Chicks love it."

"Did it work?" I asked, noting that the fourth finger of his left hand was one of the few lacking a chunky piece of gold jewelry.

"Not really," he said, with a trace of disappointment.

"Really," I said, with no trace of surprise.

"Yeah. Now I'm trying one of those dating agencies, the ones that take a ton of money up front and then try to match you up with a perfect partner. All I know is that I'm still waiting to get laid."

"Really," I repeated, this time eager to move on. "So, has Thor been neutered?"

"Shit no. I wouldn't let anyone do it to me, though there've been plenty of women who wish they could." He laughed and afforded me a smug grin. "But then old Thor only ever had one ball. One of them never grew, I guess. I thought I might breed him, but no one seemed interested in a boxer firing on only one cylinder."

I nodded, scribbled, and said, "So when did you notice his breasts enlarging?"

Mr. Measley took a sharp intake of breath.

"Couple of months ago. It's been gradual. He's been beefing up for a while, losing his tone. Not much of a six-pack left now. But then we don't go for as many walks on account of the other dogs."

"What do you mean?"

He hesitated, as though this next revelation were difficult to confide.

"They've been trying to mount him. Trying to hump him from behind, and what worries me most is that he seems to like it. He just stands there and takes it. It's embarrassing. If you tell me my dog's turning gay I'm going to have a shit fit!"

I tapped my fingers against my chin and roped in my response.

"And what about the hair loss on his flanks, how long has that been going on?"

"I'm not sure," said Mr. Measley "I haven't really noticed."

Secretly, I was beginning to get excited about Thor's case. Here, at last, was a dog that, unbeknownst to his master, had been sneaking around veterinary school libraries late at night.

"Has Thor been drinking more than usual?"

And suddenly I saw a spark in Mr. Measley's eyes. Every now and then there is a defining moment when a question that seems entirely out of left field to the owners, but is rehearsed and natural to the vet, comes across as astute and insightful, as though hitting a clinical nail squarely on the head. This was probably the first time in my professional career that I had asked a question rewarded with a refreshing hint of respect.

"Come to think of it, he has been drinking quite a lot. And pissing up a storm as well. What does that mean?"

I gave my best knowing nod as though I were keeping him on tenterhooks as I got up to examine Thor, a certain swagger in my stride.

Thor stood passively for his examination, unlike his master, who quipped sexual innuendos about how he wished he could get his hands on a camera as I squatted squarely behind Thor palpating his scrotum. What I discovered was that Thor's right testicle was nowhere to be found and that his left testicle was small and shrunken. He was balding over the sides of his body and his belly was a little distended. His temperature was slightly up and the energy he had first shown me seemed to ebb from his body until he flopped to the floor, apparently exhausted.

"So, what do you think, Doc? Is he sneaking off when I'm not looking and getting a sex change?" Mr. Measley chuckled, and I tried my best to crack a smile.

"No. Not quite. But I am suspicious that he might have an estrogen-secreting tumor."

At this Measley stood up.

"Are you saying my dog's got cancer?"

I beckoned him to be seated and calm.

"I don't know. But what I see is a classic example of a dog becoming feminized. In a dog with only one testicle, the other one is often inside the abdomen. In Thor's case, it most likely has a tumor on it that's producing female hormones. This can make him drink more, pee more, lose hair, and generally appear more feminine. But don't worry, it can't change his sex."

"So, if you go into his belly and take the ball out, will he go back to being a male dog?"

"Hopefully, yes," I said, not entirely sure. "These tumors can be malignant, so we'd have to make sure that the cancer hadn't spread."

He leaned back on the bench, prodded his chin in my direction, and said, "What's all this going to cost?"

I gave him an estimate and he told me I could do only minimal blood tests, no X-rays, no ultrasound, just surgery.

"What's the point in expensive tests," he said, "if you're going to cut him open anyway?"

And so a few days later I found myself, scalpel in hand, poised to make an incision across Thor's sizable belly. The blood tests gave me two important pieces of information: first, Thor's red blood cell count was low, he was anemic, which is not uncommon in these cases because the female hormone estrogen creates bone marrow suppression; and second, his white blood cell count was high. This struck me as strange. It smacked of an infection. I knew that Thor's temperature was slightly higher than normal, but that was all I had to go on. That is, until I stared down into Thor's open belly and got the shock of my life.

It was one of those times when you look under the drape, inspect the name tag, and make sure you have anesthetized the correct animal. It was not that I was staring at something entirely new and undiscovered. But what I saw made no sense, at least not with Thor. Before me lay a large, turgid, tubular organ sitting atop loops of bowel; an organ that did not belong. What I saw was a bulging, gray green, pus-filled uterus, the female reproductive organ, inside the body of a male dog.

Thor had what is referred to as a "uterus masculinis," an embryonic remnant that should have disappeared long before birth, but somehow persisted. No one would have been the wiser had his undescended left testicle not awoken from its slumber and begun to produce estrogen, the female hormone—ignited by a Sertoli cell tumor, if anyone is remotely interested. This surge in feminine chemicals had several effects, most of which Mr. Measley had noticed. But what he did not know, what he could not possibly have known, was that a uterus inside Thor's body started to respond to the hormones, developing an infection (hence the elevated white blood cell count) known as a pyometra (not uncommon after false pregnancies in bitches). The upshot of all this reproductive turmoil was that for the first and only time in my career I had the opportunity to perform a spay and castration on the same dog.

Now imagine what you are going to tell a man like Mr. Measley regarding the surgical findings.

"Well, Mr. Measley, you know what you were saying about Thor undergoing a secret sex change . . . ?"

"Mr. Measley, how do you like the name Thora? It's got a certain ring to it, don't you think . . . ?"

Let me just say that it was an interesting phone call. Naturally I started with the easy stuff: things went well, your dog's resting comfortably. But when it came to the details, a lot of static hovered between us. I stressed that although Thor walked both sides of the fence, the real man in him was dominant, and Mr. Measley seemed to be satisfied.

It amuses me to think that on one of the few occasions when I wasn't actually looking for a zebra, I went and found a unicorn.

When Mr. Measley and Thor returned two weeks later, all appeared to be going well. Thor's incision had healed nicely, but what struck me was that there was something different about his owner. I couldn't put my finger on it exactly. He just seemed somehow more at ease, perhaps a little softer around the edges.

"How's everything going?" I asked.

"Fantastic," said Mr. Measley. "I've been taking Thor on some short walks. He takes his time, but none of the other dogs have been trying it on with him, not like before."

I nodded my approval and then noticed that Mr. Measley was smiling.

"What?" I said.

"Oh, I'm just smiling because I met a girl. Everyone down at the park noticed Thor because of his plastic lampshade and his incision. Never realized how interested some people could be. This girl, Karen, wanted to know all about it, and when I told her about, you know, his little sexual deviation thing, she was fascinated."

"Sexual deviation will do that," I didn't say. Instead I wished him well and almost hurried him out of the room before he had a chance to spoil things by telling me how they went straight back to his place and did it.

Funny how things turn out. A dog with a feminine side playing his part in bringing out the same trait in his master.

Dr. Elliot Sweet walks toward me with long spidery strides, a frisky golden retriever bouncing by his side, blond feathery fur billowing as he trots.

"This is Whisky," says Elliot, angling his head down in my direction. "He's only nine months old but he already has a small growth on the roof of his mouth."

Elliot's tone is both sincere and incredulous at the injustice of finding this in such a young dog. As the two of us stand in the middle of the ward, Whisky tugging on his leash to the point of choking at every dog and technician that passes by, Elliot continues. "The mass is raised and firm, about five millimeters across, sitting in the midline just behind the two central upper incisors on the hard palate. It is not painful. It is not ulcerated. Whisky is eating and drinking fine and is otherwise a happy, healthy dog. Last night I had blood drawn for complete blood count and serum biochemistry, urine for urinalysis, three-view chest X-rays looking for metastatic disease, and a cross match just in case he needs a transfusion during or after surgery. Thankfully, in my opinion, the chest X-rays were normal."

He rattles off this information with stern urgency as though there isn't a moment to lose, and I have to physically shake off the intensity of his synopsis.

"Whoa there, Elliot. Let's back up a little. What exactly did you tell the owners about this little lump?"

"I told them the truth. I got right to it. Straight to the bottom line. I told them that it looks like a tumor, that most oral tumors are malignant, and that it probably requires radical surgery to be removed with clean margins. I warned them that Whisky would loose all his upper front teeth including the bone they are sitting in, and this would leave him with a droopy Concord-nose, making him look more like a tapir than a dog but that as long as he was able to eat and drink and breathe normally he would be fine."

He spoke with absolute clinical detachment and then added, grimly, "Until the cancer spread."

I took a deep breath. "Okay, Elliot. I have a couple of questions for you, the first being, how did the owners take this news?"

He shook his head.

"Devastated, as you can imagine. They are a young couple, about my age. The two of them were crying their eyes out when I told them what it was."

I nodded, imagining the scene. "And how long has this growth, as you call it, been around? How fast is it growing?"

Elliot perked up a little, obviously prepared for this line of questioning.

"They noticed it last night for the first time. Whisky was rolling around on his back getting his belly rubbed with his mouth open, tongue lolling off to one side, and the girlfriend caught a glimpse of this lump sitting behind the front teeth. They brought him in right away. I told them it was good, catching it while it was small."

I look at the carefree dog dancing at Elliot's feet and feel my skepticism rising. Time to take a gander.

I squat down and Elliot joins me as we engage in a playful wrestling match, which ultimately reproduces the owner's observation technique by getting Whisky to roll on his back while scratching his belly. The bump is exactly as Elliot described.

We get back to our feet and I'm thinking about where I should begin.

"Well, Elliot. Let me start by saying you are absolutely correct. The majority of oral tumors that I see in dogs are malignant. And when I look at Whisky's lump it does not look like an abscess or a foreign body or the result of some kind of oral trauma, so thinking that it had to be a tumor is a fairly reasonable assumption."

Elliot studies me with arms folded high and tight across his chest.

"However, before jumping into a world of doom and gloom with the owners, you might want to consider a few important factors in this case. First, Whisky's age. He's awfully young for a tumor. I'm not saying that age precludes cancer, it's just worth noting. Second, this owner only noticed the lump last night. We have no idea how long it has been there and how fast it is growing, if at all."

"But I thought that if we need to get a biopsy, we might as well cut it out as completely as possible at that time, as a single procedure, and given its location, this will mean radical surgery."

I can feel him going on the defensive, frustrated that his impressive textbook knowledge is not panning out in the real world, that I am not commending him on a job well done.

Better to let him down here, just the two of us, than in front of his peers on rounds.

"Your workup for oral cancer was excellent, Elliot. There is one small problem."

Elliot looks confused, unable to comprehend the possibility of an oversight.

"It's not cancer. In fact, it's not a tumor at all. What Whisky has is a completely normal anatomical structure, which in his case happens to be slightly more prominent than most. It is called an incisive papilla, a much overlooked little lump with a pair of tiny ducts on either side of it, communicating with the vomeronasal organ, involved in pheromone perception. The owners just hadn't noticed it until last night."

Elliot has no color to lose, but even the stubbly shadow of his beard pales to a lighter shade of gray.

"Oh, God. Oh, crap," is all he can manage.

"Hey, don't worry. Mistakes happen."

"But I painted such a horrible picture for the owners. They were so upset and now you're telling me that their dog is absolutely normal." He slaps a mighty palm against his domed forehead.

"If I were you, I would tell them the truth, that we believe the lump is an unusual manifestation of a completely benign and normal structure and that our recommendation, at least for now, is to watch and wait. Make sure you convey that there is *nothing* to worry about."

Elliot nods, but his mind is already racing ahead.

"But what about all their money I've spent? The blood, the urine, the X-rays. They were all a complete waste."

I smile. Elliot has his lesson, and now I have mine. Watching the distress and panic rising in this young and talented man, I am reminded that it is important to remember and respect how all new vets enter this world and to appreciate and savor how far we all manage to come. No one wants to put an animal through unnecessary tests or recklessly spend an owner's money, but Elliot's mistake is borne of inexperience, not negligence, motivated by his desire to help an animal, not to make a fast buck.

Without trying to sound glib, I wonder if I can help him to see at least one bright side.

"You know what, Elliot, from what you describe of these owners, I virtually guarantee that they will have absolutely no problems over the money you have already spent."

He looks down at me, incredulous, as I turn to leave, and says, "Why?"

And over my shoulder I reply, "Because you just cured their dog of cancer!"

7:48 A.M.

THE FAIRER SEX

Coffee will have to wait. My first appointment of the morning is signing in, so I decide to check my messages before getting bogged down in new cases.

Under my name, trapped in the metallic bite of a magnetic clip, two of those While You Were Out paper slips flutter for my attention, poised to add another thrilling dimension to my day. The hand-scribbled notes read as follows.

Message: Mrs. Woodman—six-week follow-up on Lunar. Just wants you to know she's doing great. Like a new dog. Never know she shattered her pelvis. No need to call. "You're the best."

This last phrase is followed not by exclamation marks of praise and admiration but by question marks of confusion and surprise. Somebody's idea of a little joke.

I smile. Maybe this is going to be a good day after all. Message Two has other ideas.

Message: Mr. Brown needs you to call first thing. Not using leg. Worse than before you did surgery. Angry and upset on the phone.

This note is covered in hand-drawn asterisks and fluorescent yellow highlighter as though I might need some assistance in getting to the crux of its sentiment. I stuff the messages in the breast pocket of my shirt and head to my examination room, figuring it would be appropriate to call Mr. Brown at nine.

I greet my first scheduled appointment of the day with a smile and a gesture for the owner to take a seat, but she makes no attempt to conceal her distress.

"Oh dear," says Ms. Sanchez, a gum-chewing, tan young woman oblivious to the winter wonderland outside in her taut Juicy Couture outfit as she bustles in on a wave of fruity perfume. "I specifically requested a woman vet."

For a second I consider coming back with the snappy retort. "Not to worry, I always carry a tweed skirt, push-up bra, and sensible pumps in my locker. I'll be back in a jiffy."

Instead, I offer a weak apology.

"Oh, it's not you," she adds, shouting over the crack of sharp enamel as my proximity in the same room breaches the "enter at your own risk" personal space of the Chihuahua in her arms.

"It's him."

Her eyes drop down to her four-legged version of Hannibal Lecter as she inches my way and whispers, "He hates men."

In fact, Ms. Sanchez has beaten the odds because nowadays the chances of seeing a male veterinarian are becoming increasingly low. What is embarrassing to me is that I failed to notice this dramatic feminization of the profession. I feel like a conspicuous tourist, bumbling forward, all pointy fingers, looking for direction, visiting the sites that mark a chosen career path while failing to stop and appreciate the significant shift in my surroundings along the way. As a boy growing up in England, my perception of veterinary medicine came from watching television images of manly men stripped to their waists in ice-whipped barns, eager to wrestle with lively livestock before tucking into a heart-stopping English breakfast.

As a veterinary student, my class was fairly evenly balanced between men and women, but with male instructors in the majority, I still felt like testosterone pervaded as the dominant hormone. Then I took my detour into surgery, purportedly one of the last bastions of onerous male egos. Even as I struggled to throw square knots and accept my initial status as nothing more than a human malleable retractor, puerile, giggling echoes of "more suction please, nurse" and "there's nothing better than a tight screw" were beginning to fade. It was only when I finished my residency and passed surgery boards that I looked up and saw my world had been invaded by a new breed of pet people, an intelligent strain considered better listeners, more compassionate, more nurturing, and infinitely more altruistic. Women had become the future of veterinary medicine because, as the dean of one prominent North American university said, "The entire profession will be women within a decade and a half. It's inevitable."

Of course, the truth is that female veterinarians have been around for over one hundred years. Back in 1903, a woman named Mignon Nicholson—perhaps named with an eye to the beef industry—became the first female vet in the United States, whereas nine years earlier, Aleen Cust became the first woman to be accepted as a student of veterinary medicine in the United Kingdom. Before you go lauding those progressive folks back in the old days, it is worth mentioning that despite completing her education, the Royal Veterinary College refused to set and examine Miss Cust, in essence denying her a license to practice. She had to wait until December 1922 to become a fully fledged member of the profession.

In fact, the American Association of Veterinary Medical Colleges noted that only 8 percent of the student body was female back in 1968, and that women were in the minority up until 1986. Now women dominate, essentially making up three-quarters of all enrollments. So what happened and what will be the result?

Yes, I realize this is dangerous territory for an un-neutered male such as myself, but I'm not exactly asking Gloria Steinem if she wants to party at the Playboy Mansion! The bottom line is no one knows for certain why the gender-shift occurred, but it is probably a combination of several recognized reasons:

- Up until thirty years ago, it was hard for women to get a place at veterinary school. They were ostracized, spawning images of ruddy-faced farmers chuckling at the fruitless efforts of a "young lass" faffing around with a "frisky ram." As it turns out, cows may, in fact, prefer a delicate feminine arm up their bottom to that of some juiced Neanderthal, and besides, the 1960s ensured that women could trade their bra for a pair of long-sleeved disposable plastic gloves and a bottle of robust lubricant.

- At about the same time as farm work began to decline, a niche in companion animal practice began to emerge. In my experience, women are just as good at large animal work as they are with small animals. The public simply was finally able to accept that strength and weight no longer provided an advantage. Realistically, was this ever an issue? I mean, how much difference can an extra seventy pounds possibly make when handling a 1,500-pound Dutch warm-blood stallion?

- In a similar vein to the teaching and nursing fields, some pundits maintain that another effect of the ascension of women in veterinary science is smaller salaries. However, any claim that gender shift *caused* a decrease in income appears to be erroneous since salaries were on the decline in the 1980s before the rise of women in the profession. Society has a track record of devaluing "female professions," and I have heard the argument that veterinary salaries can make a fine second income but relative to the cost of the education, it can prove less than stellar for a primary breadwinner. I'm hesitant to label my sex as fiscal mercenaries, but I'm sure this reality drives some men to look elsewhere for their livings. I do take solace in a recent study that showed newly qualified vets and students ranked income seventh out of eight as a reason for choosing the profession.*

But let us return to the tale of my little Mexican amigo.

"See, I got Taco from the pound," says Ms. Sanchez "and we're pretty sure he was . . . you know . . . abused."

Ms. Sanchez speaks in a considerate whisper, sparing the long-haired Chihuahua in her arms any embarrassment as she adds, "Probably at the hands of a man." Her eyes widen, chin folding like an accordion into the generous creases of her neck, a defiant "Am I right or am I right?" expression on her face.

Maybe it's me but I'm not convinced that every adopted animal from a shelter or rescue center is truly being saved from a life of interminable and unspeakable male abuse. Whatever happened to "changed apartment and they don't take pets" or "moving out of state or overseas"? Why not an honest, simple "hates men, hates kids, hates antique Persian rugs and nice new expensive furniture from Crate and Barrel"? Why not, just for once, just to be different, "hates women"? Perhaps I should be thankful that another pet has avoided needless euthanasia and simply concede to stories of our innocent four-legged friends lunging at any man reaching for a broom. Or, in the case of the charming Taco, reaching for the same air.

Ms. Sanchez and her small companion finally take a seat, engag-

---

*The influence of a friend or relative ranked eighth.

ing in an intense moment of mutual kissy-face that appears to calm both parties. I am almost embarrassed to interrupt.

"So what seems to be the problem?"

"It's his mouth, way in the back and to the side near the base of his tongue on the left. There's this big, ugly white lump."

Fabulous! Why couldn't it be a tail problem or a hind leg toenail crisis? Right about now I'd even consider some sort of anal aberration.

"When did you first discover this lump?"

"About a week ago, didn't we?"

Ms. Sanchez consults directly with Taco, who seems to have something of a taste for the sticky gloss coating her full and puckered lips.

"And can I ask how you managed to notice a lump so far back in his throat?" Not sure that I really want to know.

"My boyfriend likes to feed him peanut butter. He puts it on his nose."

"On the dog's nose?"

"Yeah, it's funny. Taco freaks out trying to get at it with his tongue. He can pretty much get all the way up his nostrils. That was when I noticed it."

I scribble in my notes.

"I see," I say, "and has it curtailed his appetite?" wanting to add "for food, raw meat, small children?"

"No, he's eating and drinking fine."

"And you've never noticed any blood in his water or food bowl? Or dripping from his nose?"

Ms. Sanchez recoils, curtailing Taco's attentive lingual examination of her earlobe.

"Gross," she says. "No. Never."

"And his general health is good?"

"Excellent."

"Up to date on his shots?"

"Yes."

"And does he like to chew rawhide? Squeaky toys?"

Taco hesitates midlick, suddenly all ears, or rather *more* all ears than he already is, at the sound of these magical words.

"God, yes, he's always got something in his mouth, always. If he gets a slipper, or a chicken bone, you'll never get it away from him, not unless you want to trade for a finger."

She laughs and I join in because I'm sure she meant to say forearm. Don't get me wrong, I like these feisty, charismatic, and attentive dogs. It's just that sometimes my interpretation of what the American Kennel Club likes to define as a "saucy expression" feels more like "Come near me and I'll rip your throat out." They can be protective, fearless little hombres, with more than a dash of habanera sauce spicing up their blood.

"Very good," I say, getting up from my chair. "Perhaps it's time to take a look."

Ms. Sanchez cracks up.

"I don't know how you're going to do that."

I offer a wan "Don't attempt this at home" smile and come around the table.

For starters, when faced with a testy patient, I like to open with a "let's be best buddies" or "breaking down the barriers" approach.

"Why don't you take off his leash and we'll let him wander around on the floor."

Ms. Sanchez complies, but Taco stands defensively at her side, barking a piercing yap that is surely an Occupational Safety & Health Administration violation in this confined space. Ignoring the pain where my eardrums used to be, I get down on the floor, maintaining a safe four feet between our respective snouts. Then again, Taco might be capable of flinging himself at my jugular, latching on and sticking straight out, his body rigid and perpendicular to my neck as Mom offers a hesitant and desultory "No . . . no . . . naughty Taco. . . . Stop that, you bad little boy."

I inch a little closer and Taco finds a deeper, throatier, postpubescent growl that's easier on the ears but far more menacing. He follows up with an Elvis impersonation, his upper lips starting to shimmer and ripple, jaw clenched tight.

This approach is obviously not going to work, so I back off and get to my feet.

"How do you think he would be on the examination table?"

Ms. Sanchez does not hesitate. "Are you for serious? He hates the table, hates the sound of his nails on the metal. He thinks he's going to get a shot."

I nod.

"But what if I were to put down a clean towel?"

She shrugs. "Maybe. You can try."

I wonder if I catch creases of amusement around her mouth and eyes, as if she might actually be enjoying my dilemma. When I return and unfurl my towel it may as well be a matador's red cape. Only her forefinger curled around his collar restrains his snapping jaws as Taco lunges, teeth out faster than the flash of a switchblade.

"See, he's not like this with women. Can't you go and get a woman vet? I'm telling you it will be a whole lot easier."

Now she's gone and done it, a sexist gauntlet slapped squarely in my face. Time to get serious. I let loose with my best, syrupy sweet Bee Gees–in–tight–leather–pants doting falsetto.

"Oh, come on now. Who's the best little man? Little Taco is the best little man."

If anyone walks in now I will never live this down.

For a second Taco seems puzzled, ears all atwitter, head tilting to one side as if he is deciding whether I am friend or foe, but when I take my chance to pet him all I see is a flash of light, hear the snap of molar on molar, and feel the displacement of air at my fingertips.

"Okay," I say, my reflexive withdrawal with both hands clenched tight beneath my chin doing little to enamor my client, "let me try one last thing."

I leave the room and return with a wooden tongue depressor, a can of cat food, and a pair of oversized industrial-strength gloves that look like they were intended to handle radioactive material. If I'm going to help Taco, I need to get a glimpse of this lump on his tongue, even if it means upgrading our contretemps from a little frisky foreplay to an out-and-out brawl.

I outline my plan with Ms. Sanchez, who agrees that it is worth a shot, and wearing my protective gloves, cautiously approach the kill zone. The cat food proves irresistible, especially when applied "peanut-butter style" to the end of his nose, and although my fingers are chomped like a cob of corn, Taco's teeth are no more than dull indentations as I finally visualize a dime-sized milky white lump embedded in writhing pink muscle.

"Okay," I say taking off the gloves. "One more thing that I'd like to try before we're all done. I'd rather not use a muzzle, so if you can just gently hold his mouth closed for a second . . ."

Ms. Sanchez brings her thumb and forefinger together, a diver's "all is well" signal, temporarily holding Taco's short snout shut as I have her turn his head away from me so I can quickly feel for the lymph nodes in his neck.

"Good. He did great. Take a seat and let's have a chat."

I pick up the record and locate the appropriate section to document my clinical findings, writing down a description of the strange lump. I note that Taco has not yet turned two and that his lymph nodes were unremarkable on palpation.

"It's not cancer, is it?"

I look up and can see that Mom is in a panic, certain that I must be hunting for the right words, Taco working the big wet eyes, in need of commiseration.

"I don't think so, but I won't know for sure until we get a biopsy."

"You don't know for sure! So it might be!"

For a split second, a vision of sliding my head from side to side while wagging an extended forefinger in a "Don't go there, girlfriend" gesture, flashes in my mind's eye. I shake it off and say, "I doubt it, but no one can be a hundred percent positive without a biopsy. Taco's young, his glands in his neck are not swollen, and otherwise he's in perfect health. I'd say it is much more likely to be something benign than something cancerous."

"So you'll take the biopsy and he'll be fixed, right?"

I notice how her grip on Taco's little body is unconsciously clamping down, suffocating him with protective fear, love, and the chartreuse velure of her sweatshirt.

"*If* I can remove the entire lump and the biopsy confirms that it is benign, then hopefully, yes, we will be all set. But my number one goal with surgery is to find out exactly what this strange lump can be so that we treat it appropriately and so that I can give you an accurate idea of whether it will be a problem in the future."

Ms. Sanchez transfers her gaze from me to Taco, comforted by his kisses attending to the tears in her eyes and suddenly, despite his animosity to me, he has won me over as a sweet and doting companion.

I am also grateful that I don't have to risk reaching over with a box of tissues.

Ms. Sanchez sniffles then smiles hesitantly and says, "But you guarantee he will make it through the anesthesia?"

This time I move forward in my chair, indifferent to the danger, so that I can make eye contact and a point.

"No. I can't do that either. Nobody can. But I can tell you that the chance of anything untoward happening in a healthy young Chihuahua is extremely slim. One thing I will guarantee a hundred percent is that I will do my absolute best for your dog."

She may not have heard all the words, but I believe the sentiment got through. I finish writing in my notes about our discussion, list some of the differentials and my plan to check with my schedule and set up the procedure as soon as possible.

"Someone will be in touch with a surgery date later today or tomorrow," I say, closing the file and standing.

Ms. Sanchez adjusts Taco and retrieves her stray Louis Vuitton handbag. I am about to hand her the file, to be delivered to the front desk on her way out, when the little alligator apparently sleeping in the green folds of his velure swamp makes one last lunge for male flesh.

"Nearly got me that time," I say with a fake chuckle, taking back the record in order to add the notation, "Extreme caution for men; will bite with enthusiasm; beware land shark," or some such warning for the unwary.

I place the record on the neutral territory of the examination table and say my good-byes, thinking, "Until next time. Adiós muchacho!"

And I've nearly escaped with all my digits intact when Ms. Sanchez pauses at the door and asks, "Any chance you could clip his nails and squeeze his anal sacs while we are here?"

In the end, the lump turned out to be a chalky deposit of calcium trapped inside tongue muscle repeatedly traumatized by busy molars and excessive chewing. The disease is entirely benign, Taco's future, rosy. Unlike the future of the individual who attemps to curb the dog's rawhide and squeaky-toy dependency!

4

· · · · · · · · · ·

8:30 A.M.

SECOND OPINION

Jester Stonewall is big—really big. Standing thirty-nine inches tall at the shoulders, he is a formidable, handsome, two-year-old harlequin Great Dane, lumbering into my examination room with a proportionally tall dad who breathes rarified air from the ceiling and a Lilliputian mom who looks like she could easily saddle up and take Jester out on a hack. The three fuss before settling, Jester's mom making a show of the imposing ream of paperwork in her arms, out in the open like a tattoo meant for me to see. The ringed notepad comes next, a deliberate flip through several pages of handwritten notes hinting that there will be many questions. I am expecting a hand-held tape recorder to document our meeting, but Mrs. Stonewall goes old school, finding a pen and signaling she is ready to proceed by dropping her printed collection of articles, anecdotes, blogs, and chat room gossip on the bench beside her, savoring my surprise as it lands with a weighty and impressive thud.

The leggy, black-and-white pony with the pointy ears has settled on the floor between us, forepaws neatly crossed, a preamble to a heavy sigh of indifference before laying an immense skull on his make-do digital pillow.

I study my interrogators. I am guessing that they are both in their late fifties, early sixties, successful baby boomers who have chosen a big dog to fill their empty nest. Mr. Stonewall squints behind lenses that could easily start a brush fire on a bright sunny day. Mrs. Stonewall does not wear glasses, but her widely spaced sheeplike eyes appear to scrutinize a point high above my forehead, making me wonder if I have something unpleasant stuck in my hair. Either she does not enjoy eye contact or she prefers a sort of visual alignment that works best with her husband.

Mrs. Stonewall begins to tell me all about Jester, and a story that centers on her veterinarian's belief that the dog has a congenital defect of the spine whereas everything she has read on the Internet points to a diagnosis of canine hip dysplasia. She makes little effort to hide her partiality, trusting that I will adjudicate, prove her right, fix the problem, and permanently vote her vet off the Island of Clinical Acumen. Of course she doesn't say this exactly, but within minutes of meeting her, I can tell she is compelled by something far greater than the piles of paper research at her side. Despite the critical tone of her words, I recognize and empathize with the driving force that is right in front of me, in the way she studies me in increments, in staccato stares that visit like a hummingbird before flicking away, giving me a millisecond of time to catch a glimpse of the true motivation in her eyes—a fear of losing the dog she loves.

Once upon a time I might have made a point of congratulating Mrs. Stonewall for coming to our meeting conversant and committed to tackling some puzzling or problematic facet of her animal's health. All too often veterinary information used to be packaged, dry, esoteric, and difficult to track down, necessitating a visit to a local library or the purchase of a pet health book. But in the last decade, with little more than a point, peck, click, and squint, the Internet has opened up a world of cheap, fast, and easily accessible data. Benefits cross both sides of the examination table. Irrespective of education and socioeconomic background, pet owners have an opportunity to be informed and subsequently more involved in their animal's care. Veterinarians can converse with a receptive client who has a better understanding of the challenges and complexity of animal disease. So why, from time to time, is the Internet being used as a weapon to confuse, intimidate, police, and occasionally trap an unsuspecting or unprepared clinician?

It would be wrong for me to make generalizations given the skewed pet population with which I interact, but my experiences with Internet-addicted owners are generally positive. I have to try to stay current, to be vigilant for new treatment options, and to achieve a better understanding of the subject so that I can justify (rather than defend) my actions. Arguably, this is a far easier task within the confines of a single specialty than it is for a general practitioner, and I have read accounts of owners verbally pouncing on the first sign of uncertainty, let alone ignorance, when armed with obscure and possibly irrelevant facts procured from the Web. It is easy to be cynical about the owner convinced that her dog has the first reported case of mad cow disease, or Ebola virus, but let's not forget her intent is motivated by a desire to advocate for her pet. Animal health care is a quagmire of clinical quicksand and all of us can slip from time to time. If an astute owner picks up on a mistake, that's fine by me—better to lose face than to lose a patient.

Part of the answer lies in the quality of the information available. Several years ago a scientific study analyzed the data available on thirty Web sites claiming to provide information on arthritis in dogs. They used regular search engines like Google and Yahoo! to find these sites and objectively evaluated their content. They concluded the sites were "at best incomplete and at worst questionable" with, in their opinion, 77 percent deemed "counterproductive or of minimal value." The researchers were quick to point out that canine arthritis is only a tiny fraction of pet-care data available online but clearly inferred that an unsuspecting public was vulnerable to misinterpretation of misinformation.

And sticking with the subject of joint disease, what better example of the inflammatory power at your fingertips than the ruckus surrounding a canine arthritis medication called Rimadyl. When pharmaceutical giant Pfizer released this drug (generic name: carprofen) in 1997, they did so in a blaze of direct-drug marketing with full-page magazine ads and prime-time television commercials that instantly transformed stiff, sedentary, geriatric dogs into spry and athletic puppies. Rimadyl was the first FDA-approved nonsteroidal anti-inflammatory painkiller for dogs, and pet owners bought it by the bucketful. Pfizer conformed to all the requisite safety and efficacy testing before it hit the market, but as with every previous drug, and all those yet to be discovered, so-called adverse reactions inevitably occur. Most dogs were given a new lease on life and side effects were uncommon and generally mild, such as vomiting or diarrhea, typical for this class of drug. But then a study from Colorado State University published in the *Journal of the American Veterinary Medical Association (JAVMA)* described carprofen-associated liver damage in twenty-one dogs, leading to death or euthanasia in four of these cases. The paper pointed out that the problem was an unpredictable peculiarity, that the drug had been used in Europe for over ten years seemingly without incident, and that most of the dogs made a full recovery after stopping the drug and receiving basic supportive care. But somehow only one finding in the report echoed around cyberspace—the discovery that thirteen of the twenty-one dogs were Labradors. No one appeared to care that all thirteen recovered from their liver disease because virtual Internet gossip had already arrived at one inevitable conclusion—carprofen kills Labradors.

Most of us would agree that listing death as a possible side effect generally constitutes negative advertising, and so the sight of chemically rejuvenated leaping Labradors faded from our television screens as fast as it had appeared. The bottom line is that around sixteen million dogs have taken Rimadyl and the adverse reaction rate reported to the FDA is less than two-tenths of 1 percent. Of that percentage, the vast majority of side effects are related to gastrointestinal upset. By any pharmaceutical standards this is an extremely safe drug, but that's no consolation when your dog is that one in ten thousand that dies. In March 2000, the *Wall Street Journal* ran an article on Rimadyl and something resonated among a small group of pet owners who were left feeling like they had been party to killing their best friends. Frustration and infuriation perfectly coincided with an opportunity to vent through a technological revolution that could warn the unsuspecting dog lovers of the world. The disenfranchised spewed their venom and sadness all over cyberspace, and who could blame them?

"To die of old age is one thing; but to die when it wasn't time is hard for those of us that are left here to live with[out, them]."

"Our beloved and trusting companions should not be, forgive the term, 'guinea pigs' for these supposed miracle drugs."

Much has been learned from our experiences with Rimadyl. It is still an excellent painkiller for the relief of arthritis in dogs, but it is not for everyone. If I have a client frightened about any product after perusing some scary blog, far be it from me to force it on their pet. The market for arthritis medication is a $130 million industry, which, if nothing else, means my patients and their owners have a choice. New drug-packaging inserts make it easier for an owner to understand the possible side effects, and veterinarians are trained to thoroughly review these details before dispensing a drug. To help avoid more subtle, subclinical disorders as a result of a medication, blood tests should be performed before, after, and periodically throughout a course of treatment. We do it for ourselves, so why not for our pets?

Over the last few years, I believe I have seen a change in client attitudes toward the Internet. Some still covet the security of an over-stuffed manila folder, but they are far savvier, understanding the paradox of discovering a miracle cure online as well as a site dedicated to its heartbreaking side effects. Sadly, and not surprisingly, negativity abounds in cyberspace. When medicine fails our pets, we want to warn others to be more cautious. The pain is palpable in these Web tributes to lost innocent animals, and it is no consolation to be labeled as the unlucky recipient of an acceptable low-risk side effect or improper drug protocol; however, for the vast silent majority, medical or surgical success provides little incentive to sit down at a computer and document a positive outcome. Sometimes the Internet can feel like a religion for agnostics who need a shoulder in times of trouble. By all means take in all the angles, but look for the bigger picture through credible sources and bear in mind, "If it don't smell, it don't sell!"

It turns out that a small number of my referrals actually discover me by going online. Their intent may be complimentary, but by offering me the kind of smile you might reserve for Paris Hilton, Colin Farrell, or Tommy Lee with the phrase "You know, you're famous on the Internet," the effect can prove a trifle disconcerting. "You have quite the following" doesn't help either because I'm thinking more along the lines of David Koresh than *Grey's Anatomy*. I'm joking, of course, because invariably their pet has revealed why they are here and the reason for their ambiguous opener. I refer to a frustrating ailment, primarily of geriatric dogs, called "laryngeal paralysis" in which the distressed patient slinks into my examination room sounding like a steam train struggling up an incline. This is a challenging area of the canine anatomy to describe, but imagine there are cartilaginous French doors at the entrance to the dog's windpipe that open wide every time the dog inhales, allowing air to get down to the lungs. In laryngeal paralysis, the door hinges have frozen up, the opening reduced to a reedy gap, making every breath a noisy and desperate gasp. The poor animal is suffocating in a room full of fresh air.

This Internet pilgrimage tends to occur in the spring because here in New England the climate often conspires to abandon an entire season, transitioning from a brisk Alberta Clipper to a Bermuda High almost overnight. Subsequently dogs that have been marginal through the cold of winter, try to pant with the first bout of hot weather and nothing happens except a life-threatening encounter with heatstroke. Too much exercise or excitement can prove just as dangerous.

These owners will have been surfing a number of Web sites dedicated to the condition, some of which offer excellent advice based on firsthand experience of dealing with these dogs before and after surgical correction of the problem. Unless the veterinarian has worked through the disease with their own dog, there is much to learn from the moms and dads who experience the majority of the patient care. The wealth of their collective experience gathered over time, trial and error, with attention to subtle nuances and indomitable dedication to their pets makes much of what they share unique and invaluable. Best of all they can be an emotional sounding board and support group, making the visitor feel welcome and part of an understanding extended family.

I assume my unwitting celebrity stems from a few successful outcomes for dogs belonging to central contributors of these sites. I should explain that there is a good surgical option, a procedure called a "tie-back," which, sticking with my previous analogy, holds one-half of the French doors permanently open so that enough air can get by without encouraging food and water to go down the wrong way on an incursion to the lungs, which can cause aspiration pneumonia. Dependent upon whom you read, complication rates for the surgery vary from 10 to 30 percent, and so I warn these owners that although their faith in me is appreciated, eventually "the House" is going to win one back. It's not Russian roulette but I imagine a time will come when the Web sites are inundated with requests to have my name withdrawn from their exclusive list of competent surgeons. Fifteen minutes is a long time in the world of laryngeal paralysis and about the same length of time it takes for a throwaway comment to be posted as fact for all the world to see. I recall a client who wondered what I thought of weaning their dog from canned food back to dry kibble following the surgery. They objected to buying nothing but canned dog food, rolling portions into little meatballs, and feeding the dog by hand for the rest of his life (sometimes I can be a little demanding with my postoperative instructions). Pressed for an answer to this ambiguous question I said something like, Oh, I don't know, maybe you could try weaning to dry food after a week or two. I thought nothing more of my comment, finished my appointments, and returned to my office to do paperwork and call referring vets. Curious to see who recommended me and what they said, I dropped in on the laryngeal site only to find the latest entries featured a heated debate sparked by my laissez-faire attitude to an appropriate postoperative weaning program. The dangerous and worrisome phrase "Trout said" glared from all over the monitor, brandished willy-nilly as both a sword and a shield. I learned a valuable lesson that day: Stick with what you know and never underestimate the dissociated power of the Internet.

As a rule, most pet owners seek a referral for a second opinion through the doctor they trust the most, their general practice veterinarian. In contrast to a pet GP, one of the challenges and disappointments of second-opinion work can be the brevity of the patient and client interaction. Consultations are like a job interview or an advertising pitch. Lose the stuttering, the nervous ticks, the open palms, and the shoulder shrugs, because this is your one chance to connect, to show off your "A" game and close the deal. There can be no distractions or foibles, no time to worry about your daughter's school report or to feel like you might be coming down with a cold, to reflect on that stupid fight with your boyfriend or wife, to need to sleep, or to crave something to eat, because you might just be their last hope. You are the closing pitcher and they seek an automaton and a sensitive, caring individual at one and the same moment.

As a result I believe second-opinion work, at least from a surgical standpoint, is far more isolating. When things go well my association with a client and patient is flitting and casual. We connect at the consultation, I might see them briefly when their pet comes in for surgery, we talk on the phone to discuss the procedure, the findings, and the postoperative care, and maybe meet one more time for a final recheck. That's pretty much it. I am nothing more than an extra with a walk-on part. If I am really lucky, they might remember my name in the same way we remember the name of the obstetrician who delivers our children. Sometimes, when spending time with my colleagues embedded in the trenches of veterinary health care, I am envious of the way in which they have years to develop a relationship with the owner and the animal. By comparison, surgeons are no more than one-night stands.

From time to time second-opinion work takes on a predestined sense of professional peril. In its mildest form it is nothing more than an innocent question by a casual acquaintance.

"My dog's lame. How much will that cost?"

"If one of my cats eats the other cat's poop, does that mean he's still hungry?"

"Why does my ferret smell?"

My inability to come up with the right answers for friends might make me appear befuddled, incompetent, and flawed by my own degree of specialization, but any embarrassment is fleeting. Not so the second opinion materializing from uncharted fringes of the family circle. The connection might be tenuous—the chain-smoking in-law whose love affair with the Marlboro Man has remodeled her vocal cords into sandpaper or the creepy second cousin twice removed who is convinced you can help his three-year-old daughter get into vet school—but that won't stop their accusatory glances and disgruntled murmurs at every Labor Day party if you fail to cure their cherished pet.

Only the pets of other vets garner greater reverence and generate greater consternation because, despite all logic and rationality, regardless of how simple and benign the animal's problem, if ever a case is going to "shit the bed," this is it. I remember being asked by a colleague to remove a simple skin lump from the front of her beagle's paw. She was in a rush, traveling home to see her family in the Midwest for a few weeks and did not want it to wait until she returned. I was happy to help her out. I performed the surgery and bandaged the dog's paw. I warned her that the skin closure had been tight, that she should change the bandage frequently to assess the hidden toes for swelling, discomfort, and quality of blood supply. She said she would and the two set out on their road trip.

Some weeks later I passed her in a hallway. She would have kept going had I not stopped her to ask how her beagle's wound had healed.

"Not so good," she said. "We had to amputate the leg."

While I was breathing in a vacuum, straining to listen over the pulse pounding in my ears, she explained in words soaked in remorse and barren of blame, of how the drive had taken longer than she expected, how she had not changed the bandage and not inspected the foot until it was too late.

As it turned out her dog did great on three legs and my surgery had only been a temporary reprieve for a tumor that could not have been completely removed without an amputation. Even so, I should have read the warning label that comes with any pet belonging to a veterinarian.

"So how long have you noticed that something was not right with his back legs?" I ask Mrs. Stonewall.

"About six months," she says, her words sailing over my head as her husband tosses her a "What have you been smoking?" expression magnified perfectly in his myopic glasses.

"More like closer to a year," says Mr. Stonewall.

She ripostes with an "I'll deal with you later" glare that lands under his chin and neither of them see the devil dancing in my eyes as I anticipate a little "he said, she said" banter.

Thanks to my experiences at the Immigration and Naturalization Service during my application for a green card, I am well versed in the art of extracting information in a hostile environment. Which side of the bed does your wife sleep on? What color is her toothbrush? Does she prefer coffee or tea in the morning? With only minor revisions in technique, I have learned to unmask the truth during a veterinary interrogation.

"Does he have difficulty with stairs?"

"Yes" and "No" at the same time. I let them fight out the answer. Yes with the flight of stairs in the house, no with the three steps out to the yard.

"Does he ever act drunk?"

I watch Mr. Stonewall ponder this question, as if he might be asking himself if Jester gets salacious, loud, and prone to throwing up. He concludes yes as his wife decrees no.

I want to know if he seems clumsy or awkward on his back legs, tending to wipe out like a cartoon dog coming around a corner at high speed, scuffing his toes occasionally on hardwood or concrete.

Mr. Stonewall now sees what I mean and maintains his affirmation, this time reluctantly joined by his wife.

I invite them to apply the dog's leash so that I can observe Jester on a walk and a trot in the hallway before returning to the examination room.

"Just pop him up on the table," I quip. No one smiles except Jester. He is an intimidating animal, a real presence in the small room, but his behavior is impeccable. Truly a gentle giant, Jester tolerates me as he would a child kneading, prodding, and stretching his body as if it were made of Play-Doh. He remains above it all, regal, palpably aloof and oblivious to the faltering sensation and reflexes in his hind legs.

I return to my seat and think about my next move. I cannot be certain, not without further diagnostic tests, but the suspicion of a congenital, anatomical narrowing of the spinal canal in the neck, a condition aptly titled wobbler's disease, would appear to be well founded. My money remains with the original diagnosis and I know this is not what Mom wants to hear. I also know that somewhere in that pile of paper data by her side there will be a treatise on the subject of wobbler's disease because it is a well-recognized condition among Great Danes and she will have been nothing but thorough in her research. I wish as much as she does that Jester's signs and history led me to a different conclusion, but from what I have learned so far, the unhappy truth appears to be unmistakable. I must tread carefully. The interrogation phase of the proceedings has passed. Now I must address my jury of two. I cannot blame Mrs. Stonewall for clinging to hope, preferring the role of Mrs. Denial over Mrs. Defeated. And, from our conversation, I suspect her husband is already Mr. Resignation. But I have to focus on young Jester, on his future, and despite the limited options and tough choices, try to make it as bright as it can be. I must deliver a closing argument that is an honest, sympathetic, yet convincing summation of the evidence, leaving little doubt that, unfortunately, the "Emperor is naked."

"There is some decreased extension in both hips," I say, "but Jester shows no sign of hip pain. I'm sure you noticed me turning over his back paws, how he seemed unconcerned about putting his weight on the skin on top and not the pads. And then when I put paper under his feet and pulled the paper to the side he was happy to splay like Bambi on ice. Both these findings are abnormal. They demonstrate Jester's conscious lack of appreciation of where his feet are in time and space. This makes him sway, wipe out, and generally appear uncoordinated on his back legs."

"But you just said his hip movement was restricted. Won't hip dysplasia make him weak and clumsy?"

I guess my equivalent of the O. J. Simpson leather glove demonstration had proved less than persuasive.

"It can, but in my experience, it would usually be accompanied by significant muscle wasting and weakness. I still get the impression that Jester is pretty buff in his back legs."

Mrs. Stonewall is silent, watching that invisible hummingbird flit between my forehead and her husband. I have no idea what she is thinking.

"Given his history," I say, "and everything I see today, my primary concern is that Jester has a neurological condition affecting his back legs. There are many possible underlying causes, but a condition called wobbler's disease requires special consideration. My next suggestion would be to get the opinion of a veterinary neurology specialist and most likely follow up with a spinal MRI."

Either the hummingbird crapped on or is nesting on my head because Mrs. Stonewall's eyes fix on this point as she declares, "The MRI was normal, at least according to my sister, who is a human neurologist."

For the second it takes Mrs. Stonewall to find the appropriate photocopies from her pile, I wonder if I have heard her correctly. Did she just tell me Jester has already had an MRI?

I take the four stapled sheets from her and read. It is all there.

The MRI report details changes in the sixth and seventh cervical vertebrae, bony and soft tissue thickening, pinching the delicate tissue of the spinal cord it is designed to protect. But what astounds me lies beyond the accompanying report from a veterinary neurologist stating her diagnosis of Jester's condition as wobbler's disease. It is the string of numbers in the top left-hand corner of each sheet revealing both reports were written over six months ago. Even with the Emperor stripped of all clothing, it would appear the truth remains unacceptable.

I keep my head down to buy a little time. Given the choice, if this were my dog, I would prefer hip dysplasia over wobbler's. Medical and surgical options carry a better prognosis for hips than necks and I have to assume that no one knows this better than Mrs. Stonewall. Her sister may be a fine neurologist, but there are significant distinctions between a neck that sticks out horizontally rather than straight up and down. Today, based on the earlier description in my hand, Jester is significantly worse. For the dog's sake, we need to start addressing his disease before it is too late.

"If I may, why don't I suggest that one of our radiology specialists look at the MRI study, to offer you an unbiased, independent opinion. We could always get an X-ray of the hips, just to be sure."

I brace myself to receive another report, but nothing happens.

Mr. Stonewall nods his approval.

"That sounds like a plan," he says, but his wife is standing.

"Yes, but I'd like to think about it first," she says.

Mr. Stonewall looks surprised, but he and Jester take their cue and get to their collective six feet.

Jester may be clumsy, but he can still get excited by an open door and a waiting room full of creatures guaranteed to be smaller than him.

Mr. Stonewall and I exchange the briefest of handshakes as he is yanked from the room by Jester. Mrs. Stonewall is not far behind.

She doesn't say another word, but to my surprise she finds a focal point smack-dab in the center of my eyes.

It's more than staring in; it's looking through, piercing and out the far side, hummingbird into hawk. It leaves me with something to feel more than something to see. Disappointment. Frustration. Heartbreak. It's hard to tell. I want to let her know that it is okay to be afraid, to allow this fresh reality time to sink in, to give me a call in a few days to talk it over some more. But she's gone and I'm left with an empty, lasting impression that I will not see any of them again. Once more the Stonewall family trial has ended in a hung jury.

I can only hope that young Jester will get another day in court.

5

· · · · · · · · · ·

9:12 A.M.

LONG SHOTS AND UNDERDOGS

White teeth and bright pink gums snap at my knees, the sharp bark cracking deep inside my head, an audible thrust and parry ordering me to back off as I open my examination room door. "No, Barron!"

The order comes from Dr. Melissa Payne and is largely ignored by the imposing German shepherd on the other end of her leash. Dr. Payne is another intern, tall and lean, apparently choosing a maximal stress diet as opposed to irregular meals of fast food. She has lived a previous life as a corporate accountant, trading her Donna Karan suit and Manolo Blahniks for stiff, freshly laundered scrubs and lemon yellow Crocs. At thirty-seven years old, with the premature infusion of gray in her "soccer mom" haircut and a blatant disregard for makeup, she stands out as the oldest of the fourteen members of her class (eleven women, three men) by about a decade. She is married but her husband lives and works in D.C. He is lonely, understanding, and supportive and determined to pick away at their combined college debt of over $120,000. They get to see each other about once a month. To her peers, she may look more like a mother than an older sibling, but it is obvious from the number of gifts and thank-you letters she receives that her maturity is embraced by her patients and their parents.

"I'm sorry, he's just mouthy," she explains, and as I wonder if she means mouthy like a cantankerous teenager or mouthy like a grizzly bear, Barron has moved on to sniffing, panting, and generally checking out the scene. He's acting like he'd rather pee on me than eat me.

I see the record for my next case sitting in a transparent plastic holder outside the door to my room, but before I can grab it, I sense that Barron is not simply passing through.

"I know you're on appointments, but I could do with some help."

I stare at her, noting the weary gray circles stamped under her eyes, an unkempt strand of hair curling around her right ear. Maintaining my best deadpan, cynical expression, I have a second to appreciate that Dr. Payne would not be bugging me if she were not really desperate, a second to capitulate, and a second in which to create a little tension as she wonders which way I am going to go.

She tries to close the deal.

"The owners were meant to drop off at eight, so I could catch a surgeon before they got trapped in surgery. They showed up five minutes ago. You're the only one who's not in sterile gloves and a paper mask."

I consider feigning disapproval as the doctor of last resort.

"I assume this concerns the creature currently sniffing at my crotch."

She apologizes and yanks Barron back.

"Tell me what you've got."

She lights up and thanks me. I smile. The reserved posturing was worth it.

"Let me introduce Barron," she says. "He is a two-year-old, castrated male GSD."

I consider the name. Slightly less predictable than the all-out Germanic Claus, Dieter, or Fritz, but only just.

"The husband claims the dog was absolutely fine up until a week ago when Barron went out to play with his kids on a pond near their backyard. Naturally this time of year the pond is all ice. The dog was chasing a tennis ball and ended up performing some kind of backward somersault. The kids said he landed awkwardly and cried in pain. They brought him home and, according to their dad, Barron hasn't walked the same since."

"What's wrong with the way he walks?"

Her wry smile almost begs me to close my eyes first as she follows Barron down the corridor like she's trailing a cigarette boat on water skis. It doesn't take long for me to appreciate the dog's unique gait and now, transfixed by this bizarre visual, both doctor and patient have piqued my curiosity and merited my full attention.

People talk about dogs with bad hips "bunny hopping" as they walk. Barron has taken this to a whole different, practically antipodean level. The dog is morphing into a kangaroo. He's not dropped or broken down on his hocks like a rabbit but his knees are flexed and his thighs appear taut, coiled, and springy. I've never seen anything quite like it before.

"And this is totally new since the incident on the pond?" I shout as she makes the turn and heads back.

"According to the husband," she says. "I've yet to speak to his wife, but the guy says Barron gets excited when he goes to the vet but at home he's pretty mellow. After the flip on the ice he went to his local vet and had his spine X-rayed. His doctor suspects the dog has a spinal injury and suggested he come here for a workup. Radiology have looked at the films but they can't be sure. There might be some disk-space narrowing. There could be a subtle dislocation of the spine, but they're reluctant to call it either way. I guess what they are saying is black and white isn't always black and white."

Barron is wired, firing on all senses as we stand next to the waiting room. It's like he's scanning the crowd for potential assassins as part of a Secret Service detail. He lets me feel along his spine making his skin twitch and ripple, but there is no obvious sensitivity or pain. The same is true of his back legs although I notice he lacks muscle mass and tone.

"So he's here for a workup?"

"That's right," says Dr. Payne. "I've booked him in for a full day of whatever you think needs to be done."

She makes it sound like a day of indulgence at a spa.

For a moment I consider Barron. Clearly the answer to his mysterious malady will not be found with a simple laying-on of hands.

"Are we on a budget?"

She shrugs.

"The husband says he wants an answer but he would prefer not filing for personal bankruptcy or taking out a second mortgage."

I stifle a smile. Unwittingly, Dr. Payne has defined two of the major challenges facing every veterinarian—diagnosis in an uncommunicative patient and the price to be paid for this revelation.

Let's be honest, many human doctors regard veterinary medicine as crude, plodding, and nebulous. Why? Well, two seemingly interchangeable words, *symptoms* and *signs,* provide much of the answer. A symptom is any sensation or change in bodily function that is experienced by a patient and is associated with a particular disease. By definition a symptom is communicated directly to a doctor. A sign is something that suggests the presence or existence of a fact, condition, or quality. A sign is a clinical finding we touch, hear, see, smell, and occasionally, inadvertently, taste. This distinction may not sound like much, but it is everything. The inability to communicate the presence of mild abdominal discomfort, to convey an appreciation of a twinge in my right elbow if I play a fifth set of tennis, makes all the difference. Animal disease is obliged to thrive and prosper, unchecked, so that it may become grossly visible, palpable, malodorous and offensive, audible or debilitating to a sufficient degree that we finally realize something is not quite right. Veterinarians spend their professional lives interpreting the language of animal signs, denied the luxury of plain, unambiguous communication.

Pediatricians may encounter similar problems with young children. Parents, like pet owners, undergo a barrage of questions that will allow the clinician to focus on a specific part of the body to be examined or palpated for discomfort or aberration. Answers generate more questions, disparities, and interpretations to be carefully weighed as the doctor runs through a mental flowchart fraught with intersections and decisions. Eyewitness testimony and credibility must be challenged, even when it comes from loved ones with the very best of intentions.

If we are lucky our senses will discover a tangible peculiarity. But so often with pets, their stoicism and desire to respond positively to our touch silences all the squeaks, grunts, and moans we want to elicit. In fact, it is amazing how well the majority of animals behave in our communal, and potentially hostile, hospital environment. They may play Freddy Krueger with the leather interior of your vehicle when they remember a specific left-hand turn three blocks from the hospital, or hide behind ascetic hospital furniture convinced that if they can't see you, you can't see them. They may howl or hiss at the evildoer in the white coat or defy the laws of gravity from within an upside-down smooth-sided cat carrier, but on the whole, with a calm approach, gentle tones, and a reassuring touch, most fractious animals will allow you to examine them. And what a treat it would be to simply step right up, demand your patient "open wide and say aaah," and nonchalantly crank on their lower jaw to inspect the back of their throat. How wonderful to insist "deep breaths only, please" or "just go ahead and drop your pants, I'll be right with you"!

Consequently, constrained by our abilities to read the signs, we may be forced to reach for the equivalent of a diagnostic sawed-off shotgun, rather than a single bullet from a sniper's rifle. We may appreciate that a problem lies in the front leg, but is it the elbow or the shoulder? Will we be forced to X-ray both joints? And will the patient pose for our radiographic pleasure or will the addition of chemical restraint be necessary? Suddenly a simple problem is proving difficult and costly to define. The average Angell client will part with $300 for veterinary services rendered, and this is trifling when compared to the cost of some of the big-ticket items. For example, hip-replacement surgery will run around $5,000, a cardiac pacemaker $3,500 to $4,500, a spinal MRI $2,000, a CT scan $1,000, a course of radiation treatment $3,000 to $4,000, and your average course of chemotherapy will cost $3,500. Right now, even poor Sage's bill is closing in on $4,000!

Veterinarians are constantly aware of fiscal restraints and accountability, and this demands a logical, methodical, and deductive approach to problem solving. There must be substantial gains from every test, whether the result is positive or negative. Every action will suffer scrutiny and must be justified for the owner, who will feel the financial impact of every test. Better our approach be more considered and less cavalier, more Sherlock Holmes and less an episode of *House*.

Regardless of our sensitivity, there remains something fundamentally repugnant and insensitive about the merger of money and animal health care, and to my way of thinking, part of the problem lies in the disparity of monetary perception between visiting my doctor and visiting my vet. Let's say I go for my annual health check. A technician takes my vitals, the doctor drifts in, we chat briefly, he listens to my chest, kneads my belly, makes a clumsy joke as he fumbles for a rubber glove, another technician takes a blood sample, and I am done, whisked away to the reception desk, where I must pay. My plastic health insurance card briefly flutters from my wallet, I part with a copayment of ten dollars, and I'm on my way. For the price of a couple of high-end lattes I get to know that I need to eat better, exercise more, and my prostate still hasn't turned into a watermelon. Employer contributions and payroll deductions could not be further from my mind because the physical effect on my wallet is marginal and painless.

Unless we lack insurance, few of us review itemized statements from our health-care visits. If we did we might be surprised by the minutia and weight of every moment and every action taken. Patients have been billed for items as minor as an extra pillow or a box of tissues. Most of the time we don't notice if for no other reason than we don't have to.

Now, walk with me to the reception desk at your local veterinary hospital, with little Woolly, your lovable Labradoodle, in tow. He's had his annual checkup and booster shot, a blood test for heartworm, and you've been handed a supply of heartworm preventative medication to be given when the test results come back. When the bill slides across the counter, it feels like we're back at the service department of our car dealership. There are numbers all over the printout, surprisingly sizable figures with totals that have us reaching for a different type of plastic that doesn't make the moment feel "priceless" in the least. We have parted with a lot more than a round at our local Starbucks. The taste lingers and it isn't anywhere near good. We may bitch and moan about fixing our car, but in the end we accept it because we know we cannot live without it. Can we really equate mending and sustaining our pets with the cost of a new muffler?

For those of us blessed with medical insurance, when it comes to our own health, what needs to be done gets done. Not so in veterinary medicine. It's like human doctors and animal doctors both play hockey, but the MDs chose "ice" and we were left with "field." They are backed by big money and get to play in prime time with coverage on premium channels. We get no sponsors and are lucky to get a Sunday-morning time slot on the local cable access. The result is that owners can be forced to answer an unthinkable question: How much is my pet worth to me?

Consider the tale of a two-year-old black English Labrador called Callaghan. His parents, Kristin and Todd, are the kind of young, attractive, well-to-do couple you expect to find dressed in ball gown and black tie smiling back at you from the society pages of *Boston* magazine. Yet all was not well between them.

They had been on vacation. Naturally, Callaghan went along and, like so many members of his breed, demonstrated a certain gusto for eating, no matter how inert the object. One day, while on Todd's watch, the scrumptious allure of his own dog leash proved irresistible.

Todd felt awful, rebuked by Kristin for his negligence and pained to see Callaghan undergo surgery to remove the ensuing intestinal obstruction. But in Todd's world of glowing academic, financial, professional, and social success, Callaghan would bounce back, the oversight would be forgiven, and the relationship with Kristin would blossom into an announcement of engagement in the *Boston Globe*, the *New York Times*, and the *Harvard Crimson*. But Callaghan didn't bounce back. In fact, he got worse, much worse, his perforated guts leaking and struggling to heal, necessitating surgery after surgery after surgery.

There are few driving forces in life greater than the emotion of guilt, and, in veterinary medicine, guilt is often accompanied by an irrational indifference to money. ER vets will tell you about the husband who accidentally reverses his minivan over the family pet sleeping in the driveway. All objectivity concerning the realities of

cost—even with the uncertainty of outcome—disappears, procrasti-
nation abandoned, replaced in an instant by a need to act, to do
whatever needs to be done to make the pain of blame go away.

When I talked to Todd about dealing with the guilt of causing
Callaghan's dilemma and his blatant disregard for the cost of the
treatment and care, he was extraordinarily candid.

"Kristin and I were both working," he said. "We have MBAs, good
jobs, no children, and significant disposable income. Not that it was
just about being able to pay. Obviously, part of it came down to responsibility, that it was my fault for leaving the poor dog with something he shouldn't chew. And, to be honest, some of it was selfish
and egotistical, my own personal resolve never to give up. But at the
time a big part of it was proving to Kristin that this was what I was
all about, that I put the importance of a relationship, be it to a person or an animal, above money."

Some of us make a point of not gambling, period. Some of us can
contrive an imaginary financial boundary, perhaps a figure we can
afford to lose, a figure we may approach but never cross, and we
can quit, cold turkey, and just turn and walk away. Occasionally veterinary medicine can feel like a bad trip to Vegas with owners forced
to calculate the dollar amount of health care they can comfortably afford to spend. Discussions about a pet's diagnosis, treatment, and
prognosis can begin to feel a bit like an insurance adjuster examining a car wreck and deciding whether the automobile is worth fixing
or needs to be totaled. Worst of all are the cases in which the vet is
optimistic, encourages the owner to make a commitment, and despite a promising start, their luck changes. The odds begin to stack
up against them, but they can't stop gambling, costs spiraling out of
control, and the only way out is to get sucked further in, raising the
stakes even higher, upping the ante to double or nothing.

And this was where Kristin and Todd found themselves, Callaghan
hanging in there, determined to fight, but unable to turn the corner as

procedure after procedure failed to resolve his leaky guts. Five surgeries came and went, five rounds of high-stakes poker with a minimum bet of around five thousand dollars a pop when you figure in the surgery, the anesthesia, and all the intensive care.

"After the fifth procedure," said Todd, "we really thought it was all over. The doctor was very honest with us and said there was still a chance that one more surgery would fix the problem but it could just as easily go the other way. I remember, so clearly, Kristin and I sitting on a bench outside the hospital entrance. We had decided we couldn't do this anymore. We couldn't see Callaghan continue to suffer. We had decided to have him put to sleep and we were taking a breather outside while a room was being set up for us to say our last good-bye. We were sitting on opposite ends of the bench, balling our eyes out, and this ten-wheeler construction truck pulls up and this enormous guy jumps down from the cab, walks straight over to me, gently places a hand on my shoulder, and almost whispers, 'Is it a dog or a cat'? He's all grubby and sweaty but he squeezes in between us on the bench and listens intently to the story of Callaghan, of everything he means to us, of everything he'd been through and how we really didn't care about the money but that it was time to call it a day. And he was so attentive, so softly spoken, it was almost surreal when he said, 'You have to keep going. You have to give him one more chance.' Kristin and I looked at each other and it was as if there was nothing further to debate. We had been told what to do. We went back into the hospital, informed the doctor that we wanted to try one last surgery, and Callaghan went on to make a full recovery. Ronnie, the truck driver, was nothing less than an angel, a talisman. I took his phone number that day and I've spoken to him on several occasions to let him know what happened."

All told, Todd reported that he spent close to $35,000 in medical bills but he was quick to point out that there was nothing heroic in what he did.

"I look at Callaghan, and it was a no-brainer investment. Some people might say 'but he's a Land Rover, he's a subscription to a decent country club,' but in my mind there's no comparison. There is something tangible between us after what he went through and I know a lot of people are not going to get it, but when I get up in the morning and I wake him up from a deep sleep, take him out into the cold air and he is instantly smiling, wagging his tail, and thrilled to be with me, I'm in awe of still having him in my life. When it comes to Callaghan, like most dogs, there is no wrong side of the bed in the morning."

Cautiously, I asked about Kristin.

"No, I'm sorry to say we didn't stay together," he said, before adding, "but I am getting engaged to my new girlfriend this weekend—in fact, I've just bought her a diamond."

I offered my congratulations, all the while wondering where Callaghan stood in this love triangle. Was the fiancée comfortable sharing Todd with the male partner in his life?

Then Todd started chuckling on the other end of the phone.

"It's a nice ring, but then again, *it* only cost thirty-two thousand."

Wow, I thought, this must be quite the rock. But why tell me how much it was worth? I had wanted to know how much it cost to save Callaghan, what motivated him to go so far. I didn't need to hear the exorbitant amount he was prepared to lavish upon his wife to be. Or did I?

As Todd continued to laugh into the phone, I realized further clarification would not be necessary. He had made it pretty clear where Callaghan stood in this new relationship.

So, is pet health insurance the key to future happiness on both sides of the examination table? Will pet insurance buffer the cost of an unexpected vet bill? Will it liberate the pet owner to choose the best treatment for their pet and not simply the treatment they can afford?

Well, if I'm to believe the hype, the answer, at least in the United Kingdom, is decidedly yes. Incredibly, pet insurance is purchased by roughly 20 percent of British pet owners and in some of the more affluent areas that figure increases to 30 percent (only 1 to 3 percent of American pet owners opt for insurance). In fact, colleagues working in private referral facilities in England have told me that the majority of their clients carry insurance. This finding struck me as bizarre for a country with a nationalized health-care system. When I was a kid, I clearly remember running between parked cars into oncoming traffic, colliding with the hood of a zippy Morris Minor, and experiencing a brief lesson in flight. I was whisked off to the local hospital, treated (i.e., given a pat on the head, a Band-Aid, and a guarantee that I was "right as nine-pence"), discharged, and I know for a fact that no bills or money were ever exchanged between my parents and the hospital. Things may have changed now, but it was always my perception that the British had little interest in, or appreciation of, the cost of health care because, understandably, the question of ability to pay never came up. Yet here they are embracing insurance coverage for their pets!

Of course the reason for the disparities in the popularity and acceptance of pet insurance between countries is complex. *Consumer Reports* once summed up pet insurance as "a form of enforced savings that almost never covers the entire bill." Their conclusion was a savings account is a better option. American veterinarians may fear third-party coverage and the trappings of managed health care. It has also been suggested that United Kingdom veterinarians can sell policies directly to the pet owner, taking a small commission on policies sold, a practice that is illegal in the United States. But perhaps it is simply the absence of negative health-insurance experiences in Britain that has rendered them receptive to the benefits of insurance for their pets.

Personally, I have found the majority of pet owners utilizing insurance thrilled by the amount of money they have saved and re-lieved that they purchased the policy. As the veterinarian I feel as though I can step outside the triangle, leave the contractual relation-ship to the owner and the insurance company, and avoid the un-sightly red tape.

The fact is, a whopping 73 percent of pet owners are willing to go into debt, according to one study, to allow treatment for their pet, and sometimes it is impossible to tell whether an owner can really afford to save their animal or not. Consider the story of another couple, a blissfully excited engaged couple, Jodi and Jeff, and their beloved maid of honor—a flirtatious golden retriever named Winnie.

With only a few months to go before the big day, Winnie was not only hit by a car, sustaining significant chest trauma, but subse-quently dragged by said vehicle, hind legs splayed apart, asphalt shearing the soft tissues of her right knee and left ankle down to glistening tendon and pure white bone.

Distraught, Jodi and Jeff, both just out of college, never hesitated to okay whatever it took to save their dog, and so, after a couple of anxious days following blood transfusions, evacuation of free air in Winnie's chest, and resolution of her lung contusions, I announced that it was time to get more aggressive about treating the wounds on her legs.

"Now that she's stable," I said, "I'd like to begin daily wet-to-dry dressings." I went on to explain that to rid her road rash of all the con-taminating grit, dirt, and hair, we would apply moist sterile-gauze dressings containing dilute antiseptic solution that when dry could be removed to physically debride the damaged tissues. I thought about the analogy of a man getting his hairy back waxed but decided against it.

"It sounds like she'll need general anesthesia," said Jodi, pleased by the report of clinical improvement but fearful to push too hard too soon.

"Yes," I said, "definitely for the first couple of times, but in a few days we should have a healthy bed of pink granulation tissue and by then we'll probably only need a sedative. Given her easy temperament I imagine it won't be long before she's fine with nothing at all."

There was a silence she wanted to make sure I heard.

"You're certain her lungs can take the anesthesia?" she asked, but what I really heard was, "Can I trust you?"

"Of course," I said, in answer to both questions. "Her chest X-rays look good. Her lungs should be fine."

And this is exactly what came to pass. The X-rays spoke the truth and Winnie's lungs were fine. She did great under her first general anesthesia and her recovery was smooth. Her life was never in jeopardy, unless, of course, you consider the fire that threatened to ravage the hospital later that day.

I happened to be with an appointment in an examination room at the front of the hospital when the alarm bells sounded. Normally people file out of the building with that blasé "must be a fire drill" look, enjoying the novelty of being ordered to step out into the sunlight of a beautiful day. Only this alarm came with the sensory bonus of a murky haze creeping down corridors and the bitter, oily smell of genuine smoke.

Most clients stood around the front parking lot hoping their vet might be willing to finish the physical examination outside. I excused myself to the rear of the building only to find smoke thick and billowing from a second-story window above the animal shelter and all manner of sick pets being led, pushed, carried, and lifted onto a large patch of grass near the back doors. I remember thinking how strange it was to see so many dogs hooked up to bags of intravenous fluids, sitting quietly and comfortably on blankets or gurneys, unconstrained by runs or cages, trading fluorescence for something that physically warmed the skin. It seemed surreally unifying, people evacuating sick animals in an orderly and calm manner as if they did this sort of thing every day. Instead of walking into the chaos of a war-torn MASH unit, I felt as if I had stambled upon a picnic in the park. It even smelled as if someone had fired up the grill.

The Fire Department appeared just ahead of the first local TV crew, and it wasn't long before photographers were scrambling for the still that would say it all the next morning.

I believe I had three cases in the hospital, and after accounting for two, I spent an anxious couple of minutes hunting for Winnie like a lost lover on a crowded train-station platform. What hindered our reunion was a transparent mask hooked up to a portable green oxygen canister, disguising my patient's characteristic snout.

"Is she okay?" I asked the technician who held the mask in place, noting how Winnie's long pink tongue licked the inside as if she were getting into the depths of an ice cream cone. "Did she inhale some of the smoke?"

I whipped out my stethoscope, kneeled down, and listened to her lungs. She sounded fine.

"Not that I know," said the technician. "Someone said she had come from Critical Care and that she might need oxygen. The tank was right here so I figured why not?"

I turned off the valve delivering the invisible gas.

"You can take the mask off her. It's really not necessary," I said, and free to sniff fresh air instead of rubber and plastic, Winnie appeared to thank me with a big grin.

It turned out that the fire was electrical in nature, caused by some ancient wiring in a storage area of the building. No animals were injured or affected by smoke inhalation, and by the end of the day, aside from the acrid smell of smoke, the incident was all but forgotten, until I spoke to Jodi the following morning.

"I thought you said Winnie's lungs were fine," she said, more disappointed than outraged.

"They were," I said. "They are. Why do you ask?"

"Have you seen this morning's papers? Page B one of the City & Region section of the *Boston Globe* and page five, Section B of the *Boston Herald.* There's a big picture of Winnie sucking on an oxygen mask as if her life depended on it."

It turned out that several photographers had spotted Jodi's photogenic and malleable pet, convincing the technician that together they might better capture a dramatic moment by accessorizing with an oxygen mask. Once Jodi understood that Winnie had only ever been at risk of media manipulation, she confessed that she had secretly enjoyed her dog's moment in the limelight.

I bumped into Jodi about a year later. She was picking up Winnie's heartworm medication while the dignitary herself, now a single-name hospital superstar, reveled in all the recognition, dog treats, and vigorous back scratches from an entourage of technicians and doctors she had met along the road to her full recovery. We got to talking and what I discovered absolutely amazed me. As a wedding gift, she and Jeff had received some thirteen thousand dollars to help them begin their new life together. And after all the intensive care, the weeks of wound management, and the numerous reconstructive surgeries, the money had vanished almost down to the last cent.

"You know what?" said Jodi, taking enormous maternal pride in watching Winnie prance around on strong, normal back legs as devotees cooed and played with her, "it was easy come and easy go. Jeff and I would do it over in a heartbeat. I can't tell you what it meant to have her walk down the aisle in front of us, wearing a pink ribbon around her neck that held our two gold wedding bands."

I smiled, humbled by her trust and the devotion to her dog.

"Besides," she added, "even after the accident and all the surgery, she's still got better legs than me!"

But let us return to the intriguing case of Barron, whose pricked ears are currently sweeping the waiting room for anomalous behavior, settling on a male cat owner squeezed between a baying beagle and a snapping schnauzer. The man looks as if he would dearly love to get both dogs together for a moment of blissful obstructive ingestion that might prove fatal to both parties. But it is the creature at the man's feet, the terrified cat feverishly scratching an air hole in his cardboard carrier into a possible escape route that has Barron eager to assist, yanking on his leash and prepared to dislocate poor Dr. Payne's shoulder in the process.

I am still debating how best to uncover the mystery of Barron's singular hind leg gait.

"Nothing about him fits with hip dysplasia," I say, "but I know I'd feel a whole lot better if we had an X-ray of his pelvis, just to make sure. And I hate repeating tests, but I think we should do our own high-detail spinal series. I suspect this whole trauma incident either exacerbated a pre-existing condition, or . . ."

I hesitate, recognizing the way my memory has kicked in, taking me by the elbow, flashing me a wink, a warning that says beware the owner who is joining the dots for you and making you appreciate an interpretation of a picture they *think* they can see.

Dr. Payne stares at me, perturbed, as though I've lost it, giving me the bulging eyeballs she might reserve for the dodgy midnight client who acts like he's taken one puff too many on his crack pipe.

"*Or* . . ." she says, stressing the verbal nudge.

"Or . . . the whole icy-pond incident is nothing more than a trap."

We lock eyes and I let my chin drift up and away for dramatic effect.

"In fact," I say, "it might be a complete red herring."

Her look is dubious verging on pitying, concerned that she is seeking clinical input from a detective in a Lifetime movie of the week. She finally attends to that stray lock of hair over her ear and I notice two empty holes in the lobes, which have forgotten the feel of fine jewelry.

"Do we have any current blood work?" I ask.

Dr. Payne checks her scribbled notes from the clipboard she carries squeezed under an armpit. It is her portable command center, listing all the in-hospital cases she must cover, their diagnostic and treatment plans, her need to call owners, her need to write orders and discharge instructions.

"Just a negative test for Lyme disease," she says.

In New England, it usually pays to rule out this troublesome tick-borne illness.

"Good, then I think we also need to run a full CBC profile and a UA."

"Already done. I also requested a thyroid panel to rule out a bizarre presentation for a hypothyroid neuropathy."

Dr. Payne may be succumbing to the allure of the rare diagnosis, but clearly she has been hitting the books in her nonexistent spare time. I give her a wooden nod and an "Okay," stretching the syllables sufficiently to let her know I think it is unlikely that hormonal imbalances are turning Barron into a marsupial, but I like the fact that she is committed and thorough.

"You think his owners will be up for all this?" I ask.

Something vacillates in her eyes, perhaps the fact that she is the doctor coordinating this case, the one running the show, the one responsible for any reckless squandering of funds. It will be her name the owners remember if all their money fails to translate into a diagnostic result.

"I'll let them know the plan, just in case," she says.

"Good," I say, "and be sure to document your conversation in the record."

I have absolutely no reason to suppose Barron's parents will be anything other than willing and cooperative as we carry out our tests, but it is always good policy to document all communication with our clients. No matter how good your rapport with an owner, it pays to remember—"If you don't write it down, it never happened!"

Barron has finally lost it. He's caught a glimpse of Jester the Great Dane sidling through the automatic front doors and the two have exchanged rival gang signs, Barron's bark exploding like a starter's gun, feet scrambling for traction on the polished floor, desperate to get a piece of him. It is all Dr. Payne can do to hold him back, needing two hands, ignoring her clipboard as it crashes to the floor.

I pick it up and hand it over when Barron loses sight of and interest in his quarry.

"As ever, Dr. Payne, you seem to have everything under control. When the results come back, find me and we'll go from there. Sound like a plan?"

She nods and purses a smile with pale, cracked lips, a smile that's difficult to read. It's like a cocktail—a splash of satisfaction overwhelmed by the flavor of anxiety, like a customer informing a bank teller she's looking particularly attractive and can she please hand over all the cash.

She says, "So you really think we can work out what's wrong with Barron?"

Her question forces me to make a translation. I think she's saying she's glad to have an experienced clinician guiding this case along but she's really worried about the mounting costs and the challenge of the diagnosis. She's saying this is only one of maybe a dozen patients in the hospital that she's covering today, that she's feeling the pressure of her significant caseload, and granted, not all of them are this confusing but sometimes she really wishes she didn't have to juggle her role as both clinician and personal accountant.

Then again, she might simply be wincing with numbing shoulder pain from Barron's unremitting game of tug-of-war.

I pick up the record for my next patient, but before I head into the waiting room I say, "Someone once said, 'the more bizarre a thing is, the less mysterious it proves to be.' "

"Who?" she says.

"Sherlock Holmes."

Her appreciative nod tells me she is seeing the bigger picture.

"But did he mention it sure does cost a whole lot more to find out?"

And sadly, I think to myself, she is absolutely right.

6

. . . .

9:21 A.M.

KISS OF DEATH

You know that feeling when you step inside an airplane and there's a solitary kid screaming his head off somewhere near the toilet in the way back? Right then, with absolute certainty, you can guarantee he's going to be seated in 27B because you're holding the boarding pass for 27A. Well, that is exactly how I feel as I step into the waiting room and call for my nine o'clock appointment.

"I'm warning you, Brian, you blow your nose right now or I'll blow it for you." The request hails from a flushed young woman juggling a screaming infant in one arm, a toddler in a baby carriage who appears oblivious, unconscious, or hearing impaired, and the defiant young Brian, whose tongue licks the candle wax dripping from his nostrils.

Although Woody Flynn, a geriatric black Labrador, responds when I call his name, he appears too weak to get up off the floor where he has flopped down. So I find a towel, pass it under and around his belly like a sling, and help him to his feet. With the Flynn clan in tow, Woody and I sashay back to my examination room like a couple of old drunks.

"This is Woody," Brian Flynn shouts, wiping vestigial mucus on his dog's head. "And these are my brothers. Billy's the stupid baby," his eyes look to the child his mother has pacified with a bottle of milk, "and this is Bobby." Brian pokes a porky little finger in his younger brother's nose just as his mother jerks him away by the arm and orders him to sit still and be quiet. To both her and my relief, Bobby sleeps on.

"I'm sorry we're late," says Mrs. Flynn, "the directions were horrible and traffic was such a nightmare and . . ."

I wave her apology away.

"Please," I say, "my sister has four kids under the age of six. I know what a handful they can be."

"Five," says Brian, looking indignant. "I'm not six I'm five."

Mrs. Flynn lets rip with a well-rehearsed Medusa glare and Brian sits back down, pulls out his Game Boy, and begins destroying aliens or monsters or innocent bystanders.

"So, what's going on with old Woody?" I ask, dipping down to the cool tile floor on which Woody has collapsed, patting a fat belly.

She is staring at her dog and I catch the distress in her eyes.

"I should probably have seen a vet a few weeks ago but what with the kids and everything I never got a chance. He's not been acting right for a while and last night he kind of fainted and passed out on the living room carpet. To be honest, I wasn't sure whether he'd still be with us this morning, but he ate a little when I fed him by hand, so I figured he can't be that bad."

Woody clearly believes that my New England dry winter skin is in need of significant salivary lubrication as I maneuver toward his head and look at the color of his lips. I keep my eyes down and apply my poker-face mask. His gums are pure alabaster white.

Gently I move my hand back over his abdomen. Woody's body is all sleepy and relaxed and I have no problem locating the miscreant. Right in the middle of his belly sits a large, softball-sized mass.

I look up at the Flynn family—Brian all concentration and dancing thumbs, Billy being burped on his tired mother's shoulder, and Bobby starting to stir and fuss, and I wonder what effect my news will have on this family. I can't be certain, but it is quite possible that the abnormal lump originates in the spleen, that it has ruptured and bled into Woody's abdomen, leaving him pale, anemic, and weak. I will suggest abdominal radiographs and ultrasound to confirm the origin and nature of the lesion. My hands are not microscopes. I want to be wrong, but most clinicians would be giving serious consideration to a tumor of the spleen called hemangiosarcoma, one of the most aggressive cancers veterinarians must face. Even after surgery and chemotherapy, average survival times for these dogs rarely exceed a couple of months. Would Mrs. Flynn want me to take Woody down that path, or was I about to face a family's painful farewell as I put their dog to sleep?

Pick up a glass of wine, mingle in a roomful of strangers, and before long someone will inquire about your occupation. The label "veterinarian" might not generate the same level of attention as, say, "secret agent" or "porn star," but revealing that I work with animals invariably ignites a superficial interest with one question, voiced in a variety of guises, proving particularly popular.

"I'd love to be a vet but I'd cry all day long. Don't you get sad when the animals die?"

And from those dubious about my surgical aptitude: "I don't know how you do your job. Putting all those animals to sleep every day."

In truth, as a surgeon, I am rarely called upon to end a pet's life. During my career I imagine that I have "put down" no more than a hundred animals (but still an uncomfortable figure to think about). Yet all veterinarians must learn to cope with animal death and the unique responsibility of performing euthanasia.

The word *euthanasia* is derived from the Greek words *eu,* meaning "good," and *thanatos,* meaning "death." This "good death" must be humane, with a minimum of pain and distress, but first and foremost it must be motivated by a determination to help the patient. It is this elemental requisite for mercy that distinguishes the act from killing, and as the enlightened Dr. Franklin McMillan, writing in the journal of the AVMA points out, "euthanasia is an act to end discomfort. Death is the unfortunate, unavoidable, and unintentional effect of achieving this goal."

Of course there are pet owners conflicted, for personal, religious, or ethical reasons, by the notion of euthanasia and by one of the fundamental tenets in all of medicine, which is, "first, do no harm." They reject an artificial termination of life preferring to seek the alleviation of pain and to provide supportive care for however long it takes to achieve a natural death. In some instances, I suppose, this approach may be tenable, but how many of us have seen family members suffer a lingering death, twisted and transformed into strangers we no longer recognize? Why do we aspire to living a fruitful life that ends with the ultimate death, the death of dying peacefully in our sleep? To me, when called to perform euthanasia on animals, I feel like I have the opportunity to provide a death that is everything it should be—a loss of consciousness and a loss of pain without the application of pain. Right or wrong, seeing an animal sustained beyond a point at which pain cannot be reasonably controlled, where organ systems fail, where secondary diseases thrive and infections run rampant, I begin to question the motives of the owner. I confess, sometimes I see futility, selfishness, and a blatant rejection of a fundamental responsibility to our pets as their caregiver. Sometimes nature can take its course and shove it. Our com-

mitment to protecting our cat or dog is life-long and sadly, sometimes, that includes protection from discomfort and pain, even if, in
the veterinarian's opinion, this means euthanasia.

Many of life's firsts stay with us as daunting, awkward, electrify-
ing, and enduring memories of who we are, and I would venture to
say that most veterinarians remember the time they had to put their
first patient "to sleep."

Mine came a few days after graduating from veterinary school. I
was in desperate need of money, so I offered to fill in for a veterinarian at a small rural practice that I had visited as a lowly student. The
owner was something of a deity in his community. Everyone knew
he was on vacation, everyone knew he had a rookie replacement,
and therefore everyone went somewhere else or did a fine job of
ignoring or putting off their animal's ailments until "the real vet" returned. Consequently the work was slow until one morning a thirty-
something woman wandered into the office, wailing into a black toy
poodle that she held in her arms.

"Peanut," she informed me, was twenty-two years old and she'd
had him her whole life. It is an impressive age for any dog but
longevity had reduced her pet to skin, bones, milky cataracts that followed you around the room, and a solitary black canine tooth jutting
from his upper lip at an improbable angle. Every time I moved in for
a closer inspection, Peanut proved he still retained a capacity for
gumming strangers to death.

Peanut had been on death row for many years, thanks to diabetes,
and his owner had done a fine job of commuting his sentence by affording him the best possible care. But now that he had stopped eating, wouldn't get up, and refused to drink, she knew in her heart
that the time had come to put him to sleep.

Now I know this should have been my cue to reassure her, to
purse my down-turned lips, narrow my eyes, and furrow my brow as
a mark of respect for her making this weighty, yet entirely appropri-

ate decision. Instead I stood paralyzed, watching the rivulets of blue-black mascara and eyeliner stream down her cheeks. I knew what needed to be done. I wanted to spare Peanut this lingering decay, but in that instant I was frightened, both by the physical mechanics and the emotional responsibility of the act. All I could see was an eight- or nine-year-old girl, playing with her new puppy, the one she got to choose for herself, the same dog who shared her pillow through high school, who whinnied with excitement when she came home from college, who detested her first boyfriend and barely tolerated the man that would become her husband. I knew none of this but I knew it all as this stranger broke down before my eyes, this fragile and sick little creature a silent and constant companion to the better part of her life. And now it fell to me to sever the bond and ensure that her best friend left her with as much dignity as I could muster.

Of course I could have played for time. I could have recommended that we run some blood test or other, take an X-ray, or have her come back another day when I would be long gone. But what struck me most as she stood before me, inconsolably crying and shaking, was her state of readiness. She had come to me feeling like the executioner's assistant, battling with the doubt, with the guilt that she might be taking the easy way out, but above all she had prepared herself for "right here and right now." Who was I to deny her this moment of grief?

These days, if I am ever asked to perform euthanasia, I begin by counseling the owners about what to expect if they have never witnessed death by lethal injection. My observations and these warnings were learned the hard way and alas, on this first occasion, I had nothing to offer Peanut's mom.

Please bear in mind that I had to work alone, without a technician to restrain the dog or to hold off a vein into which I could stick a needle. I was forced to use an owner hysterical with grief, clutching the creature tight and deep into her bosom, reluctant to relinquish the black twig that was her poodle's forelimb. Realize that my patient had not drunk fluids for two days, was utterly dehydrated, and had next to no blood pressure, making his veins virtually impossible to see or feel. And don't forget that as the owner sobbed, my target wavered as if we stood on the deck of a ship in high seas, a difficult shot for an experienced professional let alone a beginner, the stress of the entire proceeding doing little to improve the tremor in my hands.

Subsequently I have learned the wisdom of placing an intravenous catheter prior to the procedure, so that you can be assured of delivering the overdose of barbiturate directly into the bloodstream and thereby avoiding unnecessary stress and discomfort by both owner and patient. I have learned to draw up my drugs away from the owner. One client happened to notice the name of a euthanasia solution called Fatal Plus and demanded to know exactly what was more fatal than death. I also warn the owner when I flush the catheter with a saline solution prior to delivering the barbiturate, to assuage any fears that the lethal dose appeared to be inadequate or ineffective.

The barbiturates, at the concentration used in euthanasia solutions, work quickly and have several effects on the patient. Some animals will offer a deep and final sigh that can appear both belated and dramatic. Some may twitch, gasp, paddle their limbs, and evacuate their bladder or bowels. But consistently, and to the surprise of many, pets will not close their eyes in death. There can be no gracious "laying on" of hands, no gentle motion across the lids and that peaceful finality of the endless sleep we have all seen in the movies. For the most part, dogs and cats leave this world with their eyes open.

Even though there was no concealing my technical shortcomings, I feel like I was saved by a singular trait that shone through the whole tribulation. Honesty meant that I never hid my fear and I never hid my respect for what she was going through. Reassuring her and reassuring Peanut, notwithstanding the quiver as I spoke, seemed like the easy part. If only I had warned her about all the possible nuances I was yet to learn, including a final one little Peanut still had in store for me.

After driving home the plunger to my syringe and gently withdrawing the needle, I located a clean towel, drew it over the dog's chest and abdomen, and had the good sense to leave Peanut's mom alone for a few private minutes of contemplation with her old friend. When she felt ready to leave, she took my hand in both of her wet hands and thanked me, only intensifying the feeling that I had let her down, that the proceeding had been an ordeal, not a merciful and gentle good-bye. I had forgotten to have her sign any kind of consent form and fortunately I was still in too much of a state of shock to make the grievous error of demanding payment for my services at this time. She asked if I could arrange for a private cremation of Peanut's body and that she would be by later in the week to pick up the ashes. Only now as she left the room did I pull out my stethoscope to confirm that the dog was truly dead. To my utter surprise I could appreciate a slow, faintly audible, yet regular heartbeat. After all my efforts, after this woman had poured out her heart to this motionless corpse, her best friend was still only asleep; anesthetized and not euthanized.

What was I to do? Call her back and try to explain? Start over, this time for real? And what if Lazarus had blinked or sat up as she bid him farewell?

By the time I came to my senses, Peanut's mom was pulling out of the hospital parking lot.

I returned to my patient. Both veins on the front legs and both veins on the back legs were entirely blown, and with at least some of the barbiturate on board, the dog's blood pressure was virtually nothing. This left me little choice and no consolation. I took solace in the anesthetic effect of the drug. The best I could do for this fee-

ble companion after twenty-two years of life and dedicated unconditional loyalty to his mistress was to kill him properly, and painlessly,
with a small dose of barbiturate delivered directly into his heart.

Much has been written about coping with the loss of a companion
animal but little consideration has been given to the impact of death
on the person delivering the lethal injection.

Euthanasia based on the alleviation of animal pain and suffering
is not the only reason for termination of life. Consider the story of
an intern working her way through the list of walk-in emergencies
confronted by a yellow Labrador, who, based on his dazzling white
smile and frenetic tail-driven energy, had to be less than two, or else
he had found his way into a five-pound bag of coffee. The intern instantly connected with her patient. How could she have possibly re-
sisted? They chatted, traded firm noogies and deep scratchy butt
rubs for sloppy kisses of pleasure and all the while the man on the
other end of the dog's leash remained isolated from the fuss, detached and disinterested in their interaction.

Eventually the dog achieved some semblance of calm, watching
as the intern followed the red leash to an incongruous manicured
hand and black corduroy pants uncontaminated by even a single
strand of blond canine hair.

Without a word the man opened his jacket, pulled out an envelope, and offered it for the intern's consideration. The rehearsed for-
mality of the maneuver caught her off guard, inducing a nervous
smile that vanished as her eyes scanned down the lines of a nota-
rized document requesting the humane death of the perfectly
healthy animal sitting at her feet.

The intern looked up from the letter and studied the contradic-
tory strangers before her. These two did not, could not, and never
had belonged to each other. It turned out the dog was the much-
loved pet of the man's father, or should I say, late father, for the

rightful owner was now dead and gone. And, leaping from the legalese of his last will and testament was an instruction insisting that a veterinarian carry out his final request to euthanize his dog so that his canine companion could join him in heaven.

Fortunately this uncommon situation was respectfully resolved and the dog was placed in a new and loving home. But it could so easily have gone the other way. What emotional price must be paid for the euthanasia of abandoned shelter animals, of sick or injured animals whose owners cannot afford to pay for their medical care, of healthy animals with behavioral disorders or the near-term off-spring of pregnant females when they are spayed? According to Professor Richard Halliwell of the British Veterinary Association and former president of the Royal College of Veterinary Surgeons, some of the distress in putting animals to sleep may be responsible for the frightening statistic—and this both staggered and appalled me when I found out—that veterinarian suicide rates are nearly four times the national UK average. And before you go thinking that this problem is unique to the far side of the pond, consider the fact that peer-reviewed scientific articles have found a significantly increased risk for suicide in Californian veterinarians and in a ten-year period in Western Australia, one in five veterinarians who died did so by taking their own life.

Please, I am not trying to be a sensationalist and I realize that health-care professionals, doctors, dentists, nurses, and pharmacists are all at increased risk for suicide, but the proportional mortality rate, the observed death from suicide divided by the expected death from suicide expressed as a percentage, is highest for veterinarians.

It is not for me to speculate about whether the act of mercy killing plays a role, or simply the access to and familiarity of using pharmaceuticals that can ensure a quick and painless death, but what I will say is that we need to acknowledge that suicide is a problem so that we can better prepare the new generation of veterinarians with coping skills and reduce the stigma of seeking professional help during desperate times.

One thing I can say for certain, as one veterinarian succinctly put it, "We receive more thanks for killing pets than for curing them," though this thought could not have been further from my mind as I stand to face Mrs. Flynn and tell her of my concerns over Woody's abdominal mass.

"You can feel something," she says, more statement than question, never losing the rhythm of gentle back pats as she waits for Billy's burp.

"Yes," I say, instantly aware that my voice has changed, way ahead of my thoughts, setting the tone for what must come with soft, clear, and compassionate words as I share the findings of my physical examination. As I speak into the silent tension, something begins to permeate the room, an invisible and virulent contagion spreading between mother and offspring, the patting hand frozen flat across the baby's back, Bobby getting out of his stroller, headed for the trash can beneath the examination table, Brian looking up from his console, gaping, thumbs frozen—game over.

Mrs. Flynn lets the tears come now, apologizing, embarrassed, fumbling in a pocket for a tissue as the baby on her shoulder begins to wail. Meanwhile curious Bobby has discovered an abandoned canine toenail clipping and young Brian has lassoed Woody with his leash and decided he can save the family pet from my evil clutches by dragging him from the room by his neck.

I reach for a box of tissues as Mom reaches for her toddler son, stopping him from inserting the crunchy toenail into his mouth but unable to prevent the blow to the back of his head from the examination table as Bobby stands up. There is that fleeting moment of confusion in the little boy's eyes, the incredulity that his curiosity has led to this, those seconds when you think he might be able to suck it up, vulnerable to distraction and able to move on. But then the lips begin to quiver, air filling his lungs before purging an earsplitting howl of pain, and all the while poor Woody is being practically strangled by young Brian, Mom managing to snatch the leash away with enough force that a friction burn brings out the tears from the final pair of dry eyes in the Flynn family.

In this time of deliberation, heartache, and grief, the walls echo with the wail of tiny banshees, resistant to hugs, frightened by their mother's tears, and through it all, the luminary at the center of the quandary seems oblivious to the mayhem. Woody knows how much they love him, no less a brother than his two-legged counterparts, but he must feel old and tired and more than ready for sleep. His chin rests on his outstretched front paws, eyes closed, a body language that resonates in the chaos with dignity, contentment, and resignation.

I know that what remains will be difficult and draining, but all these years after a haunting rite of passage with a tiny black poodle named Peanut, I believe I can do a better job. I have tried to be impartial, unbiased in my assessment of Woody's condition, but Mrs. Flynn's reaction is not the one I expect when I am about to admit a patient for a diagnostic workup and possible surgery. We both share an unspoken knowledge that she knew it would come to this and that all along my role has been simply to confirm her suspicion and make the process of letting go bearable for her and her children. I make a mental note of the fourth finger of her left hand, the absence of a ring, a request for support from a family member or friend, as Brian begins his confused interrogation, irrational questions, shouts, screams crisscrossing between mother and sons, mother and me, verbal and emotional ping-pong at the thought of saying good-bye to the big man in the family for the last time. I do my best to comfort, reassure, approve her decision as she signs a piece of paper she never reads. She doesn't know what to do about Woody's body and suddenly the weight of this decision, its implications and finality, pulls her down and she flounders, a riptide of grief threatening to suck her out into a sea of loss and regret. It is another cue. I may not be David Hasselhoff (and you will never catch me in a red Speedo), but I'm agile with a flotation device and ready to perform the rescue, diving in with the easy stuff—empathy, reassurance, patience—guiding Mrs. Flynn through the maze of decisions and options as I pick up the phone and call down to the "ready room" for backup. A couple of technicians appear, doting on Woody, loving him up even as they wheel in a gurney, a clean blanket, and the necessary equipment to place an intravenous catheter. Their deference and professionalism visibly impacts Mrs. Flynn as I guide her and the boys back into the waiting room for a moment.

I tell her that it might be better if the boys wait outside while she and I return to the room to perform the deed, that one of the techs will be happy to wait with them before they join us to wish Woody a final farewell. My plan disturbs Brian and incites a tirade of questions concerning needles, pain, heaven, zombies, vampires, maggots, and worms. Struggling to keep him on track I ask him to tell me about some of the best things he likes about Woody and to my surprise he is suddenly lucid.

"Woody always brings you a present whenever you see him. Always."

Mom interjects that this is because he is a retriever, what he was born to do, a trait he could never and should never shake off. Brian ignores her interruption, already giggling.

"He picks up a chew toy, a sock, a slipper, mommy's bra (he shouts out this item and cranes his neck out in her direction for effect), anything so long as he can give you a present. Only last week I crept up on him in the backyard and he never saw me and when he did he looked all around for something to give me and there was nothing except one thing."

I ask to save him from bursting.

"A frozen dog turd."

I laugh out a deep breath of sadness. Somehow, even with this little boy and his inability to truly understand the concept of death, Woody has crept into his heart and managed to scratch a tiny indelible mark in his memory through a lifetime of generosity and friendship.

It is time for Mrs. Flynn and me to return to the room. Everything is prepared, every act is predictable, smooth, painless, and dignified as promised. I retrieve the Flynn boys and parade them in. None of them makes a sound, not a cry, not a word. Brian reluctantly pats Woody one last time only at his mother's request.

I whisper that she can take as much time as she needs but that when she is ready to leave, simply to head out, that we will forward the bill, my disagreeable charge for being an undertaker. She thanks me but they do not linger and I watch as the four of them cross the waiting room.

As they go, I allow myself a moment of weakness, hear the whispered second guess inside my head. Woody's life was leaking away but I was the one who stepped forward and pulled the plug. Was my timing right? Could he have had another day at home, another week? Could he have gone for one more turn around the park, had one last supper? We'll never know and to handle the reality of euthanasia I have learned to be comfortable with the ambiguity and magnitude of when to take a life. All I know for sure is at that irredeemable moment when I drive the plunger home, I will be there for the person trading the overpowering presence of love and companionship with their pet for the cold, empty ache of loss. Some vets cry with their owners and that's fine, but I never do. And believe me, at times, it's not that I don't want to. It's just that part of me feels like I owe it to the animal to be strong, to be supportive in their place, now that they are gone.

In a few seconds the Flynn family will be out of sight, but anyone who knows them can see the unnatural shift in their dynamic—baby on the hip, toddler in the carriage, Brian, in hand, walking by his Mom's side. Something is wrong with this new asymmetry. There is an empty space up front and center, conspicuous, like an empty chair with a place setting at a family dinner table. I am the one who upset their natural balance and I will accept this responsibility, file the mental picture of a happy healthier Woody in an imaginary folder, and move on.

I can't help but wonder whether young Brian will be able to admit that he misses Woody.

I wonder how long before he is asking for another dog to fill the void.

I wonder how long before he tells his friends, "Remember old Woody, my first dog?"

10:11 A.M.

DANGEROUS LIAISONS

Two separate pages inform me that my ten o'clock client has rescheduled for another date and my ten thirty is caught in traffic and running late, so, conscious of the subliminal impact of my encounter with Woody, I take the opportunity to swing by CCU and check on Sage.

At first I am excited to see her standing at the front of her run, but as I get closer, I notice how her weight is shifting from side to side, how she pitches forward and catches herself. A transparent tube delivering intravenous fluids disappears inside a fluorescent green bandage on her front leg. Color-coded sticky pads send out tendrils of electrical wire to a remote heart-monitoring device tied around her neck. A small paper bowl of water sits untouched next to her thick blue foam mattress on the floor. Seeing her in this state reminds me that there is something improbable and desperately sad about caring for a sick pet. Perhaps it is the flagrant juxtaposition of human health-care techniques with a domesticated animal trying to flout the evolutionary rules of fight, flight, or surrender to the pain and wait for death. It defies the logic of people without pets in their lives, people flummoxed by the validity and reward in caring for animals. So if I'm cornered, asked to put into words why it is I do what I do, I might try a different approach. I ask them to imagine a child walking into a classroom on their first day of elementary school, awkward, shy, prone to beet-red blushes and raindrop tears, alone, confused and, most of all, scared. And now imagine there's a kid in the class who's different from his peers, of, say, a different ethnicity, unable to communicate because he's unwilling or unable to speak the language and, for one second, just imagine how you might feel as a parent, hovering, unnoticed, invisible, watching as your child is the one taking that bold step forward, introducing himself, making a friend and helping a stranger in a strange place. In an instant you can see both sides of the equation, balanced, simple, free from criticism and cynicism, a child innocently trying to help, a child relieved and reassured, grateful to be connected by a smile, a touch. It is precisely this kind of feeling that I as a veterinarian am trying to rekindle in my working life, in a classroom striving for a connection and collaboration between two completely different species, discovering an instinctual behavior of reaching out and trying to help a frightened, sick animal with their unequivocal acceptance of your intention that can still, even now, even when I'm tired and at my most jaded, catch me off guard, spin my emotional compass, and make me proud and grateful to be doing what I do. Naturally, brandishing a bright and shiny needle can leave you on the sharp end of a verbal (and sometimes physical) complaint, but, for the most part, unlike human medicine, this exchange transpires in respectful silence, in a world of tacit clueless tolerance. It is this dependence on a different kind of language, the quintessential allure of an absence of words, an absence that, as they say, makes the heart grow fonder.

I open the gate to Sage's run, stroke her head, and she locks on me with her molten chocolate stare of uncanny endurance, understanding, and forgiveness. She is one of those gifted animals able to distill my intent from our alien encounter, to let me know it in her eyes, and yet she refuses to lie down. Sage watches as I leave the run and find her record, rifling through pages of hieroglyphics, searching for her most recent rectal temperature, and all the while I can see right through her to the burst staple line of her dead stomach.

102.4°F.

I remember to breathe. Her temperature is fine, perfectly consistent with a little postoperative inflammation. I'll allow myself to worry if we hit a toasty 103°F to 103.5°F.

"Do you have a moment?"

I recognize the voice, look up from the record, and see that Dr. Beth Maganiello has altered her hair style and color yet again. Today it is fashionably short and unnaturally black and I want to ask if it's all part of a new disguise after appearing on *America's Most Wanted* but behind her trademark pair of retro tortoiseshell glasses, I appreciate a pouty hardness that broadcasts a rare moment of frustration.

Beth is a critical-care specialist, permanently infused with a Red Bull work ethic that runs circles around her residents and interns and has her appearing in CCU unannounced in the middle of the night and on weekends just to see how things are going.

"Sure," I say, "what have you got?"

Our exchange follows a brief and familiar script and after years of working together we have our lines down pat. It epitomizes one of the greatest strengths of the hospital approach to modern animal health care—bartering knowledge between specialties for the benefit of the patient. There's no cost to the client and no paperwork generated as informal consults trade back and forth between clinicians like kids trading Halloween candy. My surgical training and skills have my plastic pumpkin swag bag overloaded with SweeTarts, and I am happy to let sticky-fingered sugar-cravers pilfer my stash, but, when I want the Almond Joy of pain control, I go find Dr. Maganiello.

Now the glasses are off and she's working the dent in the bridge of her nose with a finger and thumb, squinting, replacing the specs, and glancing over her shoulder at a dog run three doors down from Sage.

"I've just spent the better part of two hours talking to Mr. Ellis in run 33 about his thirteen-year-old ridgeback, Chipper."

"What's the problem?" I ask, and, as if on cue, she produces a set of X-rays. I hold them up to ceiling strips of fluorescent light and see the white bones of Chipper's spinal column imitating an aerial view of an Amtrak train wreck.

"Ouch! What's the neurological status?"

Dr. Maganiello shakes her head.

"Chipper went missing three days ago. He has absolutely nothing in his back legs. No motor function, no deep pain, nothing."

This is as bad as spinal injury gets—a fracture through the middle of the dog's back that has completely sliced through his spinal cord and the possibility that he has been like this for up to seventy-two hours.

"Believe me, I've tried explaining the severity of Chipper's problems, but emotionally Mr. Ellis refuses to budge from the denial phase. I don't think there's much to discuss. He says money's tight, he lives alone, works two jobs. What I need is a different approach. Someone new and objective."

I work the fresh stubble pooling in my dimpled chin. What she really means is someone tough, cold, and dissociated. Is my image in need of a makeover or what?

"Okay, here's the deal," I say. "I'll have a chat with your Mr. Ellis if you'll have a look at Sage. She's my GDV from last night. She seems really uncomfortable."

Dr. Maganiello smiles, pleased to be sealing the deal, but there's more to it, something coy, something she's holding back.

"What?" I say.

She takes the file out of my hand and begins to review the record.

"I just heard your GDV was far from routine, that's all."

Her tone is all wrong, almost flippant.

"Has someone been saying my decision to repair her stomach was inappropriate?"

I am shocked at how fast the words get away from me, their volume, how they make me sound defensive and uncertain. Have I been betrayed by Dan, the overnight technician, or worse still, my resident, Dr. Keene? It wouldn't have taken much, no more than a casual remark regarding the degree of damage to Sage's stomach, fated as watercooler gossip where oversights and screwups prove juicier and more durable than any stroke of clinical genius or miraculous intervention. Or was something said during morning surgical rounds at which Dr. Keene would have updated the other four surgical specialists on the team as to what transpired overnight?

Rounds are an essential, daily, bedside review of our in-hospital patients. They force us doctors to describe and defend our clinical actions. Criticism, constructive or otherwise, is encouraged. Common side effects include suppressed elation and abject humiliation. Whispered or inferred rivalries have an objective, open forum, in which, from time to time, gladiator egos can fight to the death. Occasionally rounds can get personal, ugly, and adrift, but, most of the time, they help to keep clinicians current, humble, honest, and forced to accept the reality of what we know and what we like to think we know, what we can actually do and what we like to think we can do. Based on Dr. Keene's morning update, I wonder if one of my colleagues has been undermining my decision to keep Sage alive?

I feel a discreet bead of sweat roll down the inside of my upper arm as I watch Dr. Maganiello's eyes, scanning the record, too focused, too robotic, and finally her furtive glance to check out my response brings the curtain down on her performance and she cracks up.

"Very funny," I say. "Did my angry rush to judgment give away the fact that I'm more than a little anxious about her?"

"I guess," she says, leaning on a counter to write her recommendations for Sage's new orders, "and the fact that you're moping around CCU, fretting about a surgical patient this early in the day. Go make yourself useful, speak to Chipper's dad for me and I'll sort out your tricky little GDV."

Amused and sufficiently reprimanded I head over to run 33 and the four shiny hazel eyes that stare up at me, equally silent and sad. Chipper lies on his side on a blue mattress, his gray muzzle resting in the lap of a big man in stained blue jeans, Patriots sweatshirt, and matching cap, stroking the dog's head with a calloused bear paw for a hand. His cheeks are pudgy and red. Some might suspect too many beers or sensitivity to the cold. I recognize the badge of tears that have dried stiff. No one is immune to the bond.

After introductions I squat down beside Mr. Ellis, pet his dog, and pull out the X-rays.

"Mr. Ellis, I need to show you Chipper's spine." I point to the displaced ends of the spinal bones, but I can tell that he isn't listening.

"Why don't you just snap them back into place?"

"I can do that," I say, "but that's not going to fix his spinal cord. He has no feeling, no nothing in his back legs. And there's really no chance that he ever will."

At this point Mr. Ellis's head recoils into his neck like a frightened turtle and he points at Chipper.

"D'ya see that? See him tryin' to move his legs?"

I follow his finger to the dog's flaccid back end, which lies motionless, a lifeless puppet without its master.

"I'm sorry, Mr. Ellis. I wish I could offer you something, but I can't. Chipper will never walk again, and in my opinion, paraplegia is no quality of life for a ninety-pound dog."

I notice how the frequency of head pats has become more frenetic.

"Even though he's been castrated d'ya think ya can get some sperms off of him?"

"Not possible," I say.

"What about some of them stem cells?"

I shake my head.

"What about cloning him?"

At this point I stand up.

"I'm really sorry. Chipper looks like a great dog. But right now I think he's miserable. I think it's time to put him out of his misery."

From nowhere anger flashes in Mr. Ellis's eyes and he pokes a finger in my direction. I notice the thick black band of oil and grease under the nail. The working man's French manicure.

"You're lying!" he shouts. "I don't believe you. I don't believe those are his X-rays. That can't be his spine. Not my Chipper. Look, see, he's trying to get up. Come on boy, let's go. Let's go for a walk."

Sometimes I am not the best judge of character. In fact, I would go so far as to say that I am exactly the sort of person behind an "I'd have never guessed my wife was a serial killer" sound bite or the total confusion at a high school reunion when my old friend Nigel turns up as Nigella. For this reason, even those people some might label as bizarre or extreme pet owners, exhibiting an obsessive and unhealthy attachment to their pet, usually strike me as being rational.

Okay, so I might be alarmed by the cat owner, described by a colleague, who elected to have her sick pet euthanized and stuffed by a taxidermist, only to return to the clinic several months later seeking a dermatological consultation for the dead animal's niggling skin disorder. But on the whole, what I see, with increasing frequency, are clients happy and proud to display the impact and virtue of the special animal in their life. Despite what you may think, I swear these three remarkable pet owners seemed like completely normal people to me.

Steve Samuels is the president of a successful real estate development company and his passion for the border collie–Labrador cross in his life prompted him to purchase, carry, and distribute embossed business cards bearing his dog's name, Sheba, with the title Adviser to the President. Although Sheba died several years ago, I wanted to discover the secret behind their remarkable bond, and given that, on more than one occasion, I had been Sheba's surgeon, I felt comfortable giving Mr. Samuels a call.

I dialed the main office number, introduced myself, stated my business, and respectfully inquired about the vague possibility of chatting with the boss about his late dog, Sheba, only to find that I had said the magic words. I was instantly credible, prioritized, and bouncing my way through the hierarchy of secretaries and personal assistants to the man himself.

As we spoke it became clear that paying tribute to his best friend came easy and felt good.

"Yeah, Sheba carried the card because she came to work with me every day. She was smart, with an uncanny ability to reason. I had some meetings where she would have to stay in my office (a room he defined as a shrine to his late dog). Every time I left the room, she would trot after me, and usually I could say 'See you later,' bend down, give her a kiss, and she would go back to the office couch. But if she decided she wanted to come along and I said 'See you later,' she would run off and hide, as though my inability to give her a kiss would force me to stay."

It turned out that Sheba developed cancer and we talked a little about the end. He confided, "I knew we didn't have much time together. I couldn't bear to be away from her but I had to go to the Bahamas on a trip. It was the summer, too hot to ship dogs in cargo."

This would have stopped most people but not President Samuels.

"So I chartered a prop plane. Sheba was able to sit up next to me. It was one of the worst flights of my life. The weather was unbelievably bad and she was bouncing in the air with all the turbulence and it took seven hours to get there but it was worth it to see her running on her favorite beach on Harbor Island, digging for those pesky crabs that always seemed to elude her."

"In the end we were in Boston when it happened. We both knew it was time. I spent an hour saying good-bye to her in the Angell parking lot. It was the worst day of my life. I went home, took out a picture of her, cut it out in her shape, hung it from a rawhide loop, and wore it on my chest, every day, hidden under my shirt. I sat shivah for a full year."

As if this level of devotion were not enough, consider another client of mine, Miss Ford and the yellow Labrador in her life, named Aspen. For Miss Ford, love is truly blind. It is also snotty, teary-eyed, and causes violent bouts of sneezing.

My consultation with Aspen centered on his bad hips, but I couldn't help but notice how Mom looked like an extra on one of those viral outbreak disaster movies. She was in her early twenties, pretty, but weary, washed-out with a wilting paper tissue never far from her eyes and nose. I asked if she had a cold.

"Oh, no," she said, "it's just Aspen."

"You're allergic to your own dog?" I asked.

"Yep," she said, snapping out the plosive "p" as though she were tired of answering this question.

"How long has this been a problem?"

"Since he was seven weeks old, when I brought him home."

"Seven weeks," I said. "But that's awful. Is it his saliva?"

I had already discovered that Aspen was a passionate licker of a dog.

"Yep."

"Were you skin tested?"

"Yep."

Unfortunately for Miss Ford, I had become fascinated by her malady and was far too curious to stop now.

"So is he your first dog?"

"Yes, but I have been around a lot of other dogs before with no problems. I just happen to have an allergy to him."

I wondered if I could find a way to ask the obvious question without coming across as insensitive or offensive.

"You said he was seven weeks old when you knew."

"Yep. It was on the ride home from the breeder. He licked my neck and face and within minutes I had these huge red welts all over my skin. I was petrified. I turned to my mom and said, 'Oh, God, I think I'm allergic to Aspen.' "

The devil's advocate in me took this as a cue to blunder forward.

"So . . . with Aspen being such a young puppy . . . you know . . . you hardly had a chance to bond with him. Did you not think that perhaps he wasn't right for you? That maybe you should take him back and buy a dog that wasn't such a . . . I don't know . . . health hazard?"

She came straight back at me.

"No. Never. I always wanted a dog. Mom and Dad said no my whole life until I was just about finished with college, and finally they agreed to buy him for me. I knew I wanted Aspen when he was three days old. I picked him out. The breeder let me come and visit every week until he was old enough to go home with me. I could look but not touch because they didn't want me to bring anything into the litter, so I never discovered my allergy. I was bonded to this dog when he was seven weeks old and after a lifetime of waiting I was not going to give him up that easily."

I guess that told me. I smiled, pleased with her response.

"So you live with these perpetual allergies?"

She laughed. "This is a good day. I visit my allergist for shots twice a week."

"And what does the allergist think?"

"He tells me I need to get rid of the dog."

"Do you minimize your contact with Aspen?"

"No."

"Do you try to avoid his saliva?"

"Not really. He sleeps on the same pillow as me. We go everywhere together. I don't care if I need an inhaler to get through the night, he's my best friend. I wouldn't give him up for anything."

I shook my head, amazed and awed by the power of a connection guaranteed to produce misery for her body and joy in her heart.

At our first meeting, when I went to address the owner of a twelve-year-old Great Pyrenees dog named Belle, I found a wallet thrust in my face, in the manner of a police detective or federal agent, open at, of all things, a Social Security card.

"Before we get started, I need you to understand how much this dog means to me."

I wasn't quite sure whether I was supposed to be studying the words on the pale blue card behind clear plastic or some faded family snapshot next to it.

"The middle name. You see it? I changed it. I made 'Belle' my legal middle name. That's how much this dog means to me."

"Really," I said, all the while thinking that Belle would have been perfectly fine as a middle name if the client were called, oh, I don't know, Jasmine Nightingale or Clarissa Rosebud, but for a man named Steven Aaron, it seemed fraught with problems.

"I had to go to probate court, before a judge. He thought I was some kind of a freak, I can tell you."

I took a step back, finally able to see around the wallet and look at said freak—a pasty, jumpy man with a scruffy goatee and pores ready to release a torrent of anxious sweat. Part of me wanted to move along with the history and the examination, but Mr. Aaron's declaration of devotion deserved more time.

"Why not just get a tattoo?"

He scoffed, as though the concept of inky needles injected under the skin was passé or for dog devotee lightweights.

"Already done that."

He started fumbling with his jeans in the back and for a moment I panicked that I would be privy to an exclusive viewing of his latest tribute, but he was simply replacing his wallet.

I'll hasten to the important details here and tell you that Mr. Aaron wanted me to perform two quite different procedures on Belle. The first concerned the tumor on his dog's paw (I use the word *on* loosely here, since about 50 percent of the foot had been replaced by aromatic, festering neoplastic tissue). A biopsy had confirmed that this was a malignant growth, a squamous cell carcinoma, by definition cancerous and locally aggressive but frequently slow to spread to other parts of the body. Unfortunately X-rays had also uncovered a troubling growth inside Belle's chest. Mr. Aaron needed me to cut out the cancer from his dog's paw, address the "squatter" that was making itself comfy among the big blood vessels next to her heart, and give him back a dog that meant so much to him he will write her name on every important document he has to sign for the rest of his life.

Some of my colleagues found Mr. Aaron, how shall I put it, a tad trying. He would eat up your time; he would call several times a day and on more than one occasion he almost completely backed off surgery. But I liked the guy. He was intense and demanding but it was clearly rooted in his devotion to his dog. It turned out that I was able to amputate a couple of digits, completely remove the tumor, and still leave Belle with a functional foot. To my relief the mass in the chest was discrete, not a metastatic disease but a different benign tumor with an excellent prognosis. At suture removal Belle was a happy, healthy dog and her master was ecstatic.

Sadly, two months later, Belle became weak, unable to stand on her back legs, and we were fearful that the cancerous tumor from her foot might have quietly spread to her spine. Belle was no longer eating or drinking and it seemed as if we had come to the end of the road. It now became clear that somewhere beyond the visible passion, sincerity, and the wacky name-changing episode there was much more that I did not understand about this man's bond to his dog. It was heart-wrenching to watch a young man emotionally implode at the thought of finally having to say farewell to his best friend, and, in the end, he was simply unable to take that final step. He realized that euthanasia was logical and responsible but at that moment he could not accept the lingering guilt of being the one to bring it to bear. Reluctantly we respected his wishes, loading Belle with painkillers and steroids and sending her on her way home. Mercifully, Belle passed away quietly in her sleep and Mr. Aaron never had to make the final call.

Many months and a phone call later, I discovered a number of missing pieces in the puzzle of this name-changing pet lover. It turned out that Steven was a child from a broken family, whose mother died suddenly at age twenty-six from an aneurysm, leaving him alone at only seven years of age. Belle was the first female love of his life. She was the mother he never had. He told me that Belle gave back every positive emotion he put into her and so much more.

Belle died on the twenty-third of December and he told me that he lights a candle for her in his church on the twenty-third of every month. Once she was gone he wanted to write down every memory he could possibly have of his life with Belle so he would never forget it. His eulogy is over two hundred pages long and he is still far from being finished.

When I returned to that Social Security card name change, he confided that there was secretly more to it. "When Belle died I added the dates of her birth and death to my tattoo."

The tattoo was on his arm, and this addendum came as no surprise to me.

"But the real reason I had my name changed was because of my own tombstone."

"I'm not with you," I said.

"I have always known that I want her ashes to be buried with me when I die. But then, I thought, who will know for sure that we are together, that a dog meant so much to me that I wanted us to be together forever? This way, by changing my name, it will be right there, chiseled in stone, for everyone to see, for everyone to know that she is down there with me."

There is one more thing to add. Shortly after Belle passed away, Mr. Aaron and his wife adopted another Great Pyrenees, who was eleven years old. I congratulated him on his desire to help out another geriatric mountain dog.

"Ah, Bianca's great," he said. "She was a rescue, totally unexpected and truly wonderful. I call her Belle's messenger, because I believe Belle was worried and sent her to keep an eye on me."

This was beginning to sound weird, but then I heard Mr. Aaron laughing before he added, "There's only problem with my theory. Bianca's totally blind!"

I mention this trilogy of exceptional pet owners because to me they embody the conspicuous simplicity and intensity of the animal bond. In our high-speed, anonymous, and entitled world of complicated and overplayed lives, true love has never been harder to find and believe in, let alone sustain. When the cure for insecurity and meaningful conversation is to slap a cell phone against your ear, hide within your iPod, or tap out a cryptic instant message, is it any wonder that we find comfort and solace in hairy, furry, and scaly companions? Far from the sleazy bar scene, blind dates, and Web sites dedicated to finding your soul mate, pets offer a relationship guaranteed free from lies, deception, and infidelity, where silence feels comfortable, where words come easily and unforced, where demands and a need for tolerance are nominal (unless that special someone tries to claim the couch for themself or insists on sharing a bout of flatulence). Imagine a marriage, with only minimal effort on your part, guaranteed not only to be successful but to endure. No prenuptial agreement. No worries about divorce. In our world of flawed, failed, doomed, and dangerous relationships, here is a chance to find true love. Here is a chance to find love without the risk.

As I see it, the only downside to this bond between animal and man comes on the wrong end of this relationship, in the losing or letting go of it all. As I look over at Mr. Ellis lovingly caressing Chipper's head, I am reminded that the joy of a lifetime commitment can also be our undoing.

Few cases demonstrate the supreme unfairness of loss better than an exceptional Weimaraner named Jake. As soon as I met Jake's mom—I'll call her Mrs. Grace—I could tell that behind the smiles, bubbly personality, and genuine concern for the profound lameness in her dog's front left leg, there was something much more at stake. It is all about the eyes, the subtle folds and creases of acquiescence that she could not completely hide. It leaked out in tiny packages; in a look, an intonation, like the glimmer of a ghost only she could see, haunting and never far away. I couldn't tell if it was pain or fear or both. It was not for me to judge, but I could tell that she was trapped under thin ice and working hard to prevent the crack that would let me fall through and reach into her world.

I ascertained that the lameness had been going on for several months, the marked muscle-wasting over the shoulder blades a testament to disuse.

"He's had every bone and joint in his leg X-rayed and no one has been able to find a thing wrong," she said.

I picked up her opening gift to me, a heavy wad of radiographs inside a large brown envelope, pulled them out one by one, and reviewed each film. She was absolutely right, every joint looked pristine, every bone smooth, crisp, and clean.

"How old is Jake?" I asked.

"Ten," she said.

"And he's been tested for Lyme disease?"

"Yes. And he was negative."

"And he's never been out of the state?"

"No."

This reply came across as wary, so I explained that I was just making sure there was no possibility of Jake's harboring some bizarre fungal disease acquired in the south or southwest of the lower forty-eight states that might account for his limp.

As I spoke, Jake studied me, eyes locked on mine as he backed his rump into his mother's knees, like reversing a tractor trailer, all experience and touch, no need to check his mirrors. Maximal physical contact with his mom was a given, and, in spite of his bum leg, he had that canny Weimaraner ability to sit perfectly square, head held high as if striking a pose that announced he was now ready to have his picture taken.

I mentally squashed a raiding party of unusual causes of front leg lameness trying to permeate my gray matter, and invited Mrs. Grace to put Jake on his leash so that I could study his gait in the hallway. Jake was more than happy to oblige, smiling, convinced that he had evaded the needless or the unpleasant aftermath of a stranger's donning a solitary rubber glove because he had become Best in Show at Westminster. Unfortunately, his moment in the winner's circle was all too brief. The lameness profound, confined exclusively to the left front leg, Jake's head fell forward and snapped back with every step like a dedicated rocker at a heavy metal concert.

When we returned to the examination room, Jake and I began to bond as Mrs. Grace appeared to physically fold into herself on the bench, as if bracing for the inevitable crash.

I ran my hands over the entire gunmetal-gray, velvet body, eventually arriving at the leg he offered for my inspection. I pinched, squeezed, splayed, and massaged the toes, inspecting the individual pads. I folded the foot back on itself at the carpus, the movement smooth, without restriction or discomfort. The same was true of the elbow and the shoulder joints. The examination was almost comical, Jake's pink nose following my hands, his eyes following mine, conveying his appreciation of my pathetic attempts at massage and that perhaps I might be best suited to a different career.

Unperturbed, I felt along the length of his bones, the lower end of his radius, the top of his humerus, those textbook locations for bone tumors. Again Jake looked, laughed, invited me to bring it on, and rolled his eyes at his mom as if to say, "I hope you're not going to give him money for this."

The joints were not in the least bit thickened or painful. Like every vet who had gone before me, I too could find nothing wrong with Jake's leg, but instead of huffing at my confusion, I kept quiet, prepared to try out a few more moves in my dwindling repertoire.

First, the regional lymph node, the prescapular, a fat, flat cherry that lies just in front of the shoulder, would not declare itself to my probing fingers, despite the muscle-wasting. This was good. This node is invariably tough to find unless enlarged by infection, inflammation, or the accumulation of filtered cancerous cells.

I moved to Jake's neck, and, taking his long head in my hands, began playing chiropractor in slow motion, pushing the neck down, up, and side to side. Once again, he demonstrated no restrictions and no pain.

I had one last trick in the bag. Holding my hand outstretched and flat, like Jackie Chan about to deliver a karate chop, I gently and slowly slid my fingers deep into Jake's armpit and for the first time I was rewarded with a disapproving response. This was not a cry. His stoicism relinquished little more than a twitch, but it seemed real and reproducible and of everything I had tried he disliked this the most.

Mrs. Grace had noticed it too, her lips pinched tight between a thumb and forefinger as if to hold a scream at bay.

I sat back down on my swivel chair and worked my heels across the floor, crab-walking the gap between us closed so that we were almost sitting knee to knee.

"Okay, let me go through my findings with you," I said. Mrs. Grace seemed so tight, so brittle that she might be about to shatter.

"When I combine my examination with all Jake's X-rays I cannot find an orthopedic explanation for his lameness."

I pressed through her look of confusion.

"Jake's lameness is real and it's not subtle. If he can't use his leg, but the joints, the ligaments, and the bones all feel and look fine, then there has to be something wrong with the muscles and nerves supplying the front leg."

Far away, deep inside Mrs. Grace's blue eyes, an emotion was vying for her attention.

"What sort of something?" she asked.

I didn't hesitate.

"Based on Jake's excellent range of motion in his neck and complete absence of pain, it would be hard to pin this on a herniated disk. But the muscle-wasting and the discomfort you noticed when I prodded in his armpit makes me wonder about the possibility of a nerve sheath tumor."

For a second there was silence in the room and Jake's head turned to face his mother. He had sensed it, something subsonic, well ahead of me, because he was tuned in and receptive, sensitive to the emotional shift my words triggered in his mom. He knew the ice was beginning to crack.

When it shattered it did so in painful smiles and proud recollections of a daughter who was only four years old.

Was.

The only word I caught as I fell in, the cold burning, unable to stop my last inhalation from turning into a gasp.

Was, as in past, as in lost, as in gone, forever.

Her daughter had been a beautiful, happy, innocent little girl with a tumor, a sarcoma, highly malignant, growing in her armpit, and, as Mrs. Grace spoke, she cupped the inside of her left armpit, her left arm limp, a movement that seemed to mimic the dog by her side, and right then I saw it, the thing she had been hiding, the thing she had feared yet probably suspected all along, that she had been dealt the exact same, awful deck, not once, but twice, with a beloved daughter and now a beloved dog, and in that instant I knew I was in serious trouble, the numbness beginning to set in.

The description of the two-year battle was understated, dignified, and perhaps a little cathartic. Mrs. Grace relaxed slightly, an easing savored by Jake, who felt that it was appropriate to take a snooze. During much of what she said, I stared at Jake, imagining his tissues when she talked of surgery, seeing his skin raw and weeping from another round of radiation, hearing him wretch from another dose of chemo. Here is the danger of doling out all that carefree, irresistible, unconditional love for our children and our pets. Chances are our children will outlive us. We believe we will not have to bury them, praying that we will be spared the unbearable grief of their loss in our own lifetime. Not so our pets. We pour our heart and soul into the animals in our lives, insisting that they are our children, that we love them no less than if they shared our DNA, and we do this with a certainty that for all this joy, we are guaranteed to lose them, to bury them, and somehow, to face life without them once again.

By the time she had finished her story, I realized that the past tense was nothing more than syntax. This brave child would always be by her mother's side and what is lost is left for those of us who never got to meet her.

As I tried to compose myself, I realized I was out of my depth. She had revealed a bruise, a real shiner that would never fade, let alone heal. She could try to cover it up, hide it from prying eyes, but it was always there. It wasn't Jake's fault, it wasn't mine, but right then, as I told her my concerns about the underlying cause of her dog's lameness, I felt as if I had pounded my fist into her until she was black and blue. Hardest of all, she tried to help me with a smile, the smile of a seasoned professional in the unfairness of pain.

Mrs. Grace and I agreed on a plan. Jake would visit with one of our neurologists and undergo another detailed examination. This is a different and more complicated dance than the one I had performed with Jake, full of handstands, wheel-barrowing, hemi-walking, pinching, knuckling, and jerking to the rhythm of a rubber mallet hammering for reflexes. The upshot of the assimilated information was affirmation of my suspicion regarding an aberration of the nerves supplying the left forelimb, most likely a nerve sheath tumor of the brachial plexus, that Mississippi Delta of fleshy white nerves buried deep in the armpit.

To help localize the problem further, we would perform electromyography and a nerve conduction study along with an MRI. Electromyography is performed in conscious people and involves sticking needles through the skin, into the underlying muscles, measuring the patterns of electrical activity provoked, and determining the response in muscle groups supplied by specific nerves. As you might imagine, most dogs are resistant to the pleasures of imitating a voodoo doll, and therefore general anesthesia is a prerequi-

site for electromyography and MRI, something the more claustro-
phobic among us might prefer to the terrors of being confined inside a tight and resonating magnetic coil.

Detailed imaging revealed an abnormally shaped nerve, unique
and unusually thickened. Best of all it was situated in a desirable
location close to the limb. Why desirable? Because nerve sheath tumors can occur anywhere along the length of the nerve, including
high up on the neck, adjacent to the spinal cord, making surgery
challenging and less likely to achieve a successful resection of
the primary tumor. This location afforded a good opportunity for
amputation.

At our next meeting Mrs. Grace came with reinforcements. Jake
led the way, now completely unable to bear any weight on the leg,
followed by a daughter with a Barbie doll in tow, marching straight
over to my computer and asking if I could hook her up to Disney's
or Nickelodeon's Web sites so she wouldn't get bored. I was still
thinking about the little girl's late sister as I shook hands with the
husband, Mr. Grace.

There was no examination. There was really not much of a discussion either. They might have told me that they were not strong
enough for this, not up for all they knew Jake must endure, that they
had opted to put Jake to sleep and who was I to tell them otherwise.
But they never did. Just like they never had to spell out how much
this dog meant to this family in anything more than their incredible
willingness to travel the same painful road, this time with a sick dog
and not a sick child.

The word *amputation* seemed to come up only once, in a negative
context, inconceivable and unworkable. Instead, they wanted me to
try to remove the nerve sheath tumor, to perform an excisional
biopsy, to cut out the lesion as best as possible but to leave the leg intact. They understood the possibility of failure, recurrence, and the
fact that Jake might never use the leg again, particularly since the

EMG had been inconclusive with regard to which specific nerve was affected. For this family, this was what made sense. This much they could accept.

And so I did the surgery, approaching the nerve tributaries from in front of the limb, sliding under the shoulder blade to find the culprit, fatter and unnaturally creamy compared to its pure white counterparts. I cut out a piece as large as I could, striving for the largest margin I could manage, and watched as the leg twitched and jumped for what I imagined would be the last time.

There was some comfort in the fact that I could not make Jake much worse than the non-weight-bearing state he had achieved before surgery, but to my surprise, the following morning, I dared to hope that he was actually a little better, occasionally capable of tapping his toes to the ground.

My warnings and skepticism were repaid two weeks later with a chance meeting in a hallway with a fully weight-bearing Weimaraner that I recognized only by virtue of a large skin incision in front of his left shoulder. It turned out that Jake was trotting off to his first radiation treatment with virtually no trace of lameness.

I checked in with Mr. Grace a year later to discover that Jake had never skipped a beat on the return to full function. After the resounding (and if I am being honest, completely unexpected) success of the surgery, they had decided to pursue radiation treatment to minimize the chance of local tumor recurrence.

"He's doing great. Still drags me for a walk and loves playing with our new puppy."

Mr. and Mrs. Grace had gambled over ten thousand dollars on Jake's treatment, and despite the cost, the odds, and everything they had been through, they know that this time they have beaten the house. I didn't have to tell them that the winning streak may not last because they let me know their understanding in that parting phrase, "new puppy." Here we go again. Even for a family who endures greater pain than I can conceive, the rewards and strength of the bonds with the animals in their lives proved irresistible, irrepressible, and more than worth the risk.

Sadly, two months after this phone call, I discovered that Jake had begun a precipitous decline in limb function. The tumor had returned and this time Mr. and Mrs. Grace elected to put him to sleep, an event that coincided almost to the day with the dedication of a children's playground to their late daughter.

Dr. Maganiello is back in run 33, her hand resting on Mr. Ellis's meaty shoulder as the man weeps uncontrollably. Have I done my job? Should I feel good about bringing him to his knees and bullying his frightened mind into a state of acceptance?

I look over at Sage, see her finally lying down, swallowed whole by the foam of her blue bed, and I wish faith were all it took to make her better. I never ask myself how I cope with fear and failure and loss and pain. Best not to. It has become so integral, so expected of me, it dissolves into the job, melts clear away even though it's still there, and every so often, under a certain unexpected light, individual cases make it stand out like fine particles in a stirred solution.

People have suggested that clinicians can become desensitized in order to survive. Maybe. I know you can learn to harden your heart with a greedy, detached consumption of cases that go wrong and cases you cannot win, like an addiction to pastrami with extra mayo, but the damage is cumulative and you can ignore the harm they do only so long. With time and introspection I think it's better to strike a healthy balance, bracing for failure and disappointment, distilling the positives and lessons learned and the irresistible possibility of victory the next time.

But as Sage sleeps, for the first time since meeting her I recognize that her effect on me is rooted in something more than sordid professional pride in the job I have done and the decisions I have made. It goes beyond her seductive personality and the understated charm of her owner because together, whether I like it or not, they have disturbed my past, picked at a guilty scab, and slowly it is beginning to bleed as I recall the suffering of another dog and another man in another life.

8

· · · · · · · · · ·

10:22 A.M.

MINOR COMPLICATIONS

Praying that my pager's silence will allow me to catch up on a couple of phone calls, I head back to the surgery department only to be intercepted by a frazzled Dr. Payne.

"You got a second?" she says, falling in with my pace and direction.

"Sure, does this concern your mouthy German shepherd, Rebel or whoever it is?"

She knows I'm joshing, rolls her bloodshot eyes, and I see raspberry ripple in vanilla.

"His name is *Barron* and so far *your* diagnostic plan has produced a whole lot of nothing."

I return the sullen gesture.

"Okay," she concedes, "*our* diagnostic plan." She continues. "His hips look fine. Radiology says the spine is clean, no disk space narrowing, no fracture, no dislocation, nothing."

"No evidence of infection. Discospondylitis?"

"No. Unless you want to take a peak at his spinal cord with an MRI, they can't find a lesion to account for his weird gait."

I don't make any effort to suppress a yawn.

"Is this case boring you?"

I apologize, trying to fight the slow stretch of my lower jaw.

"Far from it. I'm just knackered from last night."

In her face I see the need for clarification.

"Sorry, English colloquialism meaning 'I feel a little tired.' What about the blood and urine?"

"Well, he's not diabetic and he's not hypothyroid."

"Cushinoid?"

She shakes her head.

"Nothing to make me want to do an ACTH stim. Everything was pretty unremarkable," she says.

"So where does this leave us?"

"I don't know," she says. "I thought you were the one with all the answers."

I know she's not being critical or vindictive, but her snippy comeback reveals the gravity of her personal accountability to Barron and his owners. These cases can be as frustrating as they can be rewarding. Dogs like Barron often bounce from one veterinarian to the next because it can be hard to maintain the confidence and trust of the owner in the face of negative results. Exasperated or disgruntled owners seek a fresh opinion, new tests, and then another and another until finally the lucky, timely vet comes along with the ability to take a step back, gather and interpret all the previous data and, in doing so, see the big picture and nail the diagnosis. The secret is to make the owners believe that you are this vet—the last vet standing.

"Don't worry," I say with a sardonic smile. "I still have a cunning plan."

Dr. Payne remains serious and skeptical, and in her increasingly cadaverous features, I see her millstone of anxiety, exhaustion, and, if it were possible, the danger of caring too much. I wonder what her husband really thinks about all this further education, the physical effect it is having on his wife, his marriage, and whether it is really worth it. They probably went into their forced separation believing they could put up with anything for a year, but looking at her now I wonder if she wishes to recant. An internship is not for the faint of heart. All of us serve our time and almost without exception none of us would ever wish to repeat the experience. It is hard labor during which sensitive souls survive not by suppressing their feelings but by gently setting them aside for later. I want Dr. Payne to nurture her compassion and alacrity and learn to defend against her vulnerability.

"It's going to be fine, Melissa. Really. As my daughters keep telling me, just 'chillax'! When I get a chance I'm going to take another look at Kaiser."

She concedes a smile and says, "Please, stick to the British slang. And the dog's name is Barron."

"Him as well," I say. "I'll give you a page when I'm done."

And with that I duck into nonsterile surgery to check in with Joe, my liaison, lifesaver, and lifeline to the outside world.

Joe lives in a room affectionately referred to as "the fishbowl" because of its central location in the department with large glass windows that afford the occupant a fenestrated 360-degree view of the anesthetic induction room, surgical prep area, the surgical scrub sinks, and the operating rooms. From his command post Joe mans the phones, scheduling our appointments, organizing our paperwork, and generally bringing order and discipline to the chaos of the working day.

Joe is perfect for his job. His voice is a silky NPR baritone, melting even the most cranky of clients with a patient, accommodating, and upbeat manner. Over the phone he is a dashing, forty-something anchorman inspiring confidence and trust. In person, he's just a kid with doughy skin, Brezhnev brows, and ornery Velcro for hair, yet he is blessed with a talent for handling people who love animals. His niche may be the microphone and not the camera, but he's praised by owners and veterinarians alike for being one smooth operator.

When I walk into the fishbowl, Joe sits alone, expressing his side of a testy dialogue hissing in his headset, fingers playing allegro across the keyboard, windows zooming back and forth on his flat screen as he tries to find an appointment for an anxious client. The maestro of the multitask rolls his eyes at me while his mouth fires off a calculated buttery remark.

I take a seat next to him, scratch out a note asking him to take a look at my schedule and set up a date for me to biopsy that tongue mass on the enchanting Taco Sanchez, and slide it his way. He nods his understanding, keeps the beat of the conversation with a credible laugh, and I dial the number for Sage's veterinarian on the Cape. This is a courtesy call to let him know what has become of his patient as well as an opportunity to air my fears.

"Boy," the vet says, chewing on a breathy pause, "I hope you can pull her through. She's all he's got and he's such a wonderful old man."

I promise to keep him up to date with Sage's recovery, thank him for his time, sever the connection, and feel the protracted prickle of his words like a mohair sweater on a humid August afternoon.

I move on to my second call.

"Hi, Mr. Hartman. I hope I didn't wake you up?"

"Not at all, I've been waiting by the phone. How's my girl?"

He sounds perky, almost nonchalant, as though I'm the dog-sitter and he's just checking in to make sure all is well.

"Sage is resting comfortably. Her temperature is normal. She's not interested in drinking but that's okay. She's on intravenous fluids to make sure she doesn't get dehydrated."

"It's good that she made it through the night, right?" he asks, and I can tell he's fishing for what he wants to hear.

"Yes. It is. But it's early days. In fact it's only been a couple of hours."

"I know, Doc. I know. But if things continue to go well, when do you think I might be able to bring her home?"

Now he is beginning to worry me. For all of last night's silent nods and shock absorption in his wizened eyes, I wonder if he has isolated himself from the unthinkable. I don't want to hurt his feelings but I cannot feed him false hope. I want to get to the real reason for my phone call without revealing the motive. I want to offer him the chance to visit Sage during the CCU visiting hour starting at eleven thirty. Ordinarily I might have advised against it. Some animals can be adversely affected by a fleeting interaction with their owner during their hospital stay. It is a bit like visiting a son or daughter in summer camp and inducing a bout of homesickness. The pet is confused when he or she is abandoned for tests or treatment, and at your next meeting, the hospital visit, forgives your neglect and insensitivity because they anticipate going home with you, convinced you cannot make the same mistake twice. Imagine their disappointment, incredulity, and sadness when you abandon them for a second time at the end of the visit. Sometimes it is better to make that next visit the one in which you spring them from their brief incarceration at the time of final discharge from the hospital.

"Let's not worry about that for now. I want Sage home as much and as fast as you both do. But we have to be patient. There are a lot of things that can go wrong over the next few days."

He mumbles an acknowledgment that I know best, that he trusts my judgment, but I can tell I have burst his bubble.

"The reason I am calling is to see if you were coming in to visit this morning."

"I'll be right down," he says, his voice almost bipolar in its ability to trade compunction for keenness. "Do you think I should bring something for her to eat? She loves cold cuts of turkey breast."

I have no doubt that food is the last thing on Sage's mind right now, but I am happy to indulge this optimistic placebo. After all, what does he have to lose?

"Why not?" I say. "I think it will be good for her to see you." And then, after a pause, I add what is really on my mind.

"Good for both of you."

When I put down the phone, the fraud in me wonders if I should have told him the truth. Sage, thankfully, is out of it, her narcotics have kicked in and she is asleep. I doubt that she will notice who comes to visit, but I don't really care because I want him there for my own selfish reasons. I know Sage is brittle, she could go either way, and if things take a turn for the worse, I would hate to think their parting moment was that harrowing, rushed good-bye as she was whisked off to surgery.

I want them to share a quieter moment together, now, while I know they still can.

Just in case.

I get up from my seat and Joe waves a jazz hand in my face, scribbling a note on a yellow Post-it and handing it over. The note says, "Did you remember 'Hugo' Brown?"

And suddenly I see the horror of my negligence reflected in his sour grimace, the original phone message burning a hole through my left breast pocket. I promised myself that I would get back to Mr. Brown at nine and now it is, I check my watch, after ten thirty.

The record for my next case is waiting for me in my examination room, but I choose to ignore it, close the door, and pick up the phone.

Perhaps I should backtrack. Hugo Brown is a boisterous two-year-old male rottweiler who likes to go for long walks in the woodlands of Vermont. Three weeks ago he was running off leash, cried out in pain, and limped back to his dad unable to put any weight on his right hind leg. An examination with a veterinarian in a small rural practice outside Woodstock confirmed swelling and pain of the right knee, no obvious broken bones, and a strong suspicion of a torn cranial cruciate ligament. A ruptured cranial cruciate ligament or, in human parlance, a torn ACL, is the most common disorder seen by veterinary specialists with an interest in orthopedics. When the case came my way and I confirmed the diagnosis, I had no hesitation in recommending a procedure called a tibial plateau leveling osteotomy or TPLO. This is an incredibly popular treatment option for young, energetic larger breeds of dog. It is, however, more invasive than other, simpler options, involving significant dissection of soft tissues, cutting bone, and necessitating the application of a stainless steel plate and screws. Consequently postoperative complications, though uncommon, can be more problematic. I try to explain the details of a normal recovery as well as one hundred and one possible disasters that might go wrong during the procedure or in the weeks following the surgery so that the client is fully prepared for all eventualities.

As I pick up the phone, dial Mr. Brown's number, and listen to the ring tone, I can't help but wonder if poor Hugo is the lucky beneficiary of number one hundred and two.

During my years as a veterinary student at Cambridge there was an exclusive society named The Chess Club whose maxim boasted that they would never lose a game of chess. This infallibility was assured because, as a thinly disguised gentlemen's drinking club, they never played a game of chess. In much the same way, any surgeon who claims he never makes mistakes is either lying or an impostor.

Our professional lives are spent dancing on a fragile, omnipresent fault line like reluctant seismologists waiting for the next big one. It is inevitable, not a question of if, but when, and the bigger question is how will we handle the mild tremor of a petty mistake and our state of preparedness for an impending catastrophe?

Things can go wrong for a veterinarian from the very first moment you pick up a crisp manila file, step out into a crowded waiting room, and call for your client, because a great deal of peril lies hidden in a name. Sure, you can be fairly confident that Java, Mocha, Cocoa, or Hershey is going to be the chocolate Labrador bungee jumping off the end of his retractable leash in an attempt to reach the stranger downing a jelly doughnut. Frosty, Casper, or Angel is bound to be the white longhaired cat cowering at the back of her carrier. But even among your common or garden variety Max, Lady, Buddy, Brandy, Duke, Misty, Muffin, Lucky, Rocky, or Buster, danger prowls.

Consider the following dilemma surrounding a sixteen-year-old cat that goes by a name similar to Moe Hay. Moe came in for extensive dental work, an outpatient procedure but one that, pets being pets, necessitated general anesthesia. The case had been set up through another staff clinician, so the dentist had not met with Moe's owner in person. All he knew was that they would return in the afternoon to pick up Moe, at which point he would meet with them to discuss after care.

Unfortunately, Moe underwent a stroke about an hour after her recovery from anesthesia. She was stable and being carefully and skillfully nursed in the CCU when word got back to our dentist that Moe's parents were in the waiting room. Eager to apprise the Hays of Moe's situation, the dentist strode into a bustling waiting room. He thought he was being shrewd by starting with the last name, "Hay," but as he stood before the throng in sweaty scrubs, anxiety and trepidation contorting his features, the masses mistook him for a frustrated employee asking if they would all just keep things down a bit before he went out of his mind. In short, he was ignored.

Changing his tack he hurried to the reception desk, apprised them of his quest for Moe's parents, and was directed to a mother sitting quietly next to a teenager feasting on a large fibrous muffin. He approached, made his introduction as Moe's doctor, and, appropriately, cut to the chase, getting into the details of what had happened to Moe and how sorry he was but, with the appropriate care, having caught the complication quickly, there was a good chance that Moe would recover. What he could not have foreseen was the impact his news would have on the daughter, the shock causing some doughy clump to get lodged in her airway, inducing a coughing fit that stopped just shy of the need for a Heimlich. Clearly the possibility of anesthetic-related complications in a sixteen-year-old cat had not been properly discussed given this girl's degree of surprise at his news.

"But he's in great shape. And he's only six," she said, her words syncopated between mouthfuls of half-masticated bran.

"Six?" thought the dentist, wondering if there had been some kind of a typo, some inky slash, some erroneous smudge that had made him add a decade to the cat's real age. The cogs slowly turning behind the dentist's eyes became incrementally visible to mother and daughter alike.

"You're talking about the cat being anesthetized for the constipation problem?" asked the mother.

Unable to contrive a more nimble riposte than "not exactly," the dentist apologized for his mistake, surprised that both mother and daughter disproportionately lauded the news with laughter and tears of relief. Obviously more than one Moe was in the hospital that day and when the real Mr. and Mrs. Hay stepped forward, they were concerned but completely understanding of what had transpired. They were aware of the anesthetic risk before consenting to the dental work but felt comfortable that they had made the right decision given the pain and discomfort their cat was experiencing with his mouth. As it turned out the real Moe was discharged some three days later, much improved and likely to continue to be so.

Perhaps this should be a lesson to us all that we should abandon naming our pets with the safe, the bland, and the familiar and strive for something altogether unique and risqué. Consider the inspired choices of Mr. and Mrs. Bolton with their African gray, Michael; Mr. and Mrs. Hiscock and their bouncy golden retriever puppy, Zipper; Mr. and Mrs. Dick and their pointer, Wrigley; and Mr. Gross and his iguana, Izzy. I'm not suggesting anything gratuitously controversial like Barabbas, Hitler, or Stud (sadly, all of which I have encountered), but something more along the lines of a wonderful shepherd mix named Spot. After pawing my way over every hairy inch of the latter's black fur, I could not find a single blemish that in any way resembled a spot.

I turned to her owner. "But she's not got any spots. Not a single one," I said.

He offered me a weary look and said, "I don't really think she cares. It's just a name. Get over it."

And of course he was right.

So let's assume that our client has responded to our name-calling as opposed to sizing us up, maintaining their silence, and slinking out of the building unnoticed, and decided to follow us into the examination room. These first minutes of introduction are critical as we strive to set the right tone, to reassure, inspire confidence, demonstrate our compassion, and resolve to get to the crux of the problem. Cavernous faux pas lurk for the unwary, poised to swallow us whole, tongue-tied and floundering before discarding us like flotsam on the deserted beach of the insolent and the inept. Few things may prove more dangerous than labeling a pet as a specific breed or worse still inquiring as to the genetic heritage of the arresting and unique "mutt" only to discover that this prized and highly expensive import hails from some backwater of the Russian steppes or the foothills of Andalusia and has a pedigree far longer than your list of hard-won credentials. In my experience, and you would think I might have learned my lesson by now, this insult carries no less weight than asking an overweight woman if she is pregnant.

Sometimes, even experienced clinicians fail to recognize the booby trap in their midst as a colleague of mine discovered while selflessly working a few weeks of the summer stranded on an agree-able little island in the Atlantic called Nantucket.

Hot off the last crop duster to land at Memorial Airport, Tanya and Steve, and their six-month-old terrier, Rocco, headed directly to Angell's satellite clinic and Dr. Doug Brum.

Tanya stood about five foot two in the high heels she wore with her traveling sweats, and the easy tears and bloodshot eyes told of a harrowing trip from the West Coast with Rocco, the sick little puppy in her arms. When I probed Doug for specific details, he suggested Tanya seemed no more than nineteen or twenty, funda-mentally attractive but with a hint of something sultry, promiscu-ous, even illicit, lurking near the surface. Her speech slurred, her body swayed as if she had never left the turbulence of bumpy air, and curly pink fingernails grappled for his forearm, more for bal-ance than reassurance. If he was being honest, she appeared to be completely stoned.

Taking Rocco from her, it was obvious to Brum that the puppy was extremely sick and in need of emergency surgery for an intes-tinal obstruction. In fact, Rocco was so weak, dehydrated, and most probably septic that he offered the couple a grave prognosis, pes-simism leaped upon by a bespectacled Steve who made up for his girlfriend's sleepy ganja intoxication with a manic, jittery insistence that Dr. Brum *had* to save little Rocco's life.

In fact Rocco made a remarkable recovery from his surgery, and, to her credit, young Tanya made a point of visiting her puppy twice a day during the next week. She was attentive, caring, and devoted, traits that did not escape Dr. Brum, together with her propensity for wearing skirts so short that they revealed the lower portions of her buttocks and stringy little tank tops that allowed him to appreciate the beauty of her big brown eyes. Dr. Brum insisted that at no time did anything flirtatious or unprofessional pass between them unless Tanya's gift of a homemade apple pie when Rocco went home seems inappropriate.

The story should have ended there, had it not been for an e-mail Brum received nearly a year later suggesting he might hustle down to his nearest newsstand and catch the story of his interaction with Steve, Tanya, and Rocco in a recent issue of a major pornographic magazine. It turns out that Steve is a seasoned writer of adult entertainment and Tanya, a professional actress in the kind of films that don't appear at your local movie theater. According to the article Dr. Brum had become physically enamored by the sight of young Tanya. "It is obvious from the bulge in Doug's pants, that he has more than Rocco on his mind."

And, when Tanya heard that Rocco was starting to improve, Dr. Brum was supposedly the recipient of the sultry promise, "If you can save my Rocco, I'll give you the best thank-you gift you've ever received."

I am assured that Doug's wife found this literary summation of her husband's lack of professionalism more amusing than offensive, but it serves as a poignant reminder that sometimes sharing a common language with our clients can be more hazardous and open to interpretation than the unspoken interactions with our patients, guaranteed free from confusion.

Of course, in the scheme of miscues, this ranks as one of the more innocuous and entertaining scenarios. However, far more serious troubles can arise, and here, perhaps, we should make a distinction between a mistake and a complication in the eyes of a pet owner. A mistake feels like nothing more than a misunderstanding, something reparable and, best of all, forgivable. Okay, so you may be down a fruit basket or a bottle of wine come the holidays but at least you won't have to appear in front of the State Veterinary Board. Conversely, a complication feels altogether more sinister. It feels negligent, almost reckless, and, correctly or not, wholly irreversible.

A complication can be defined as a secondary disease, an accident, or a negative reaction occurring during the course of an illness and usually aggravating the illness. I like the word *accident* in this context. To me it suggests "unanticipated," even "clumsy," but, in fact, the vast majority of complications are not the result of ineptitude. How can they be if we can foresee their advent and impact? These days, a significant part of a consultation resembles one of those irksome television advertisements for the treatment of acid reflux, asthma, or insomnia. By pointing out more things that can go wrong than right, it is hardly surprising that my clients rush off to chug down a handful of purple pills, huff on an inhaler, and need chemical assistance to sleep at night. I was reviewing one of the latest surgical textbooks and turned to a description of a procedure called a total ear canal ablation, a surgery intended to relieve intractable ear disease by carefully cutting the entire cartilaginous ear funnel down to the base of the skull and free of its surrounding tissues. It may sound like medieval torture but in experienced hands it is possible to say goodbye to incessant head shaking and the inexorable smell of sweaty sneakers caused by bacteria thriving in the warm and inviting folds of an expansive cauliflower ear. This surgery can literally transform the quality of life for both owner and animal, but it is not without risk. Let me quote from the appropriate section of the textbook on postoperative complications.

"Complications are seen in 29–68% of animals. . . . Facial nerve paralysis occurs in 25–50% of dogs after this procedure and is permanent in 10–15% of all dogs. . . . Draining fistulas will appear in 1–12 months after surgery in 5–10% of animals."

Yikes! I turned the page and the list kept on going. For clarification purposes I should explain that the facial nerve emerges from the skull adjacent to the ear canal and curls around the ear cartilage en route to the lips, eyelid, and muscles of facial expression. Permanent damage to the nerve leads to flaccidity on that side of the face but more importantly destroys the ability to blink and lubricate the cornea of the eye. A draining fistula is usually a discreet opening close to the surgical scar caused by failure to completely remove all the infected and wax-secreting tissue during the procedure, leaving the dog or cat with a permanent supply of sticky green hair gel oozing or plastered on the side of the head. I will spare you the details on sloughing the ear, damage to the balance centers of the brain, and interfering with normal pupil function. I stopped reading after respiratory distress and the need for a temporary tracheostomy.

Veterinarians need to discuss the risk for complications, but we must resist creating so much fear that our clients would rather avoid the procedure altogether. Generating textbook doom and gloom may ensure that all your bases are covered while guaranteeing that most sensible pet owners, that is, those with more than a brain stem, decide against surgery. Vital medical statistics in a reference book can pounce upon snippets of data and present them in a concise and readable manner, but they can be taken slightly out of context. Some of the original data may be several decades old, with small numbers of cases, performed by surgeons of varied experience and expertise. My sense with total ear canal ablation, during and after my surgical training, is that the long list of potential problems is real but rarely comes to fruition. Here again is the dilemma of experience. Hopefully, like most surgeons, my potential for error is inversely proportional to the number of times I practice. Early on in our careers, every procedure is a minefield, the movement of the scalpel blade, the snip of the scissors, a clumsy size-eleven boot stomping on the brink of disaster. Only with repetition can we find a reasonable balance between fear mongering and the assurance of a fairy-tale ending.

In much the same way, I'm reluctant to chalk up another complication if the outcome was a potential or inevitable consequence of the original disease. I can live with the dalmatian owner who is upset because after the dog's surgery I was unable to perfectly align his spots. When I have done my best to achieve perfect anatomical alignment of a broken joint and the animal goes on to get some degree of arthritis, I try not to beat myself up, although one owner had other ideas. One year after knee surgery on her Labrador, she called to report her disappointment that the dog displayed significant limitations in the amount of daily swimming he could perform.

"I'm sorry to hear that," I said. "How much can he do?"

"Sadly we're down to six hours," she said. "We used to do eight."

Either there's no pleasing some people or I failed to give her a reasonable expectation of her pet's future athletic prowess. Of course, like most performances, things rarely go exactly as planned. We forget our lines, miss cues, improvise, and fudge, but we work it out, and most of the time the audience is oblivious to our minor mistakes. When our blade trembles off the fibrous, avascular white midline of the belly, the appropriately named *linea alba*, and catches the nearby bleeding muscle, our work may be technically suboptimal but it will suffice. After every orthopedic surgery that implants a metallic object, we critically appraise our handiwork on the postoperative X-rays, hoping for our moment of instant gratification but more often than not learning to do it better the next time. Was that screw too long or too short? That pin too thin or too thick? Are we being pedantic or will there be consequences to our subtle technical errors? Most of the time these complications go unstated because they have no bearing on the big picture. What does it matter if my fracture repair is more Salvador Dalí than Claude Monet if they both go on to heal equally well? Do I really need to worry an owner about the fact that I nicked a major blood vessel during surgery when the amount of blood lost does not require a transfusion and is of no clinical consequence to the animal? I am not being dishonest or even economical with the truth when the normal imperfections of trying to repair a biological system ensure that most of what I do cannot proceed like a Martha Stewart cookbook.

Sometimes it would be nice to blame the animals for the problems we encounter. I imagine that most human surgeons rarely give a thought to their patient's desire to lick and slobber over a fresh incision, and I don't buy into the proverbial dog's mouth being cleaner than a human mouth, because either way, no saliva is best. And don't get me started on the scouring-pad action of the feline tongue.

Similarly, after restoring the normal anatomy of a dislocated elbow or a simple radius fracture with a cast, wire-coat-hanger-assisted scratching of a niggling itch seems innocuous compared with gnawing on enough fresh fiberglass that the limb is once more dangling in the breeze. And if chewing is not your pleasure, why not consider dipping your cast into a pool of fresh urine? Why listen to your physical therapist on that road to recovery if jumping off the couch or catching that pesky squirrel proves irresistible?

To be fair, as veterinarians, if animals and owners deviate from our written and verbal instructions, then we must take the blame. We must anticipate the troublemakers (on both ends of the leash), be clear and concise as we define parameters and boundaries, and closely monitor the situation for potential violations. Sometimes house arrest, Elizabethan collars, and sedatives (again, on both ends of the leash) can only do so much. Accidents will happen. If we have all tried our best, we should all be able to live with the consequences.

Responsibility for the mistakes caused by nurses or technicians might be harder to swallow, but again, the animal is under our care and we are the ones who will be apologizing to the owner. I still remember a brisk, autumnal morning, a weak sun struggling with its ascent, casting stubby shadows over my shoulder as I walked toward my first day of employment at a new hospital, long before I arrived in Boston. I was less than fifty yards from the main entrance and parking lot when I noticed a girl weaving through honking traffic, dancing in my direction, and waving for attention. I checked over my shoulder, certain that her harried expression must be aimed at someone close behind me, but I was alone.

"Do you want any business?" she asked, patting her chest as she caught her breath.

I studied her, cars whizzing by, perplexed by her turn of phrase. And then it dawned on me. She wore no makeup, greasy and disheveled hair licking around a bone-white face with despairing eyes set in gloomy gray sockets—what the glossy, aromatic magazines from the late nineties might term "heroin chic." Only this was the genuine article. She was just a kid, probably no more than fourteen or fifteen years old, and when I finally took in the leather miniskirt and stiletto heels on which she tottered, the nature of her services hit me full in the face.

"No," I replied, starting to walk on. "Not today. But thank you very much."

There was no time to be embarrassed by my own unnecessary politeness, for in front of me I saw my new boss stepping out of his car. "Oh, my God," I thought, "what if he thinks I'm soliciting a hooker on my first day." I physically shook this troubling image from my mind, increased my pace, and was just about to step into the zone in which shouting "Good morning!" might be considered socially acceptable, when I heard the girl calling in my direction. Her cries caught both our attentions and I was forced to turn around and see her swivel her hips and push her bottom in my direction while wrinkling her nose and biting down hard on her lower lip.

"Fifty bucks," she shouted, using her index finger and cocked thumb to rhythmically gesture to her backside.

I turned back to my new boss wondering if he might misconstrue her outburst as the result of an earlier haggling dispute. Who would want to employ a man unable to control his primeval urges before eight o'clock in the morning?

"Ah," he mused, locking his car, "prices have gone up."

He glanced in the girl's direction and added, "I see you've met Tracy. Don't look so worried, my boy, we know all about her. She's not around much during the day. Not unless she's in real trouble. For drug money, I mean."

I regained muscular control of my rubbery lower jaw and we started toward the hospital entrance.

"She's just a kid," I said. "It's terrible."

"I couldn't agree more. Drugs are a big problem in this town, particularly heroin. But they're not our problem. No one's going to raid our lockbox for narcotics or ketamine on my watch." He nodded once as though stamping his authority on the subject. "Closest they get is sneaking in to use the bathrooms. Not in a professional capacity, you understand. Unfortunately the hospital happens to be on the edge of a new and rapidly expanding red-light district. For some reason 'the johns,' " he pulled out his "quotation fingers" as if to reiterate that he was hip to the trendy jargon, "started using this area about a year ago, but it's mainly at night, so fortunately most of our clientele never have to see it."

Suddenly he reached for my elbow and tweaked it so that I lurched in his direction.

"Be careful where you tread," he said.

I looked down, expecting my shoe to be hovering over some land mine of a ripe dog turd. Instead the dry crunch of red and gold leaf litter skipped a beat as I dodged a used condom.

He smiled at my dismay.

"Don't worry, you get used to it."

"Right," I said, wondering about the finer details of my contract and whether I had written in an escape clause.

But he was right. It wasn't a problem. The hospital's symbiosis with the local prostitutes went almost entirely unnoticed, aside from one midnight emergency in which I pulled my car behind another vehicle and found my headlights illuminating a solitary figure in the driver's seat. I presumed it must be the pet owner waiting for me to arrive until a head with flowing blond hair floated from his lap into the neon glow and offered me a greeting that suggested that I might want to park elsewhere. This was the only hiccup in the hospital's unblemished moral reputation during my first six months of employment. That was, until a troubling turn of events with an ordinarily cheerful and reliable technician named Leah.

It was not Leah herself who brought me the bad news but one of her fearful and mumbling assistants.

"What do you mean she's lost one of my patients?" I said.

"She didn't mean to," the assistant replied. "It was an accident."

I considered her over the top of my glasses—cropped orange hair and makeup from the Cleopatra school of excessive eyeliner. I made little effort to hide the irritation in my glare.

"I'm sure it was, but what exactly do you mean by 'lost'? You mean she can't find the correct run, that the patient has been incorrectly labeled? What?"

"I mean 'lost, lost.' As in gone, run away, nipped off, done a runner, no longer in the building, and last seen headed in the direction of the city center. He somehow slipped his leash while Leah was taking him out to pee before surgery."

Choking back a throatful of expletives I asked, "Which dog?" praying that it might be some enormous sloth of a Labrador, a paraplegic dachshund, or else an amputee.

"It's Fly, the greyhound."

My heart sank. "And where's Leah now?"

"Running after him," she said.

Without thinking—obviously without thinking—I said, "So, is Leah a good runner?"

Leah's assistant did not need to reply. She possessed a remnant of surly teenage attitude that she employed to full effect with a facial expression that said, "The dog's a greyhound, you idiot, do you really think it matters?"

What the hell was I going to tell the owner? Moreoever, who was the owner? The surgery to remove a small lump from the skin on Fly's belly had been arranged weeks in advance and I could not put a face with the last name. Was she a nervous, flighty, paranoid reflection of her dog, or was he a no-nonsense hood with a penchant for semiautomatic weapons and a lifelong subscription to the NRA?

I imagined the traffic, this poor dog, confused, frightened, coursing his way into certain danger. What if something happened to him? What if a car hit him? Was it remotely possible that Leah could catch him? That even now she might have him in tow, poised to walk through the front door at any second?

In a moment of clarity I realized there was nothing to decide. I asked the assistant to round up as many people as possible and head into town, on foot and in cars, to try and find Fly. I would join her shortly, but first I had an important call to make.

With adrenal glands reduced to the size of raisins, I picked up a telephone, dialed, and heard a woman's voice on the other end of the receiver.

"Good morning, Mrs. Trembley, this is the doctor from the animal hospital." I could hear my voice overcompensate. I was way too peppy.

"Actually it's Ms. Trembley," she corrected. "How's my baby?"

"Good. Great. Super. Doing very well. I just wanted to let you know that we will be doing surgery this afternoon, not this morning as previously planned."

"That's okay. Thank you for keeping me up to date."

"Yes, you see, there was an unexpected emergency."

"I understand," she said. "These things happen. But you are still planning on doing Fly's surgery today, aren't you?"

"Yes, of course." I let the silence hang between us and then added, "Ms. Trembley, may I ask how you came to the hospital this morning?"

It was her turn to hesitate.

"By car, why?"

"I see. And Fly likes to go for rides in the car?"

"He doesn't get sick, if that's what you mean?"

"And does he happen to sit up front, perhaps attentively noting the route, the traffic lights, the intersections, the parks and playgrounds he passes en route, thereby formulating a mental roadmap by which he might navigate his way home should he ever happen to escape from an animal hospital in a strange and remote part of town?"

Of course our conversation went quite differently. Trying to pin my woes entirely on Leah may have felt good at the time but was totally unprofessional. The dog was under my care. I was responsible for his security and I had failed both pet and owner. So I told her the truth. The dog had escaped, it had been an accident but we were doing everything in our power to capture him and bring him back.

To my surprise Ms. Trembley took the news relatively well, saying she would come over right away to help with the quest for Fly.

By the time she arrived, Leah had returned, pathologically flushed and sweaty but still carrying an empty leash.

"I'm so sorry, someone left the back gate open and he must have slipped his leash. He was so fast."

"It's okay, Leah. Where do you think he is?"

She thumbed over her shoulder, pointing toward the parking lot.

"He's out there, just down the street. But you can't get near him. He's freaking out, buzzing you as he sprints past."

When Ms. Trembley arrived my memory kicked in and I felt a little more at ease, remembering her as a pleasant client who had listened attentively and appreciatively to my warnings about general anesthesia with sight hounds. She was dressed in a sweatshirt,

147

sweatpants, and sneakers, as though prepared for a workout, and so, together with Leah and me, she set out to corral the flash of fur and light that was Fly.

We hadn't been out there long before it became apparent that far from being in distress, young Fly was actually enjoying himself, sticking to pavements and grassy islands around the parking lot, skillfully avoiding traffic at every twist and turn, and panting and laughing at our lethargic lunges whenever he stopped to catch his breath.

Ms. Trembley took considerable comfort in this observation, and after thirty minutes of grasping at displaced air, she suggested that she might have better luck catching him if we left her alone.

It was nearly three hours later when I got a call to come up to the front office. There, on a leash, stood Fly, smiling like a naughty schoolboy. Ms. Trembley's expression, on the other hand, was less than pleased.

"Thank goodness," I said, dropping to one knee to offer Fly a rascally pat on the head. As I stood, I followed Ms. Trembley's stare, out beyond the parking lot, to a car pulled up to a young girl in high heels and a miniskirt. A girl I had not seen for some time.

I looked back at Ms. Trembley and I understood.

"Ah," I said, unable and ashamed to maintain eye contact. "You must have met Tracy."

"Yes. You could say I've made her acquaintance." Her words slipped out crisp and clipped. "But that was later." The sarcastic inflection was clearly intended to invite curiosity and I did not see how I could fail her now.

"Oh, really?"

"Yes," she said. "Why don't you ask me how many times I've been propositioned? Go on, ask me."

I cringed.

"Seven times. Seven disgusting perverts wanting to know exactly how much I charge not to use a condom!"

She shouted this statement, much to my chagrin and to the obvious pleasure of a young couple with a caged cockatiel and an elderly man holding a Westie on a leash.

I was speechless. What could I say? "Actually the going rate is around a hundred bucks." I don't think so.

"And to top it all, your friend Tracy came over for a little chat. Such a charming young girl, full of so many colorful ideas about what I might do with myself."

"Yes, I too found her to be most pleasant. Perhaps sweatpants are not best suited to that line of work. Did she give you her list of the better pimps in town?"

Of course I said no such thing. I felt dreadful that this poor woman, after all her tolerance, patience, and understanding, had been subjected to the horrendous degradation of solicitation while trying to secure the very pet that we had so easily managed to mislay. Rarely have I been so humiliated. Rarely have I stooped lower or groveled for longer than I did on that afternoon. I assured her that hospital security would be swiftly and comprehensively overhauled, that shy of digging a tunnel or disguising himself as a particularly muscular borzoi, Fly would not escape again.

Unlike Tracy, I gladly performed all services for this customer entirely free of charge.

From my perspective, true complications are the mistakes you never saw coming, or by the time you do, they are a speeding freight train that you can chase but rarely catch. True complications are like hurricanes. Every year we alternate between male and female names for the storms that whirl up the Atlantic from June to November. From time to time the havoc created is so memorable and cataclysmic, the name is retired, its legacy embedded in our psyche. The names of certain patients have the same effect, retired in my memory as a disaster. They barrel into your life, unstoppable and destined to cause mayhem and frustration. Through no fault of their own, the name will forever instill fear, disappointment, and permanent regret.

Of course there are some complications that are inescapable, unambiguous, entirely and irrevocably our fault and ours alone. The lawyers might prefer to impress us with their snappy slogan *res ipsa loquitur*, or "the thing speaks for itself," but clinicians use the term *iatrogenic*—a complication induced in a patient by a physician's activity, manner, or therapy.

Now, these are exactly the kinds of mistakes the sensationalists love to focus on, flinging accusations of negligence and malpractice. I'm talking about problems so detached from the original disorder that they can only be iatrogenic in origin, and arguably the most clear-cut mistake that can be made by a surgeon is leaving a sponge or metallic instrument inside a patient's body. Coarse, cotton sponges are invaluable in virtually all surgical procedures to mop up extraneous blood and allow visualization of the anatomy. They come with blue metallic strips embedded deep into the material so that they are visible on an X-ray, and typically, in our packs, we start out with ten sponges, which I routinely count at the beginning of a procedure (it's not a good feeling to go hunting for a missing sponge because there were only nine at the start). Recently I heard about one resident, battling his way through a bloody procedure, who sought an intraoperative consultation from an experienced surgeon operating in an adjacent suite. The surgeon joined the resident at the table, gave an opinion, and returned to her procedure, only to hear cries of dismay when the resident's final sponge count did not add up. The resident was adamant that the original tally was ten and now he could only account for nine. The patient was closed up and while remaining under anesthesia, transferred to radiology, where an X-ray confirmed that the sponge was categorically not left inside the patient. The animal could now be woken up, but still puzzled by what had happened, the resident returned to the surgeon, once more seeking her opinion. Only now did he notice the bloody wad of a single surgical sponge stuck like bubblegum to the bottom of one of her clogs.

It has been reported that a foreign object is retained in a human patient in the United States once in every 15,000 operations, which means I should have been guilty of, seen or heard about, far more than the one case of a retained sponge referred to me as a hunting exercise. Consultation with my colleagues yielded similar experiences, and no one reported a single incident of a metal instrument being left behind. How can this be? Human surgeons have nurses dedicated to a sponge and instrument count. Are human surgeons more lackadaisical, more clumsy, more prone to intraoperative bleeding? I think not. Perhaps the secret of our apparent superior surgical prowess actually lies in the fact that veterinary procedures are relatively simple by comparison, with less risk, less stress, and fewer distractions. By virtue of our patients' size, abdominal and thoracic cavities are smaller, thereby providing fewer places to play hide and don't seek. Also, most of my patients are not thinking about beach vacations and bikini styles. Consequently I can indulge in a larger incision that affords me greater visibility than working through a vanity-driven keyhole.

I recall an urban legend of my student days that serves as a warning against complacency in the operating room. A young surgical wannabe joined a veterinary practice and quickly tired of spaying cats, claiming the procedures were tedious and beneath him. His boss insisted that he must master the basics before moving on to more difficult surgery and so the frustrated young surgeon offset his boredom by trying to perform feline sterilization as quickly as possible, timing himself against the clock until he felt so accomplished that he challenged his boss to a spay race to prove just who was the superior and worthy surgeon. To his surprise the senior clinician accepted the duel, and so it was that the two men stood back-to-back at adjacent operating tables, scalpels hovering over shaved and surgically prepped kitty bellies, awaiting the starter's orders. A minute into the race and our young gun was in serious trouble. Trying to keep his incision small to save precious seconds during the closure meant that he would have to snag the uterus using an instrument called a Snook hook, a skill he had mastered during training. Yet suddenly here he was pulling up nothing but fat and loops of small intestine. By the time he had decided to enlarge his incision, the senior partner was throwing his closing stitch and declaring himself the winner.

The young doctor was both humiliated and incredulous that he had not even come close to making a race of it. The senior partner smiled and said, "If you learn nothing else from this experience, let it be a keener sense of preoperative evaluation."

The young man made it clear he did not understand.

"Take a closer look at your patient," said the senior partner. "You've been trying to spay a tomcat!"

There can be no greater affirmation of your failure as a surgeon than an amputation for a fracture repair that went wrong, and it makes no difference if the odds were stacked against you at the outset. We make our judgment calls and like some of the best umpires in the world of sports, without the benefit of hindsight, rewind, and slow motion, every so often we are bound to get things wrong. Amputation for fractures are often a rubber stamp that lets the world know that your best efforts were not good enough, that you were unable to convince the body that it needed to heal, that you were not up to the task, not quite the surgeon you thought you were.

Here's a perfect example. Toto is as sweet a full-figured four-year-old cat as you are likely to meet, and shares her disposition and lengthy white hair with her slight and fragile old mom. One day Toto decided to go for a stroll. Apparently she hadn't noticed that Mom

lived in a seventh-floor apartment, an omission that cost her a fractured jaw, lung contusions, a broken left front leg, and a broken
right hind leg after sky-diving from an open window.

In December 1987, a scientific article from the Animal Medical
Center in New York documented the fate of 132 cats that leaped from
assorted tall buildings over a five-month period. And no, that wasn't
a typo—132 cats in five months. I don't know about dogs, but it must
have been raining cats in Manhattan that year. The paper offered fascinating insight into so-called High-Rise Syndrome (a title applied to
animals falling two or more stories), describing the different injuries sustained and how to best treat them. Amazingly 90 percent
of the cats survived, but what surgeons like me with an eye for
minutia and obscure detail remember about the paper is the importance of the lucky number seven in their findings. It turns out that
if you look at the severity and frequency of the injuries, there is
roughly a linear relationship with the number of stories you fall up
to the seventh floor. This seems intuitive—the higher the jump to
the concrete down below, the greater the trauma sustained. But then
the results went a little wacky. Greater than seven-story jumps actually resulted in a decrease in the rate of fractures. Only one cat out of
twenty-two falling from above the seventh floor actually died as a direct result of his or her injuries, and there was only one broken bone
in thirteen cats falling more than nine stories. One pioneer of this
evolution of cat into flying squirrel dropped thirty-two stories onto
concrete and was released from the hospital after forty-eight hours
having sustained nothing more than mild lung bruising and a
chipped tooth.

So how is it that cats can successfully play Spider-Man, leaping
from tall buildings virtually unscathed, whereas you and I are guaranteed to die landing on a hard surface from greater than six stories?
The authors of the article speculated that the secret lies with the cat's
unique desire to right itself during flight, twisting and contorting

their springy little bodies, able to get their legs underneath and extended, ready to take the impact of the fall. Most of this preparation for landing and placement of limbs in the full-upright position is thought to be a reflex response to acceleration as our furry projectile tries to reach terminal velocity (roughly five stories and sixty miles per hour). Once this point is reached, the body cannot go any faster, balance centers in the brain no longer perceive acceleration, and perhaps reflex rigidity abates, leaving the cat relaxed and able to spread out in a horizontal manner like a skydiver sans the goggles and parachute, unwinding into free-falling acrobatics. With legs stiff and extended, bones break on impact. With legs horizontal and relaxed, impact can be distributed over a larger area, which means fewer fractures. Perhaps Toto's mom wished she'd taken that apartment with a better view on the tenth floor.

But I digress. The first time I met Toto, she completely sucked me in. Who could resist a white fur ball wearing chubby teal green boxing gloves on one front leg and one back leg, pulling herself forward in a cage before rolling onto her back and saying, "Quit feeling sorry for me and give me a scratch"? She appeared insensible to the severity of her trauma, as though her nirvana would be complete with a warm lap, the click of knitting needles, and the aroma of Earl Grey.

When the admitting doctor asked if I could repair Toto's legs, he wafted the X-rays under my nose and the challenge of multiple-limb trauma proved irresistible. Having signed me up he dared to throw in his caveat. "Did I mention that Toto left a calling card on the pavement where she landed?"

I made a "let's have it" beckoning motion with my right hand.

"Yeah, a three-centimeter piece of bone, part of the shaft of her left tibia. The owner brought it in with her. But that was three days ago, so we tossed it in the trash."

I took a closer look at the X-rays. Three centimeters may not sound like much but in a cat that's a whole lot of contaminated nothingness.

"Don't worry," said the admitting doctor. "I prepared the owner for hind-leg amputation and she was fine with that."

And there it was, the schoolboy dare, out in the open. But was I man enough to take it? If I fixed the front leg and removed the back leg, this happy-go-very-lucky feline would do great, but was it the best option for the cat? Amputation would be a whole lot easier for me, but given the choice between trying to repair a fracture and lopping off one of my limbs, I know what I would prefer. Anthropomorphism is rarely the best impetus and part of me worried that I was being motivated by the challenge, but I tried to focus on the big picture. Reduced to one back leg, Toto would be forced to throw more weight forward, potentially jeopardizing the repair of the broken front leg. If I could restore her as a quadruped, wouldn't this improve her chance to heal? And besides, veterinary students are taught that cats only need the ends of their broken bones to be in the same room to heal. Discounting the segment on its way to the nearest landfill, there was still a good chance I could mend the break.

So I repaired both legs. The radius and ulna fracture came together nicely, and I moved on to the tibia, supporting the defect in the shaft of the bone with a combination of plates and screws together with an external scaffold of skewering pins. Then I packed the gap with fresh, healthy bone graft scooped like little balls of raspberry gelato from Toto's left humerus. Everything went great, looked great, and the cat did great until the follow-up visit and X-rays six weeks later. Toto was fully ambulatory, Mom thrilled, and the front leg completely healed. But my graft in the tibia had disappeared. In fact, the ends of the bone seemed to have melted farther back than when I'd performed the surgery.

There are three ways we can classify the failure of bone to heal. A malunion is where the bone heals but in the wrong way, making a limb twist, bow, or bend, impairing normal function and range of motion. Toto's tibia was perfectly aligned but appeared reluctant to heal. Therefore at six weeks I could optimistically hedge that this was nothing more than a delayed union, a bone that was in no hurry to heal, as opposed to an explicit definition of failure—a nonunion.

I convinced myself that I was overprotecting the tibia with too many metal implants, that Toto was walking around on so much hardware, her little body happy to trade stainless steel for new bone. So I removed the external scaffold and waited another six weeks.

At the next visit, Toto was as precocious and content as ever, but as she came out of her carrier to greet me, I noticed how she carried her back leg as if she were double-jointed, the paw buckled underneath her belly. Then I caught the glint of light bouncing off exposed steel where the plate had stripped off the lower segment of bone and burst through the skin. Mom seemed as surprised as I was. She thought it was part of the repair, not least because Toto made no complaint, beating out a tune like a Caribbean steel drum band as she danced across my metal examination table.

To my way of thinking, there was nothing left to decide. I had tried to save her leg but I had failed. Bone had vaporized, the screws had loosened, and everything fell apart. Time to accept my nonunion and an amputation I should have elected from the start.

Although such brazen complications have a tendency to leave a surgeon wary and unsettled, who better to slap you upside the head than the patient herself? At her final suture removal, Toto was racing around, leaping on chairs, playing in the sink, and making it quite clear that I should learn to lose my pride as easily and as graciously as she had learned to lose a leg.

Given the inevitability of mistakes and complications, the importance of the animals in our lives, and the increasingly litigious tendencies of our society, you might wonder how any veterinarian manages to sustain a career. To my way of thinking, the secret lies in the evolution of arguably the most important skill a veterinarian will ever possess—the art of good communication.

It has been suggested that bad communication, miscommunication, or a blatant lack of communication accounts for up to 80 percent of legal actions taken against veterinarians, and given the ubiquitous nature of mistakes and complications, it makes sense to vaccinate against this possibility by learning how best to convey, argue, defend, advocate, and console. These days an endearing bedside manner is much more than a gentle pat across a cherished threadbare pillow. Acquiring good communication skills is like a shot during flu season. You still might catch a cold, but the effects are far less severe. And as for those high school students who tell me they would rather be a vet than an MD because they prefer to deal with animals and not to deal with people, I let them know they have it all wrong. Veterinarians get to work *with* animals. We get to work *for* people.

I am not trying to belabor the importance of good communication because I think I am an authority on the art. There are legions of clinicians out there far more gifted with a sixth sense that allows them to connect with the entire spectrum of the pet-owning public in a way that seems instinctive and pitch perfect. I have tried to define what it is and where I can buy some, but the best I can come up with is that for all the honesty, compassion, and trust they manage to squeeze into a brief encounter, more than most they appreciate the importance of when to just shut up and listen. None of us can know exactly what each individual owner of a sick pet is feeling and going through, but with little or no effort on our part we can really hear what they have to say and strive for that elusive and essential quality called empathy.

As Mr. Brown's phone rings for the fifth time, I think about the burden my postoperative instructions place upon my clients. No stairs, no rough-housing, no licking the incision, no slippery floors, no jumping on furniture—I rattle off orders like a drill sergeant, orders that would challenge the mental health of a motivational speaker, let alone a rambunctious puppy. Recovering pets must share homes with family members forever cursing my existence and the impossible rules I make them live by.

Having said this I am forever amazed by the lengths to which people will go to optimally recover their sick pet. They will move a mattress downstairs, sleep on the couch, carry a 150-pound dog upstairs (and not bill me for subsequent consultations with their chiropractor), lay sod on a deck or porch so the dog doesn't have to go down steps to pee and poop in the backyard, build ramps, disarm doorbells, try Venezuelan hot sauce to deter licking (note: this will not stop most Labradors), buy carpeting to protect against slippery, hardwood floors, purchase a harness, a log carrier, a Radio Flyer, a cart, or whatever it takes to ensure safe and limited mobility during a surgical recovery.

After the sixth ring I hear "Hello?"

"Hello, Mr. Brown. I am calling to check in on Hugo. I'm sorry to be calling so late in the morning, but I got trapped in appointments."

My tone is positive, upbeat, all "I'm sure it's not as bad as all that." Air builds in my lungs as I await the rejoinder.

"That's okay," he says and he sounds genuine. "The problem is swelling. But fortunately my dog thinks he's a Newfoundland."

"I beg your pardon," I say. I don't have Hugo's record in front of me, but I could have sworn he's a rottweiller.

"He's been doing well, perhaps too well for a dog only a week home after surgery. Yesterday I found him at the top of the stairs. I reckon he'd gone up and down a couple of times because his knee blew up like a balloon and his ankle went all watery. He stopped using the leg altogether and that was when I called. But then I remembered what you said about applying cold packs or hot packs and how some dogs like Newfoundlands are often more tolerant of the cold. Well, so was Hugo. He's much better this morning. Didn't you get my message? I called first thing to let you know."

Mr. Brown has a few more questions, just small stuff and I am happy to answer, knowing that Hugo is a name I will not have to worry about, a storm that, for now, has lost strength as it makes landfall, downgraded to a forgettable tropical depression.

Somehow I manage to restrain myself, because at the conclusion of our conversation all I really want to say is "And you're doing a heckuva job, Brownie!"

9

· · · · · · · · · · ·

10:47 A.M.

SUPERSIZED!

There's a note clipped to the medical record for my final appointment of the morning informing me that my patient needed a bathroom break and will be back in ten minutes and suddenly that elusive caffeine fix is finally within my grasp, so long as I embrace the lunch-room coffee machine trading seventy-five cents for an eight-ounce cup of boiling watery pig swill that they swear is fresh brewed.

"You look like shit," says Scott, a burly redheaded radiology technician dressed in the royal blue scrubs of his department. "Up all night?"

"GDV," I reply, passing the cup back and forth between my hands so as to avoid the need for skin grafts on the tips of my fingers.

He gives me a sage nod. No need to say more. Then he makes a show of scratching his chin.

"Clients enjoying the early George Michael stubble you're sporting this morning?"

I shake off the quip and make to leave, but Scott's not through.

"Hey, hold up," he says, reaching for a carefully folded piece of paper in his pocket that he passes to me. "Here, you'll get a kick out of this."

I meet his eyes, convey my doubt, look down, and gasp at the image before me. It is a digital photograph printed on regular A4 paper of Scott struggling to carry a cat of mythical bodily proportions. A pinhead of a pointy feline face is attached to an unruly sprawling mass of fur, all extraneous appendages in the form of limbs or a tail engulfed by the enormity of the cat's belly.

"Who, or should I say, what, is this?"

Scott smiles. He likes the effect his picture has on people.

"This living legend is a little cat called Chunky Bear. He came in last night and he weighs a little over forty pounds. I reckon that's the equivalent of me topping off unseen bathroom scales at around seven hundred pounds."

Scott's hands begin banding around like a boastful fisherman talking about the one that got away in an attempt to do justice to the sheer volume of this corpulent creature.

"And get this," says Scott, " 'the Chunkster' was in for a skin fold infection, just like the ones people get who are morbidly obese."

Feeling guilty about keeping my last client waiting, I return his digital proof of Big Foot.

"I went online," Scott shouts after me. "The *Guinness Book of World Records* says the current living record holder is only a few ounces more. Makes you think, doesn't it?"

When I return to my examination room a supervisor informs me that my client is still not back, and so, succumbing to the tug of "believe it or not" curiosity, I sit down in front of the computer terminal to locate the phone number for Chez Chunky Bear. This cat is a train wreck and like everyone else who saw the picture, I can't help but stare. There has to be more to the story. Obesity is the most important nutritional disorder facing twenty-first-century pets, and I want to know how Chunky came by his name and whether his human parents are trying to offer him the feline equivalent of another "wafer thin mint," manipulating his size on purpose so that he might have a shot at the heavyweight title. Perhaps he was adopted later in life, by which time his portliness had earned him a fitting name? If so, why did the owners hold back? Why not go whole hog by calling him Lard-Ass, Bloated Tick, or that other timeless classic, Fat Bastard?

With these and many other equally pertinent questions in mind, the phone begins to ring. Chunky's owner and/or coach seems extremely pleasant and appreciative of my interest in her cat. She tells me she bred his mother and claims that Chunky was a cross between a Maine coon cat, a breed noted for its large proportions, and a feral cat (perhaps a panther or a mountain lion, I helpfully suggest).

"When he came out his head was about the same size as his mom's," she says. This troubling gynecological image haunts me as she explains that his original name was Raven (short for "ravenous" I imagine), but she changed it to Chunky Bear when he was still a svelte and lithe thirty-five pounds.

Around that time she moved into the city and Chunky resigned himself, with no great difficulty, to being an indoor cat.

"He might make it to the stoop," she says, "but there he just plops down."

"So he must eat a lot of food?" I ask, bracing myself for an exhaustive list.

"Not really," she tells me. "He only eats diet dry food, a cup or a cup and a half a day."

"What about the dozen eggs, five pints of whole milk, and half a dozen steaks?" I want to add, but instead I say, "What, no people food?"

"No. He's not interested." And then into the silence of my incredulity she adds, "Really. He's just a big cat. Big boned."

"Big boned," I reply, realizing too late that my slowly rising into-nation has given away my skepticism. I try to move on.

"Does he do much in the way of exercise?"

She pauses to think about this.

"He likes to lie around and watch TV," she says. Then she adds, "He walks around, some." And then enthusiastically, "He jumps down. Always down, never up."

"Really," I say. "The whole house must shake."

She laughs and adds, "Yes. Sometimes I think it's my boyfriend walking into the room."

I really want to inquire as to the size of her boyfriend, but some-thing holds me back.

"You know," I say, "Chunky Bear is almost big enough to get into the *Guinness Book of World Records*. Another can of tuna a day and who knows, he could be famous."

Her scream in delight pierces my ear, and when I can hear again, she is rattling on about the current record, what it might take to get him up to a good competitive weight, and who she should contact to get the appropriate media attention.

"Seriously," I say, "I was only joking about the extra can of tuna."

But she is no longer listening.

"Everyone loves him. All my friends come to visit, just to see how big he is. They think he's so cute."

And this is precisely my point. In the world of cats and dogs, obe-sity is not only acceptable, it can actually enhance an animal's ap-peal, transforming them into something akin to a stuffed, or even overstuffed, soft and cuddly toy. This is a far cry from our world in which judgment and prejudice against the overweight members of our society runs deep and develops early. Consider this example: A group of Yale University psychologists visited three kindergarten classes, each from different socioeconomic backgrounds, and of-fered children a chance to win a doll. The children's choices were, however, limited to dolls missing a limb, sporting a disfiguring skin condition, or dolls that were fat. So which dolls were the last to be selected? That's right. The fat dolls were perceived to be both "ugly and lazy."

Even in the health-care profession, the very people dedicated to helping individuals with weight-related disorders, sadly, often lack empathy. The majority of seventy-seven physicians surveyed in one study considered the obese "weak-willed, ugly and awkward." And in another report, doctors stated they disliked treating obese people because they were "self-indulgent, hence, at least faintly immoral and inviting retribution."

So why are pet owners so accepting of their pets' weight problems? Well, for one thing, pet gluttony, for the most part, is the owner's responsibility. If we succumb to the silent heart-wrenching stares that whisper, "You really don't need all of that juicy steak now, do you," then we are to blame, and blame is something most of us do not enjoy. Making our pets happy makes us feel happy. We reach for the kibble, rustle up a little magical percussion, and hey, presto, instant gratification all around.

Why do we even bother to share our food with our pets? Take my own Labrador as an example. How can a creature with such an exquisitely sensitive and overdeveloped sense of smell have such dreadful taste in food? Every morning I feed her the same, monotonous, desiccated, dusty nuggets that she devours with precisely the same enthusiasm, literally inhaling the entire meal in seconds. If I do toss her a piece of meat or a crust of bread, the routine is exactly the same—grab, swallow, and a look that says "What was that?" What ever happened to taste, savor, or, dare I mention, chew? What a waste of a perfectly good set of teeth!

Offering too much food is instinctive, a way in which we ingratiate ourselves to our mute friends. But it is only part of the problem. Failure to burn adequate calories is the other big player. For humans, televisions, computers, and automobiles carry a burden of responsibility. But pets are not accountable to these trappings of a comfortable life, and therefore, once again, we are to blame if exercise is wanting in their lives.

Unfortunately, many owners are unaware, or in complete denial of obesity problems with their pets, and this is when my life becomes difficult. Of course I am oversimplifying obesity and there are many significant metabolic, reproductive, hormonal, and genetic reasons for packing on the pounds that I am purposefully avoiding. But with an estimated 45 percent of the dog and cat population considered overweight or obese, rarely will I buy into the old chestnut that "He's just got a slow metabolism" or "We think it's a problem with his glands."

Historically, I have often found myself trapped in an examination room attempting to convince the overweight owners of an overweight Labrador (or "Fatador" as they are sometimes fondly labeled) that their dog's arthritis really would benefit from shedding a couple of (dozen) pounds.

"You really think he's fat?" They say, both incredulous and offended.

"Well," I offer, gently, "Beef certainly would benefit from a little dietary discretion. But then again, so could you."

It is this last, unsaid sentence that I believe many sensitive owners really hear. This type of discussion can be awkward and occasionally embarrassing territory. Despite my most valiant attempts to keep my dieting instructions practical, even lighthearted, and my eyes focused solely on the animal in front of me, I frequently come away with the impression that owners think I was pointing fingers at them and not their dog, as though I have grouped both parties together for a lecture intended to benefit all. Like so many humans who attempt to diet, my experience with dogs and cats is that they usually fail. I perceive that some of these clients leave me appreciative of the information but saddened that I have burdened them with the responsibility.

I recall one client entirely comfortable with that anthropomorphic theory of the pet resembling its master or, in this case, mistress. Mrs. Katz is a wonderful woman. She is warm, sensitive, brimming with ingestive skills and incredibly attached to her Persian cat, William. She is, by her own reckoning, "a fatty," and then again, so is her cat. It turned out that young William had a hernia that required surgical correction and so it came as something of a shock when, during our discussion about the pending procedure, Mrs. Katz did not hesitate to whip up her tent of a sweatshirt, exposing an ample belly studded with stitches and bearing the ocher hue of recent surgical bruising. She proudly pointed out the healing incisions from her six, count them, six, abdominal hernias, repaired four days earlier. For the record her husband was in attendance throughout the exhibition; he sat wearing a goofy grin and nodding like one of those bobble-headed dogs. He left me with the distinct impression that his wife had pulled this stunt before.

I like to think that my face only gave away a sense of incredulity at the sight before me. I like to think I masked the expression of utter revulsion, but I'm really not sure. They don't teach this stuff at vet school. I mean what is the polite response to a flabby flash from a virtual stranger of the opposite sex?

My first encounter with canine obesity took place when I was a ten-year-old boy. My grandmother had come to live with my family during a period in her dementia when running into the neighborhood in search of her dead mother still occurred at an alarming rate. Unfortunately she had sufficient marbles to insist on bringing her canine companion, a dalmatian dog named Rex. Ordinarily this should not have been a problem but we were far from being an ordinary household, because as I mentioned earlier, we were already living under the rule of a wonderful but dominant alpha dog, our German shepherd called Patch.

At the time, I was woefully ignorant of the dalmatian's prestigious history as an endurance breed, popular as carriage dogs in eighteenth-century England. Had I known that Rex possessed enough stamina to keep up with a horse, I might have appreciated his need to blow off more steam than a lady with a walker could satiate. I might have understood that Rex needed a personal trainer to offset his tendency to become ornery. Instead, I thought Rex was an overweight, deranged, spotty dog, upset because his crown as top dog had been toppled by the senior canine in our household.

And so it came to pass that the king was forced to become a lowly prince. Feeling dejected and alone, the king found sanctuary in the form of food. Rex would devour any food, anytime, anywhere, and through a combination of binge eating and inadequate exercise, he managed to pack over one hundred pounds onto a body designed for about half that amount.

The king's behavior began to take a turn for the worse when he decided that if he must be subservient to another dog then he must become dominant over people, including my grandmother. He perfected the precious trait of lunging at you, with much drooling, growling, and gnashing of teeth, should you deign to leave any room occupied by his majesty. Consequently, when the time came to vacate a room, it was necessary to create a distraction. Initially this took the form of a ball or chew toy tossed as far away as possible. But it was not long before the wise king twigged the inanimate decoy ploy and refused to be moved. When food bribes were implemented they proved extremely successful, however repetitious they became. Unfortunately the caloric burn created by these short spurts of energy did little to offset Rex's expanding girth and it soon became clear that drastic steps would be needed to derail his ascension toward morbid obesity.

Placing Rex on a diet had several effects. First, the speed with which Rex retrieved the lure, devoured it, and pounced at your heels forcing you to close the door on his snarling snout, dramatically increased. Second, there were never enough pieces of old cheese or leftover chicken in the refrigerator. Third, Rex became something of a cheese connoisseur, increasingly demanding of more mature and flavorful cheeses than the cracked and crusty ball of Edam we usually tossed his way. Last, and most important of all, the dog did not appear to be losing any weight.

With hindsight, it was not surprising that one day his psychosis finally snapped. I had come home from school and like most boys my age was irrationally famished and in need of food. I entered the kitchen and Rex greeted me, playing innocent and doe-eyed. Getting in was the easy part. I moved to the refrigerator and felt his gaze as I rooted around inside. I made my selection and backed toward the kitchen door, a desiccated dreg of cheddar in one hand, a fragrant slice of fresh Stilton in the other. The routine was always the same as I faced off against one hundred and one pounds of dalmatian. Rex would retract his head and neck into his body, as if ready to pounce, while his lips rippled and quivered to display his fine ivory dentition. Now, dalmatian breeders reading this might chuckle at my naive observation and say that he was merely expressing what they jovially refer to as a "smarl," a hybrid of a full-toothed smile and a snarl, clearly with the emphasis on the friendlier of the two gestures. If this *was* Rex's intent, then let me suggest that in his case I change the emphasis to that of a "snile."

From here on out I had my moves down pat like a highly trained commando. I would pretend to pull a pin out of the dry cheddar ball with my teeth before tossing said ball over-arm like a hand grenade into a far-flung corner of the kitchen. Next, with absolute faith in the power of my decoy, I would reach for the door handle, resisting the temptation to look back at this guardian of Hades, and commit to making good my escape.

As always I followed the plan to the letter. What I did not realize was that Rex had decided that he wanted the Stilton, and no sooner had I turned for the door than I felt the piercing sting of his canine teeth sinking into the succulent flesh of my young buttocks.

I was too shocked to scream, but fortunately I did drop the Stilton, giving me enough time to lock myself in the downstairs bathroom. Entombed in the bathroom, nursing my swollen rump and unable to fully inspect the damage, I waited until my father came home before being carted off to the hospital to have my bottom inspected by a professional.

Obviously something had to be done about Rex. The Stilton saga revealed how our whole family had become completely subservient to a fat spotty dog. Poor Rex was in need of a family that could give him more attention, more freedom, and much more exercise. He needed to be top dog. He needed to be coronated once again.

My father telephoned a local veterinary practice for advice and was put in contact with some sort of canine rescue group happy to place Rex with a retired couple (hopefully retired from the British Special Air Services or the Military Police) who had recently lost their dalmatian to cancer. Apparently they had no other dogs, no children, and lots of land on which Rex could shed the pounds. So Rex's abdication from our family worked out well for both parties, and whenever I came home from school there was always a plentiful supply of cheese and chicken in the fridge.

For a refreshingly different yet somewhat disturbing outlook on obesity I must recount the tale of a veterinarian's own dog, a rascally two-year-old Jack Russell terrier named Wally.

Wally's problem was all too common for this increasingly popular and highly active breed of dog. Given the slightest crack in the front door, Wally would hurl himself, Indiana Jones–style, through this fissure, bolting down the front path before disappearing into the neighborhood with a triumphant bark as he went.

"It drove me absolutely nuts," said his owner. "No amount of calling his name made any difference. I could tell he was laughing at me, giving me the finger as he trotted off down the street."

"How did you get him back?" I asked.

"Well, I'd get out the car and cruise around until I spotted him. Imagine curb crawling for hours while your neighbors are thinking you are some kind of pervert, and all you can do is curse the day your kids first set eyes on the little fur ball. What I really hated the most was having to be all sweet and nice when you finally caught up to him, otherwise the little shit wouldn't get into the car."

"I see," I said, nodding in the sympathetic way that only a fellow parent of a Jack Russell might. "You must have gone through an awful lot of treats."

"Not really," he said. "I used bread. He always came for bread. Don't ask me why but it seemed to work. The trouble was that the very next day he'd be at it again; slight crack in the door and bang, he'd find the gap and was gone like shit off a shovel. Out I'd go with the bread again."

"Wheat, pumpernickel, sourdough, rye, challah?" I inquired.

"What?"

"Nothing," I said. "So what did you do about the problem? I mean, you couldn't go on chasing this dog every night."

"Exactly right," he said. "So that was when I invented . . ."

He deliberately paused as if waiting for a drum roll.

"The Jack Russler." He spoke like someone announcing an act on a talent show. And then, as though he had given careful consideration to its salability, added "The Jack Russler is a unique and affordable method of restraint for even the most wayward of our canine friends. At one time I was even thinking about applying for a patent."

"Really," I said, "and what exactly is it?"

"Well," he said, almost conspiratorially, "it's actually a two-liter Coke bottle full of sand, attached by a metal chain to his collar."

I nodded and tried not to hide my alarm. Not exactly under threat of industrial espionage, I thought.

"That sounds a bit," I wanted to say irresponsible and likely to get you reported for animal cruelty, but I managed, "drastic. I mean how does Wally get about?"

He studied me as though I were a complete idiot.

"He doesn't. At least, not at first. See you have to carefully titrate the amount of sand so that he has some mobility, but not too much. Believe me, it's a fine line between serenity and abandon."

"I'll bet," I replied, having no idea what he was talking about. "And did it work?"

He dropped his gaze and muttered, "Not really. The clever little bastard quickly learned how to get the better of me."

"How so?" I said, trying to sound surprised.

"He would pretend to be dragging his bottle behind him, as if the weight were too much, and then, as soon as I lightened his load a couple of grains, he'd bolt for an open door as if the bottle weighed nothing, pausing momentarily to turn and look me in the eye. I can read that look. He was saying, "Screw you, buddy," before he bolted down the street."

I tried to conceal my smile and asked, "So then what?"

"Well, I was at a veterinary meeting, wandering among the booths in the exhibitors hall, looking at all the latest stuff they've got and there was a guy selling shock collars. So, I thought, why not? I asked him for two, and he inquired as to the size of my dog. When I said it was a Jack Russell, he looked alarmed. I said, you don't understand what I'm dealing with, that I don't just need to shock him, I need to physically drop him to the ground. I think the high pitch in my voice might have made him nervous and I noticed that he was studying my name tag. I decided a shock collar might not work after all and started backing off. I'm pretty sure he didn't catch my name."

"So you went back to the bread."

"No way," he said, smiling. "Problem solved. I elected for a more natural solution."

"And that would be . . . ?"

"Obesity, of course. I just took the bread thing to the next level. Wally gets to eat whatever he wants. He's happy and as a result significantly slower than he used to be. When he heads for the door I can usually wrestle him to the ground before he makes it halfway down the drive."

"Exactly how heavy is he?" I asked.

"Not sure," the vet replied. "As long as I can rest a six pack of beer across his back, I know I'll have the better of him."

I confess that the image of an obese Jack Russell terrier, fed the antithesis of a low-carb diet as an alternative to appropriate dog training, did not sit well with me. Clearly his owner was actually condoning gluttony in his own pet. And so, several months later, I found myself paying this vet an impromptu visit.

It was Friday at lunchtime and I found Wally's dad in his office, sitting down to a big bowl of green salad. Even seated behind his desk, I could tell that Wally was not the only one who had been packing on the pounds.

"Sorry to interrupt your lunch," I said.

He beckoned me in around a mouthful of chewed cud.

"Looks . . . good," I said. "Or, at the very least, healthy."

He nodded, swallowed hard, and continued to work his jaw.

"We order pizza for everyone, every Friday. But I'm looking after myself. I only ever order a salad. Which reminds me."

He reached into a drawer below his desk, pulled out a pill, popped it in his mouth, and washed it down with a swig of bottled mineral water.

"Lipitor," he said by way of an explanation. "My doctor says I've got to watch my cholesterol."

I feigned surprise and thought of using "and speaking of obesity" as a segue but went with, "So how is that Jack Russell of yours, young Wally?"

"Fine," he said, repeatedly jabbing at his arugula until he had accumulated a worthwhile wad.

"Is he still overweight?"

I had to wait for the slapping mouth noises to subside before he replied, "Not at all. He's right back down to where he used to be."

"What do you mean?" I said. "What about the bolting for the front door? What about the escapades in the neighborhood?"

More stubborn mastication.

"It's no longer a problem. For some reason, all I have to do is show Wally a slice of bread before he goes out of the house and it's enough to ensure his return. He doesn't even eat it. And on the rare occasions he wanders farther afield, he's learned to recognize my car. I pull up, open the door, and he hops right in. No bribe required."

I imagined this crafty little dog, happy to be back in shape, and wondered if he was actually trying to tell his master something.

"When Wally wanders off, do you always have to go and find him by car?"

The leaf-laden fork froze in front of his open mouth.

"What are you trying to say? You think my dog is looking out for me, trying to get me to do more exercise?"

Giraffe lips sucked the vegetation down to white plastic.

"Wally may be devious," he said, "but he ain't that clever."

I left him to finish the dregs of his salad as I caught up with his partner in the practice, and after a further fifteen minutes was heading out of the building when I passed the staff break room. The room seemed quiet and empty but I sensed movement behind the half-open door. Peering through the gap at the hinge, I saw Wally's dad, alone, rifling his way through a stack of empty pizza boxes until he found a cold unloved slice of pepperoni in the bottom. Surreptitiously, almost tenderly, he held the greasy triangle up to his lips and began to devour it.

I could have walked on, but thinking about what Wally would have done, I popped my head around the door, waved my hand, and said, "See you later."

And as our eyes locked—him seeing the satisfaction on my face, me seeing the stringy mozzarella stuck to his—a single, liberating word blossomed in the silence between us, a word I wanted to scream, a word his priceless expression simply could not deny.

"Busted!"

I walked off, pleased and in no doubt as to who was the real top dog in his family.

10

· · · · · · · · · ·

10:56 A.M.

THE FINAL STRAW

Ms. Jessie Wicks greets me with all her trademark warmth and affability, as though the delay in seeing her Bernese mountain dog, Jacob, has been a blessing and a wonderful opportunity to socialize with all the other sick animals in the waiting room.

There is nothing I don't like about this woman, from her ratty, woolen hat that I have never witnessed off her head and the grubby red ski jacket that she wears permanently zipped up and Michelin-man style to the crusty white streaks of leftover toothpaste at the corners of her mouth and the mysterious grocery bags always hanging by her sides. She has to be sixty. She is intelligent yet certifiable, articulate yet reclusive, unemployed yet "loaded to the gills," and she will gladly lay down her life for her mountain dog.

When I first met Ms. Wicks, I was physically bowled over by her exuberant, jolly, and powerful one hundred and forty pounds of tri-colored silky fur and energy. Jacob savored life. He panted, drooled, pounced, and pranced around the examination room like no other nine-year-old "Berner" I had seen, despite the obvious lameness in his right front leg.

"My vet tells me that Jacob has bone cancer, so I want you to take off his leg."

Not exactly my typical discussion about the delicate and highly emotive subject of amputation. More than most common surgical procedures, amputation incites enormous trepidation in pet owners. This is perfectly reasonable and normal, but consider the following questions: When was the last time you saw a dog pick its nose? When was the last time you saw a dog arm wrestle, paint, or play the piano? Do you really believe three-legged dogs become ostracized by their friends and spurned from cocktail parties? Do you think they get branded with a handicapped sticker and forced to use a ramp or purchase a stair climber?

If you believe the answer to be no to all these questions, and appreciate that cats and dogs do not have these psychological issues, then the decision to amputate a limb becomes a whole lot easier. In the case of Ms. Wicks, any discussion on the subject was moot because, with a greater clarity than most, she already understood that vanity is not a doggy deadly sin.

Back at our first meeting she had shown me a series of X-rays of Jacob's right shoulder. Even to an untrained eye, the alignment of scattered radiation seemed all wrong; solid white lines of bone replaced and eroded into a rotting, moth-eaten frame; so delicate it might crumble or fracture at any time.

"We did a biopsy to be sure," she told me. "Osteosarcoma. Average survival time without surgery—five months. Average survival time with amputation—five months. Average survival time with amputation and chemotherapy—fifty percent to one year, twenty percent to two years."

She had handed me the pathologist's report on the biopsy and I read it, trying to absorb the cold rationality of her understanding. Osteosarcoma might try to hide behind a clinical, emotionally inert and pathologically descriptive label, but it is a bitter, foul, and pernicious crab, hungry to feast and have its fill before scurrying off for seconds.

Long before this tumor has finished munching its way through solid bone, causing pain that laughs in the face of anything less than a potent, full-bodied narcotic, its microscopic cellular offspring have hitched a ride in the bloodstream and decided to throw an impromptu party in the nearest available warm and cozy capillary bed, which, in most cases, happens to be the lungs. By the time of diagnosis, tumor has spread in virtually 100 percent of dogs, even if modern diagnostic tools are unable to find it.

I should point out that the osteosarcoma story is somewhat different for cats. Where dogs contend with a promiscuous party animal that wants to get around town, cats suffer more of a parochial pariah—lonely, self-destructive, and a homebody. Feline osteosarcoma tends to be locally aggressive and slow to spread to other parts of the body, meaning that amputation alone has an excellent chance of proving curative. Unfortunately in dogs, making a difference against this formidable opponent necessitates a combination of amputation with chemotherapy. It is the migrating microscopic progeny, and not the primary tumor, that will kill. This metastatic disease is what we have to beat.

"I understand what he faces," she said, "but the Swiss have a saying about these dogs. 'Three years young dog, three years good dog, three years old dog, everything else is a gift from God.' "

My only reservation with Jacob had been his size and the fact that he already possessed a case of horrible arthritis in both hips and his remaining front left elbow. Nevertheless, limited by other alternatives, we went ahead with the amputation and Jacob appeared to recover well.

About a month or so later the photographs started to appear. They arrived in a plain white envelope, with no accompanying note or letter except for a line of barely legible scrawl on the back of every picture describing the scene.

At first I was thrilled to receive a visual update of how our patient was thriving in the aftermath of losing his leg. There was "Jacob with gnarly pig ear," "Jacob with squeaky toy," "Jacob with dinosaur bone," "Jacob in snow," "Jacob with massage therapist," and lots and lots of "Jacob asleep."

As the months went by, the frequency of the mailings increased, and by the one-year anniversary of Jacob's amputation, I calculated that I must have received over three hundred photographs.

That was when disaster struck. The scheduled X-ray checkup of Jacob's chest revealed two golf ball–size nodules in his lungs. Despite the chemotherapy, the osteosarcoma had spread.

"Can you be positive that the tumor in Jacob's lungs is due to the osteosarcoma?" Ms. Wicks had asked.

I answered her truthfully. "Not absolutely positive. But we know it wasn't there three months ago. Chances are extremely high that it is metastatic disease."

She took a deep breath and I remember bracing myself to argue against her suggesting that Jacob be put to sleep right there and then. But instead she came back with, "I want you to take the lumps out of his chest. I know that this is done in people and that Jacob's outlook is better because he is over a year out and has less than three lumps in his lungs."

And that was when it hit me. It lay beyond her awesome understanding of Jacob's disease and the frightening amount of information available on the Internet. Instead, it was something I had seen, over and over again for the last twelve months, but never, up until that moment, truly appreciated. The photographs—the visual diary of a woman's undying adoration of her sick dog—repeatedly demonstrated a single and unifying feature. In not one photograph was

Jacob actually standing. In not one photograph was he doing any-thing other than lying down or being propped up on his sternum. Not one frame had captured the merest hint of motion, and if this really was the case, then what would his quality of life be like after I cracked open his chest?

There has never been a better time to believe in a brave new world in which our own desires and expectations apply equally to our pets. Current thinking dictates that if it makes me feel better, it must make my pet feel better. If I put my child in day care, then why not my dog? If I'm drinking designer water from a bottle, then so is my cat. The same doctrine applies to health care, as both a blessing and a curse, challenging owners to face painful and emotive end-of-life decisions. Owners given a diagnosis of a terminal illness in their pet have viable alternatives to the needle and the blue juice. The ability to alleviate the effects of disease and pain for some period of time, despite being unable to achieve a cure, defines palliation, and the de-sire for prolongation of animal life has never been greater. For some clients, the possibility of one extra day with a cherished companion is priceless. For others, survival rates that promise to extend life for less than a year are unacceptable. Occasionally, and always after careful deliberation, a push for active euthanasia, as in the tragic case of Mr. Ellis and the catastrophic damage to his poor dog's bro-ken spine, feels like a clear-cut and humane decision. But more often than not, there is no single and obvious course of action. Whichever way you cut my words, at that precise moment when I tell owners the bad news, I'm delivering a death sentence, firing point blank into the bystander in the room. The shock and emo-tional impact of this bullet may have only just pierced the skin but it is tumbling toward their heart where it will tear and rip and lodge. Could there be a more difficult time to make such a complex and far-reaching decision?

I have rerouted the small intestine of a bassett hound with stomach cancer to give the animal an extra six weeks. I have peeled paralyzing tumors off the spinal cord knowing for certain that they will be back with a vengeance in less than three months. I have placed permanent catheters in cancer-ridden bladders to offset the incontinence, the makeshift diapers, and the splashes of urine scald painting skin a sore and angry red. And I have cut out tumors from the skin only to find them twice the original size before I have had time to take out the stitches. For me, it doesn't matter whether I agree with the premise behind the palliation, so long as it remains ethical and humane. What matters is my impartial ability to deliver possibilities and expectations. Veterinarians are purveyors of information, narrators of speculative medical scenarios, full of options with endless diversity from which an owner may choose. If this includes past and personal experiences, so be it. I must accept that no one knows my patient better than the innocent bystander. Their decision may be agonizing, complicated, influenced by previous loss, social isolation, experience with terminal illness, thoughts on natural death versus euthanasia, money, and so much more, but in the end it is theirs to own and I will respect it.

But what if I decided to say, "No, enough is enough. Your animal is suffering and needs to be put to sleep"? Can I insist, after all, that an end to animal suffering is mandated in my oath? When I put this question to my professional bodies on both sides of the pond, I was hardly surprised to receive a variety of vague and woolly responses. How do we define when an animal's quality of life sinks from acceptable to unacceptable, from misguided albeit well-intentioned care to abuse and even cruelty? Perhaps the Royal Veterinary College did the best job of cutting to the chase in its *Guide to Professional Conduct*, which states, in part, "The veterinary surgeon's primary obligation is to relieve the suffering of an animal but account must be taken not only of the animal's condition but also the owner's wishes and circumstances" and "veterinary surgeons can only advise their clients and act in accordance with their professional judgment." I'm sure the language is not meant to emasculate, but I am reminded first and foremost that I am employed in a service industry, where overt neglect and torture will not be tolerated, but where most everything else falls into an ethereal catchall that can be open to interpretation.

In the quest for answers to these difficult questions, I have been frequently rewarded by the perspectives of the respected veterinary ethicist and philosopher Bernard Rollin. Without demeaning the intelligence and emotions of our companion animals, Dr. Rollin points out that although humans may be able to understand and endure a negative short-term medical or surgical experience because we recognize and desire the future benefits, our pets cannot. They are trapped in the now and all the side effects and unpleasantness it may bring. "We have no reason to believe that an animal can grasp the notion of extended life, let alone choose to trade current suffering for it."

I don't believe he's saying it's time to abandon chemotherapy and radiation treatment and the next great thing to come shooting out the medical breakthrough pipeline, but that we must be able to justify the merits of what it takes to help our pets and the outcome we can hope to achieve. He helpfully suggests that early in the human-animal relationship we take the time to list and document all those wonderful idiosyncrasies that let us know, unequivocally, all is well with the world. Silly little things, like the way your dog rolls over and pees in front of strangers, how she trembles for an hour before the first crash of thunder, how your cat likes to sleep in the linen closet, and how she prefers strawberry to vanilla ice cream. Don't panic, I'm not suggesting that there will be an inquisition during the first visit with your new puppy, kitten, or rabbit, and somewhere between toilet training and dental hygiene, quality of life issues will slide into the conversation. I'm just saying it is something to think about before the relationship with the veterinarian has progressed from being the formal Doctor Last Name, to a more personal Aunt or Uncle First Name status. In this way, with everything written down, we will have a point of reference, something tangible to consult when facing questions about quality of life, something to challenge the inevitable skirmish with that easy, fair-weather friend we call denial, and perhaps save ourselves some of the hurt and betrayal that lingers long after our one true friend has gone.

If asked by an owner whether I believe a treatment option is reasonable for their animal, I frequently pontificate about a fifteen-year-old black standard poodle named Noodle. Based on body weight, severity of lameness, and exercise regime, Noodle was a fine candidate for knee surgery. Her age gave me pause, but thankfully for both people and pets, age is not a disease. There is no expiration date on veterinary care. That being said, the reluctant revelation of a concurrent battle with malignant melanoma had me reigning in her mom with a diplomatic version of "Whoa there, Seabiscuit."

"She's doing great," I was assured. "She's in complete remission and her most recent blood work is normal. Her leg is the only thing holding her back."

That and an average survival rate of a couple of months tops, I thought to myself. But I shushed this inner pessimist and began unloading information—sadly, much of it steeped in negativity and chilling statistics. Mom remained calm, lucid, rational, and not to be dissuaded, so I complied, performing my gig in the operating room, enabling the gambler, spotting her a final loan because she was convinced Noodle could beat the bank.

It wasn't the lottery and nothing miraculous transpired overnight, but it turned out that Mom was on the money. Noodle went on to live another two years of pain-free, playful, and unrestricted life and in doggy time that's a huge chunk of living. She serves as a reminder for me to slow down, step back, and take in the bigger picture because, when you least expect it, emotional and financial risks can sometimes pay big dividends.

Every time I admit a case to the Angell Critical Care Unit, I am asked to confront the owner with one unavoidable question—how far would you like us to go to save your pet's life? The question is posed out of necessity, out of practicality, to expedite our actions at a moment of crisis, but the words always leave my lips cold, with an unnerving tingle of pessimism tagging along for the ride as they poke like an insistent finger demanding an objective answer that hopelessly oversimplifies the animal's significance. I am talking about codes, clearly defined and reproducible protocols for the purposes of resuscitation. Three simple colors: red, yellow, and green. In the event of cardiac and respiratory arrest red means stop, no resuscitative efforts should be made. The animal should be monitored but allowed to die naturally. Yellow stipulates standard techniques to revive the patient's heartbeat and breathing while resisting the urge to slash a scalpel blade down and through the muscles between the ribs, cranking open the bloody rent, and blindly attempting to manually squeeze some life back into the heart. This variation on the theme, this attempt to do everything and stop at nothing acquires the ultimate go color of green.

Unfortunately my rare personal experience of the code green, open thoracic cardiac massage and defibrillation, has failed to produce a single survivor that left the hospital (a critical-care specialist told me that she can recall only three cases living to discharge in a fifteen-year period). Naturally there are countless variables that come into play, but even in one "optimistic" study, the results suggest that only about 4 percent of dogs and a little more than twice that percentage of cats (tangible evidence of the feline capacity for extra lives) will scratch and scramble their way back from the white light and recover from their so-called crash. Whatever the exact numbers may be, the outlook in this worst-case scenario looks pretty grim. Sometimes the difference between a code red and a code green can feel like the difference between not buying a lottery ticket and your chance of buying the winning numbers, that is, virtually nothing.

Although there are only three possible answers to my question, red, yellow, or green, the label that will be applied to the animal's permanent record is open to interpretation. Does code red mean the owner is a realist, appreciates that the chances of survival in an arrest are slim, that the condition that precipitated arrest must be severe, that the body is saying it is time to go? Or is it a bloody smear of condemnation that says I do not care enough? Does code green mean I am totally dedicated to my animal's well-being, I will take any odds if there is the slightest chance you will survive, or does it mean I cannot bear the thought of being without you regardless of what you must endure?

Forced to decide whether to accept or deny treatment, whether to sustain or curtail their pet's life, owners may turn to their vet for advice. In this situation I often speak candidly about my hard-earned personal experience with our first family dog, our German shepherd named Patch.

As a thirteen-year-old dog, Patch slowly surrendered to a progressive paralysis in his back legs. I was just a teenager at the time, and like my father, resigned to our family vet's opinion that the stumbling and weakness in his rear end was due to the chronic effects of hip arthritis. With the benefit of hindsight and my own veterinary education, I realized that in all likelihood the cause was an insistent incurable neurological disorder of the spinal cord called degenerative myelopathy. It was as if Patch's body were controlled by two actors trapped inside a pantomime dog costume, with the guy playing the head and the front end all alert and coordinated, while the guy playing the rear was all stoned and wearing roller skates. From Patch's belly forward he was a normal dog—bright, eager to please, and utterly without pain—defying time gracefully, had it not been for the Jell-O in his back legs.

This refusal or failure of the two halves to communicate is the animal's downfall. Head and front end may have purpose and direction, but the straggler in the rear keeps holding them back, literally dragging the dog down. In our backyard Patch would scramble forward like a soldier advancing under enemy fire before collapsing, unable to move, barking for assistance to hoist his withered back end and restore his balance by setting his feet like a surveyor's tripod. One time an animal control officer even paid a visit after receiving a phone call from an anxious neighbor concerned about the German shepherd who must have been hit by a car and broken both his back legs.

Childhood time stretched months of deterioration into years, as if this long good-bye wasn't long enough. And then I came home late one night to find my father in the kitchen, Patch sitting on his haunches, inching away from a paper towel and the steaming turd hiding below the luxuriant brush of his tail.

My father looked like a thief caught with his hand in the till, he and the dog sharing a moment of surprise, confusion, and embarrassment. Neither of us spoke but something passed between us, the men-folk of the family, that it had come to this, that we could deal with the inconvenience so long as we kept the accidents secret from my mother and sister. After all, it wasn't as though Patch was incontinent, not in the true sense of the word. Patch knew that he wanted and was going to have a bowel movement. It was simply his inability to squat, posture, and move away, and for a while our cover-up appeared to be working with my father securing the early and late shift while I destroyed the evidence at lunch break and after school.

In the end bleeding and infection proved to be an indomitable snitch. Regardless of the soft blankets and comforters, trading up concrete and asphalt for carpet and grass, the falls, the scrapes, and the pressure sores began to take their toll. Skin ulcerated, bled, and opportunistic bacteria thrived in wounds that braced for daily beatings. As hard as my father and I tried, there was always a bloody streak or tissue stencil on the linoleum that we had missed.

The knock on my classroom door came late one morning, some forgettable snot-nosed kid informing the teacher that I was to report to the headmaster's office immediately, a request guaranteed to produce a crescendo of oohs directly proportional to the crimson glow of my cheeks. In the eyes of my peers, I was already guilty of an abominable crime.

Our headmaster, Mr. Brian Harris, was a formidable, neckless ogre who stood at least eight feet tall. Behind his back everyone fondly referred to him as Bomber after the British Air Marshal Bomber Harris, the man ultimately responsible for the infamous fire bombing of Dresden in 1945. The nickname said it all, a tribute to our perception of his hard-line approach to school discipline during an era when corporal punishment was not only acceptable, it was encouraged. His very presence and mythical penchant for a trusty wooden cane was more than enough intimidation for far tougher kids than me.

I trudged down empty corridors, resigned to my fate. No one ever received a summons to Bomber's office for a gold star or a pat on the head. The hitchhiking incident during the cross-country run had all but blown over, it was my friends and not I who had been caught smoking behind the bicycle racks, and as for burning down the caretaker's garden shed, the charge of arson had been dropped for lack of evidence, or so I thought.

Bomber's secretary usually greeted me with a suppressed smile that belied the pleasure she took from overhearing a well-deserved thrashing. But this time she ushered me into an empty office, gesturing to a rotary telephone with the hand-piece liberated and abandoned on a large ink blotter at the center of an orderly oak desk.

"It's for you," she said, her tone polite, almost obsequious, and I watched her leave and close the door. For a second, I wondered if Bomber was hiding behind a bookcase, about to leap out, brandishing his fiendish twitch like Zorro. But it was just me and the telephone, alone and incongruous with the smell of old books and dry sherry. I felt like an actor on an empty stage who has not only forgotten his lines but why he was there in the first place.

"Hello."

"I'm so sorry, son."

My father's words were suffocated by sobbing and jabs to his diaphragm that stole the air from his lungs, butchering his speech into a gasping, dismembered apology.

"I had no choice. The sores, the infection . . . I couldn't see him suffer anymore."

I stood in silence and listened to an emotional implosion, the dam of months of anticipatory grief that had surrounded and defended my father's heart finally broke and he was being washed away in a flash flood of sorrow. I felt the piercing pain of the decision to put Patch to sleep, the immediate emptiness left behind, and the unforgivable guilt of acting alone, without discussion, delivering the Judas kiss that finally denounced our dog as a lost cause.

I left school without saying a word to anyone, walked home, and, together with my father, quietly buried Patch in our backyard.

I never shed a single tear that day, crying unthinkable for a boy of my age. Better to trade the pain of loss for the pain of blisters on soft hands from digging the grave. I never blamed my father for taking the easy way out. Instead, like so many others, I succumbed to the dead weight of guilt.

Right now, another German shepherd and another devoted father have entered my life. I can deny the similarity, after all their individual diseases epitomize the distinction between chronic and acute, but the essence of the bond between Sage and Mr. Hartman, between Patch and my father, is undeniably the same.

I cannot make the same mistake with Sage as I did with Patch. Sure, back then, I was a clueless teenager, but even so, to my way of thinking, I was party to a selfish prolongation of life. I conspired with my father to tolerate an existence that took a proud, loyal, and protective animal with superior athletic prowess and reduced him to a withered, humiliated, and needy creature. Like it or not, I helped Patch lose his dignity. The last year of this poor dog's life takes up more real estate in my memory than the first twelve years combined.

Ms. Wicks wanted to do everything she could for her Berner, Jacob. Her desire for me to perform metastatectomies, as they are called, in this case removing the spreading cancer from individual lobes of the lungs, was based on accurate, credible, and current data. Part of me might have felt like I was crossing the line, but there was nothing experimental about the procedure.

That was nine months ago, and today's visit is simply one more satisfying backhander in the face of the pouting cynics. Jacob was loping around and having fun, documented in color stills for my viewing pleasure, within days of his thoracic surgery.

"How's the man been getting on?" I say, ear canals cleared to dock with my stethoscopic earbuds.

"Really good," says Ms. Wicks with an understated pride that is downright charming. The circular diaphragm of the scope leaps around the quadrants of Jacob's chest like a winning move in checkers. I am all ears, listening to the breeze while Mom continues to chat, a character in a silent movie.

"I'm sorry?" I say, having missed a question.

"How's he sound?"

"Fine. No muffles, no squeaks, no crackles. Normal air sounds in all fields."

Ms. Wicks does not smile. She simply nods. She knows that to-day's definitive hurdle still remains—chest X-rays—and right about now it must seem like the bar is set for a pole vault and not a high jump.

Radiology is quiet and they can take Jacob without delay. I process the paperwork and leave them with his medical record, the size of a telephone directory. No need for sedatives. Jacob's warm and mal-leable demeanor makes him the perfect patient, and besides, he is a regular, known to all on a first-name basis. He understands the drill.

I leave Ms. Wicks alone in the waiting room, stolid and staring into an uncertain future. She has everything to lose and I feel like I am scrutinizing her decisions, holding them up to the light and hunting for flaws. She knows the sand in the hourglass is reaching that critical point where the core of the vortex seems to gather mo-mentum, boring a hole for the final drop. She knows that ears are easy to deceive, that X-rays are less forgiving.

I wait with my hand hovering at the mouth of the automatic film processor in radiology, bracing myself for a bag full of Titleists where a healthy set of lungs used to reside. I'm as nervous as an innocent man waiting for a verdict. I need more proof that we did the right thing because I'm still not convinced that I am innocent.

The three films of the chest, left lateral, right lateral, and ventro-dorsal, emerge and line up on a viewing box. When I was in school, they taught me that it is impossible, for the most part, to distinguish between the shadow of a cross section through a large blood vessel and the earliest indication of a tumor, until the latter has reached a size of half a centimeter in diameter. So I set about hunting for dots, scrutinizing the darkness for big and shining stars I hope I cannot find. Truthfully, I already know what I see. I collar a radiology spe-cialist, ask for an opinion, and my suspicions are confirmed. Jacob has hopped away to find his mom and now it is my turn.

In the waiting room, Ms. Wicks is on her feet, reading the radi-ographic synopsis written on my face. The woman who coined the phrase "Dogs are not four-legged creatures, they are born with three legs and one spare" is unable to speak but her eyes tell me my findings come as no surprise. So I squat down, embrace the drooly jowls in my hands, and tell a remarkable animal, "I'll be seeing *you* in three more months."

11

. . . .

12:01 P.M.

EXOTIC DETOUR

Visiting time is already in full swing and as I head for CCU I kick myself for not seeing the problem sooner. It is the whole purpose of their meeting, the best medicine I can offer, the physical contact between Mr. Hartman and Sage, and it never occurred to me until now that the two of them cannot touch. She is flying Morphine Air to la-la land and although she is aware and responsive to her environment, she probably can't get to her feet no matter how hard she tries. And based on last night's demonstration, Mr. Hartman has all the flexibility of the Tin Man on a Pilates mat. Stubborn arthritic knees will veto his best efforts to get down to her level. I dearly want them to connect and if he cannot lay a hand on her body, if she cannot smell him and feel his touch, their meeting will be futile.

As I approach I can see that I needn't have worried. Mr. Hartman is sitting in a chair at the entrance to Sage's run. Propped up on a series of blankets and towels, the big girl herself relaxes, head out-

191

stretched, a furry Rubenesque model taking a break between poses, her eyes closed. Best of all, knotty blue fingers are savoring the delicate velveteen touch of a shepherd ear, speaking their secret tactile language, a coarse Braille that reminds the sender and recipient that they still both have each other.

Standing with them is Dr. Keene, and I am pleased that she has taken the time to chat. No doubt she is the one who found a way to facilitate the unique correspondence between dog and man, and I make a mental note to commend her efforts.

I can overhear them talking. Dr. Keene is trying to excuse herself and all the while Mr. Hartman is waving a pound of fresh, thinly sliced honey-glazed turkey breast in a Ziploc bag that, apparently, will only go to waste if she doesn't take it. Eventually she concedes, presumably because she sees no alternative, and leaves with her impromptu gift and a fading farewell of his unnecessary apologies for failing to provide a loaf of bread.

This is my cue to step forward, the hands on the face of my watch waving like a nervous prompt, a reminder that I don't have much time. Tinkerbell, my first case of the afternoon, is about to go under anesthesia and I promised Dr. Payne that I would take another look at Barron, her German shepherd with a penchant for kangaroo impersonations. But for some reason, I stand perfectly still, unseen, a big fly on an institutional green wall taking an unscheduled moment to do nothing but watch.

I never get to step back and take in the contented nothingness that exists between people and animals. Most of my interactions take place during emotional peaks and troughs—tearful hellos and good-byes, the sudden impact of stitches and incisions, bandages and casts, drains and catheters, trauma and cancer, three legs and not four. I miss everything in between, everything that counts, all the wonderful, convivial silence, the accumulative fundamental background noise that motivates and drives these extremes. And staring at Mr. Hartman and Sage sharing only space and time, I bear witness to another of these unprecedented relationships. Be honest, how many couples do you know that have nothing to say to each other, waive all distractions, and remain perfectly at ease with the simplicity of togetherness. If we were watching the same exchange among ourselves, the innocent touch, the lingering eye contact, the whispered sweet nothings, I guarantee it wouldn't be long before someone shouted, "Hey, buddy, do us all a favor and get yourselves a room!" And this is not restricted to the giddy, steamy, trembling thrill of new love. This has been around for some time. It has depth and intensity. If I knew the other visitors in the room, the headless bodies squeezed into a bank of cat cages against the wall, the dismembered legs and feet sticking out of all the dog runs, I'm sure I would read the same signs, but right now all I see is an old man and his dog breathing each other in, sharing molecules and savoring every breath.

"Excuse me!"

The words squeeze between the grinding teeth of a stout technician trying to get past me with a large bag of dog food. Her stare is chilling, liquid nitrogen in her eyes, incredulous that a doctor be seen lollygagging, daydreaming in CCU. Her frustration brings me back, an instant reality check like the concussive blow of a deployed air-bag in a crash. I veer out of her way and mumble an apology. I must be more tired than I thought.

"Hello, Mr. Hartman."

We shake hands, a bizarre Masonic squeeze with his left hand because his right hand refuses to stop patting Sage.

"How do you think she's doing?" I ask.

His smile is big and directly wired to his eyes and I can tell that he is thrilled simply to have her near.

"Pretty good," he says with enthusiastic nods. Sage senses the appearance of a new arrival, pink third eyelids sliding back like a nosy neighbor taking a peek from behind a lace curtain, and I earn a single tail swish of acknowledgment before she succumbs to the charms of her ear massage and goes back to sleep.

"Not interested in the turkey, but that's okay, right?"

"Absolutely," I say. "I'm hardly surprised that she's not hungry. I just knew she would feel better having you around."

"Yes," he says, and then, "I'm glad I came."

He turns his attention back to Sage, and it's as if I am no longer there. Mr. Hartman is like a sleeper on a train ride, somehow able to dispel the sensory distractions all around, able to dream, to reminisce, and soak up everything this creature embodies.

I am a third wheel. This is their time, a glimpse of normality. I make my excuses, promise to call later, and leave them alone, telling Mr. Hartman that he should pretend to be unable to get out of his chair if anyone tries to kick him out. I figure this is not too far from the truth.

Leash in hand I head over to J ward and walk up to the run with Barron lunging at the bars, all frisky and territorial. The intravenous sedative for his spinal X-rays from earlier this morning appear to be all but forgotten, no more effective than a swig of cough mixture.

"Easy, Otto," I say, letting him smell me through the bars. "Let's go for a walk."

"His name's Barron," says a technician breezing by with a bowl of food for another dog, transporting my patient's state of unrest into a full-blown frenzy.

I thank her for the clarification as I lasso the insistent, twisty snout intent on a prison break and head outside into the snow.

Cold air has a calming effect on Barron and after an interesting yellow tribute in the compacted snow to the work of Jackson Pollack we are able to go for a long walk in the parking lot.

At first Barron is dancing on his back legs, eager to take the leash in his own mouth with that clever watch-me-walk-myself look in his eyes. But within a few steps his back legs start to mutate, to tighten and bounce in unison, and this time, right by his side, watching closely as we keep on walking, the problem becomes so blatantly obvious that I am more shocked and embarrassed for not seeing it sooner than I am relieved to have defined what is really going wrong. Barron's bizarre kangaroo posture is not the result of increased muscle contractions clamping down on the hips and knees, but the result of certain muscle groups getting so weak that those remaining are working overtime to prevent his body from collapsing to the ground.

I try to keep him walking, but in less than a minute he does exactly what I hoped he would do. Reigning in my excitement, I get back inside the hospital, grab lunch, and page Dr. Payne.

"I need you to call Otto's mom and dad right away," I say with a crunchy mouthful of Doritos and the fizz of residual Coke.

She's so tired of my running joke she doesn't even bother to correct me about the dog's name.

"Why? What's got into you, you sound weird."

Anticipation is getting the better of me.

"Try speaking to the wife. She might prove to be a little more objective. This whole icy pond incident just doesn't fit."

"You think the kids are covering something up?"

"Slow down there, Woodward and Bernstein. I suspect there were gait problems long before young Rebel auditioned for *Stars on Ice*. From what we've learned, the timing of the fall and the onset of this problem appears to be nothing more than coincidence. You got a pen?"

"Yeah."

"Then write this down. Ask whatever you feel is pertinent, but I need the answers to the following three questions."

"Go ahead," she says.

"One—has Barron been throwing up? Two—how do they store

his dog food? Three—and this is very important—does their house have a problem with ants?"

I hang up before she has a chance to ask why.

Tucked into a corner between the fishbowl and the scrub sinks is a compact work space frequently visited by an eclectic potpourri of creatures and the doctors and technicians who care for them. Right now, the team are in a huddle, a tight little scrum, animated, enjoying a private session of "show and tell," and I'm curious to see what all the fuss is about.

I've already changed into scrubs, Tinkerbell is about to go inside the OR and I should be setting up my surgical gown and gloves, but, as always, I can't resist wandering over and finding out what Dr. Joey Ramirez is up to.

Dr. Ramirez is a second-year resident in exotic medicine from Venezuela, and when I say "exotic," I don't mean that he uses enchanted potions or has a talent for lap dancing. I mean that his specialty embraces all those weird and wonderful small companion animals that are not cats and dogs.

Joey has his back to me, his body squeezed up against a small examination table, and there are two female technicians packed tight, one on either side of him, with a large anesthesia machine opposite, sealing the quadrangle. Their three heads are angled down as if focused on a crystal ball. Joey may not be tall in his high-heeled, Tom Cruise–approved cowboy boots, but he has broad shoulders to ward off voyeurs, making me step in close to breach their circle.

"Whatcha up to?" I say, instantly breaking the spell for the dreamy-eyed techs.

"Hey, Buddy!" says Joey, only it sounds more like "A, Body." In truth his English is impeccable. I reckon he simply enjoys impersonating Antonio Banderas with a thick, suave accent.

"Perfect timing, we're about to perform a radical surgery."

Dr. Ramirez shuffles aside to let me in and I breathe in his familiar cologne and notice his beard has been trimmed back to a black Machiavellian goatee, sharp and tight against his almond skin. His patient fills the palm of his right hand.

"This is Brad," he says.

I glance down and see what I believe to be a turtle. It's got an olive shell stenciled with pale yellow hexagons, four stumpy legs, and a long, thick tail. What else can it possibly be?

"He's a red-eared slider," says Joey, pointing out the Porsche red stripes on the side of Brad's little head.

If Brad has ears, I can't see them.

"He's been getting into trouble with the women in his life."

The technician showcasing her oral acrobatics by clinking the metallic bauble from her pierced tongue against her front teeth, emits a shrill laugh, as her powder blue eyes bore into the man she would love to get into trouble with.

"What sort of trouble?" I ask.

Dr. Ramirez unleashes his perfectly bleached smile and I feel the women at our sides melting into the table.

"Well, like any mature slider, Brad enjoys an active sex life. His problem is he can't keep his pecker in his pants. He keeps trying to mount his girlfriend and he won't take no for an answer."

"Don't tell me," I say. "Brad's girlfriend is Angelina, right?"

"Actually, I am told, this one is Jennifer."

More high-pitched giggles and I begin to wonder if I am being set up.

"After repeated warnings, how you say, Brad bit off more than he could chew. Or should I say Jen bit off as much as she could chew."

At this he points out a sad and desiccated nubbin of scaly tissue protruding from a slitlike vent in the slider's tail.

"That's a slider penis?" is what I really want to say, but I manage to stretch my question into "That's all that's left of Brad's penis?"

Appalled that the female slider equivalent of a fake headache had proved ineffective, I add, "So how are you going to fix it?"

Now it is his turn to laugh at me, his own harem quick to follow suit.

"I'm not. I'm going to help Jennifer out by lopping it off completely!"

The ubiquitous question for a veterinary surgeon at any high school career fair is "What's the weirdest thing you have ever operated on?" My paltry list of blue moon patients—iguana, Indian Rock python, bobcat, beaver, and box turtle—is sure to disappoint because, undoubtedly, they are hoping for something utterly improbable like a stick insect, slug, three-toed sloth, great white shark, or woolly mammoth. In short, what they crave is a creature categorized as "exotic."

I don't know how the exotics doctors do it. At veterinary school I had a hard enough time keeping the "big six" straight—horses, cows, sheep, pigs, dogs, and cats—with all their anatomical, physiological, and pathological idiosyncrasies. Our understanding of this diversity has been cited as the skill that sets our profession apart, generating a piece of forlorn bravado that dares to suggest that vets possess superior talents to MDs, who are blessed with the luxury of studying a solitary species. These days, doctors with an interest or specialization in exotic medicine have taken the pursuit of diversity to a whole new level, in fact, from an evolutionary standpoint, they are taking a huge taxonomical step backward. The "big six" may hail from different "orders," but at least they are all mammals. The exotic repertoire includes creatures of different "classes," meaning fish, amphibians, reptiles, and birds, and that is before getting to the loosely termed collection called "pocket pets." All I can say is there must be some pretty baggy clothing out there because included with the obvious mice, hamsters, gerbils, and guinea pigs are creatures that will definitely be a tight squeeze next to my pocket protector such as African hedgehogs, sugar gliders, rabbits, chinchillas, ferrets, and rats.

When I was at veterinary school, exotic medicine and surgery comprised a miniscule portion of the curriculum. In fact, I believe I graduated with only two worthwhile factoids of exotic information.

1. Fish get a disease called "white spot" caused by a parasite named *Ichthyophthirius multifiliis.* Diagnostically the disease is easy to define, the fish get white spots all over their body, and when you come across this disgusting sight you are apt to remember the synonym for the disease—"Ich"!

2. Most mammals can make their own vitamin C. Guinea pigs, like us, cannot. Unlike us, guinea pigs prefer to avoid scurvy by eating fresh, commercially milled pellets rather than citrus fruits!

So much of my time (at least 95 percent) is devoted to cats and dogs that I love the opportunity to shake it up a little with a spinal fracture in a rabbit or a tumor excision in a snake. The quirks and foibles of exotic animals give them their unique appeal, offering an intimate, Roswellian moment in which we can call upon our fundamental skills and desire to heal with our hands and apply them to an unfamiliar life form. Exotics are evolutionary marvels with bizarre internal plumbing of impossible blues, greens, and yellows, outlandish organs, and aberrant structures suspended, traversed, or masked by slick membranes, sacs, and ligaments. I had no point of reference for closing my first reptilian wound in a blue-tongued skink—scales tough, unforgiving, demanding coarse sutures thrown more like a cobbler than a surgeon. I was unprepared for the cluster of sunny yolks—a glistening, overflowing bag of delicate marbles—that greeted me in an egg-bound green iguana, and I was agape at the complexity of a bladder stone removal in a box turtle where the procedure hinges, pun intended, on cutting a window into the shell and taking a peek inside, like looking under the hood of a car. For surgeons like me, exotics are a welcome and educational distraction. When I work with Dr. Maganiello in Critical Care, I am trading surgery for her medical insight and acumen. When I work with Dr. Ramirez in Exotics, I am trading surgery for a desire to satiate my curiosity.

Some species of exotics are less amenable to a visit from their curious surgeon than others. Take, for example, the third most popular pet in the United States. Hopefully most of us will have pegged the top two as being cats and dogs, respectively, but would you have guessed that the animal coming in at number three, with somewhere between eight and fourteen million of these creatures in this country alone, is the parakeet, the most popular breed of pet bird in the world. In England these miniature parrots are known as budgerigars or budgies, an unfortunate epitaph derived from an aboriginal phrase meaning "good to eat." Presumably at one time these delicate birds were vulnerable to the attentions of a wayward boomerang. Truth is, they are vulnerable to even the most delicate and familiar touch. Under anesthesia they have a monitor-defying heart rate of six hundred to seven hundred beats per minute, a subdued machine gun, virtually impossible to record. Parakeets can die of cardiac arrest simply by being picked up, let alone a surgical intervention.

And then there is *Mustela putorius furo*, literally "stinky mouse-carrying thief," more commonly referred to as the domestic ferret. These whiffy, whimsical weasels are sadly one of our more popular visitors to the operating room. They have a high incidence of tumors, particularly of the hormonal variety, associated with the pancreas and adrenal glands, and it has been suggested that this predisposition stems from excessive inbreeding, a little too much heavy petting while swimming in a small gene pool. Curious to learn more, I visited the hospital library and sat down with a couple of the definitive works on all things ferret. These were gold-standard text-books full of factual, thoroughly researched but essentially dry and crusty data, so you can imagine my surprise, flicking though the opening pages, when I discovered a section that seemed wholly out of place in an academic volume. Despite my unprecedented yearning for scientific information, I had found myself quickly (and to be honest, rather easily) waylaid by the subject of ferret-legging.

Apparently ferret-legging is a centuries-old English sport (I might have guessed) in which the contestant stuffs a pair of ill-tempered ferrets down his pants. To ensure maximum hanky-panky several restrictions apply:

- The pants must be baggy enough to ensure optimal ferret slinkage between both legs.
- The ankles and waistband must be cinched tight and secure to prevent their premature escape.
- White pants are preferable to demonstrate the contestant's blood loss.
- No underwear of any description is permitted.
- Ferrets should have a full set of sharp teeth. I found no reference to their claws, but I suppose all pain is relative.
- Neither the competitor nor the ferret can be under the influence of chemical intervention. Dutch courage in its various forms (e.g., frantic tokes on hydroponic marijuana or excessive quaffing of best bitter) will not be tolerated.

The aim of the game is quite simple. The winner is the person who can keep the ferrets in their pants for the longest period of time.

The section even included a reference to an article in *Outside* magazine by journalist Donald Katz. Katz originally reported on the Lance Armstrong, Tiger Woods, Michael Jordan of the sport, a seventy-two-year-old retired miner from Yorkshire named Reg Mellor, who was able to endure the carnivorous melee for an unbelievable five hours and twenty-six minutes.

I reread the statistic in the textbook, perturbed by the author's use of the word *impressive*, imagining a live ESPN special from a bustling smoke-filled pub, capturing every squirm and nip of this pandemonium in the pants.

Unfortunately the final sentence shattered my illusion, the author doubting whether this unusual spectator sport would catch on in other parts of the world.

Exotics have always had a loyal fan base, but their appeal has expanded to include the modern workaholic. Constrained by time or money or residential restrictions but yearning for camaraderie that is practical (and harboring an occasional desire to be noticed in public places with an unusual animal), this latest stripe of devotee finds that exotics, whether they walk, hop, scuttle, scamper, or slither, make fabulous alternatives to your pedestrian pets.

Unfortunately, some cynics fail to appreciate the love for an exotic animal, unable to accept their place as an integral member of a family. Faced with a broken bone in a rabbit, they would rather reach for a bottle of chardonnay, garlic, and their favorite Jacques Pepin recipe for lapin than their check book. A former veterinary technician, who was great with cats and dogs, but disliked exotics, summed up this sentiment in the expression "if you can flush it, you should not cut it" whenever a patient was incapable of leash walks, house-training, answering to a name, and could easily negotiate the u-bend of a toilet.

Thankfully this outlook is becoming obscure. It is no longer unusual to perform a cat scan on a rat (a so-called rat scan). Frogs and fish can undergo abdominal ultrasound (the animal is placed in a Ziploc bag in water and the ultrasound probe placed directly on the bag—hopefully they won't swim around too much). And consider this story about a four-year-old male Toulouse goose curiously named Q. When I discovered the bird was labeled with a single letter I felt sure he must have been named after the endearing gadget guru originally played by the late Desmond Llewelyn in the James Bond movies. It turns out I highlighted a generational crevasse with his owners, Mr. and Mrs. Picard, because Q was named after a character I had never heard of on a popular TV show I had never watched called *Star Trek: The Next Generation*.

Q lived on a farm with the Picards, two hens, a rabbit, two ducks named Daffy and Donald, and four cats that somehow tolerated all the feathery temptations in their midst.

Shortly after the New Year, presumably a time when most poultry celebrate seeing the back of the holiday season, young Q was strutting around his domain, minding his own business, when he was mauled in a random attack by a mysterious drive-by canine. The dog was long gone by the time Mrs. Picard responded to the squawks and honks in the yard, the paw prints in the snow difficult to pin down to a specific model.

The resultant injury to Q's left wing was so severe he was rushed to our emergency room and it didn't take X-rays to confirm a broken humerus, the feathers, skin, and muscle ripped from shards of bone like the work of a hungry knight at a medieval banquet.

I know I have exhausted the culinary references, but forgive me when I say that draping off a broken goose wing for orthopedic surgery feels like, well, preparation for a Dickensian Christmas dinner. Feathers were plucked from adjacent to the wing, leaving bruised and puckered goose bumps, flesh untrussed, a thorough rinse in tap water traded for a frothy antibacterial preparation guaranteed to destroy far more than salmonella. For those of us unfamiliar with avian surgery it felt surreal until my sterile surgical field was in place, a window through which to focus on the job at hand, fixing the fracture, reconstructing the damaged anatomy, striving to return function to Q's enormous wing, and suddenly the image of me wearing a chef's toque vanished, and I was back in surgery wearing a bouffant cap.

The mystery dog had already made the surgical approach for me, the ends of the bone stripped of muscular attachments, two pieces of cracked white china overriding and displaced. With cats and dogs I am familiar with the shape and contour of many bones. Like returning to an old jigsaw puzzle, I have a sense of where the pieces go. But at first glance this goose bone was different, foreign, lacking any characteristic curves, ridges, or interdigitations that would confirm a perfect fit. It wasn't until I noticed the tiny half moon defect on one broken end that I was grateful to the dog that put Q and me in this situation. By finding an identical imperfection on the other end, I was able to line up both pieces to restore a complete, empty circle, a punched-out bone defect corresponding perfectly to, I imagine, a canine tooth from the perpetrator of this heinous crime.

The rest was straightforward, and Q, the goose, made a remarkable recovery. When I decided to check in on his progress, some six months later, I considered my opening question to Mrs. Picard carefully, so as to set the tone for our conversation.

"So you're not one of those freaks that dress up in homemade sci-fi costumes to attend conventions in Vegas?"

Mrs. Picard laughed, confirming that she and her husband were simply fans of the television show at the time they were searching for a name.

"We've had him since he was a gosling. He was raised by hand."

"And how is he getting on?"

"Fantastic," she said. "He's just a little needier than before."

"How so?" I asked.

"Well, he doesn't like to go outside for walks on his own anymore. He'll come tap his beak on the door when he wants to go. He follows my husband around everywhere. He's just like a dog."

I had a sense of how much Q's medical care had cost and felt compelled to ask, "Why? People must ask you the same question. Why invest all that time and money in a goose, of all things?"

They obviously had, and I felt like she had the answer rehearsed.

"There was a time when I would have been skeptical myself," she said. "But he's my child. We don't have kids. He'll let you hug him and kiss him. Q's my little boy."

And, of course, she is absolutely right. Exotics are simply another form of animal life with which to bond. Where there are those that see quick incisors, razor-sharp beaks, and venomous bites, many see affection, companionship, and a love that defies fiscal prudence. Whether you spend five thousand dollars on a dog or a goose, the emotional drive to save a silent companion remains exactly the same.

Dr. Ramirez has Brad's scaly tail in his left hand, a butterfly catheter in his right. There's no tourniquet to raise a vein, no delicate palpation to appreciate its secret pathway below reptilian skin, he just knows where his target should be and drives the needle home, inky blood leaking into the transparent tubing to prove he has hit his mark.

"Why don't you just box him down?" I ask. General anesthesia on small exotic creatures is always a challenge and it can be helpful to place the animal in a warm, transparent plastic box and feed in anesthetic gas to minimize the stress of handling and catheter placement.

"Good idea, only one slight problem," says Joey, injecting the milky white intravenous anesthetic agent. The tongue-pierced technician spins Brad around and Joey slides a tube into his airway. To be honest, it's hard for me to tell whether the slider is asleep or not.

"Sliders are good at holding their breath," says Joey as what remains of Brad's manhood is prepped for surgery. "We put him in a box for an hour, pump in the gas, come back, and he's still wide awake. Intravenous is best with sliders."

I frown my way into an approving nod. Makes perfect sense. I love this stuff.

Ramirez quickly applies a pair of surgical gloves and opens a simple pack of instruments. I make no attempt to hide my surprise.

"Whoa there, fella! You look like you're not planning on taking Brad inside the OR."

"I'm not," says Joey, applying a sterile clamp across healthy tissue at the base of the penis, picking up a pair of scissors, and with one swift snip, it's already all over.

Gasping would not be a cool thing to do right now, so I simply say, "But what about all his internal plumbing? I mean if Brad were a cat or dog, I'd be having to reroute a lot of piping to make sure he could still pee after a penile amputation."

Joey places a number of fine stitches, oversewing the stumpy remnant, before tucking it back inside the slit in Brad's tail. He snaps off his gloves and they switch off the gas. It's all over in minutes.

"Don't worry, my friend," he says. "The slider's penis is an intromittent organ only. It's purely for sex. It has nothing to do with urination."

We step back from the table, and he makes a point of glancing over at his two fawning technicians before our eyes connect, mano a mano, and in a suggestive whisper he says, "Like me, Brad can still enjoy smelling all the flowers in the garden. Only now, he cannot water them!"

12

. . . .

12:41 P.M.

BITTEN!

Standing over the scrub sink, soapy froth dripping from my elbows, I notice a stranger in crisp, oversized scrubs with traces of teenage acne letterboxed between his mask and cap. An OR technician points to me and the stranger sidles over, pimples twinkling on a rosy, embarrassed forehead.

"Do you mind if I watch you do the surgery on Tinkerbell the cat?"

He speaks with the awkward hesitant style of teenagers who are in a hiatus from communicating with adults.

"Not at all," I say. "You visiting for the day?"

"Yeah."

"High school student?"

"Yeah."

From time to time high school students will visit the hospital, trying to determine the merits of a career in veterinary medicine.

Sometimes they are self-motivated. Sometimes they are pushed by ambitious parents. Either way they often gravitate toward the action in the operating rooms, enticed by the prospect of blood and gore, a mandatory test to make sure they have the right stuff.

"Senior?" I ask.

"Uh-huh."

I work the scrub brush between my fingers before spiraling the bristles into my palms.

"See anything interesting this morning?" I ask.

"A dog with a broken leg."

The dog in question was 180 pounds of Neapolitan mastiff with a fractured femur that had shattered into tiny pieces.

"How did you get on watching orthopedic surgery?"

The first time inside an operating room can be a daunting experience. Combine a gruesome surgery with heat from the overhead lighting, the novelty of standing for an extended period of time, a hunger for lunch, and you have the perfect recipe for a faint.

"No problem," he replies, sounding as dismissive as a surgical veteran.

"And what did you think of all those pins and wires and plates and screws? Playing with all those power tools?"

I had noticed the postoperative X-rays of the repair hanging up in radiology when I was waiting for Jacob's chest X-rays to be developed. Bone had vanished behind an outrageous and audacious scaffold of surgical stainless steel. The fracture fixation was a brilliant work of art.

"Pretty cool."

I nod in agreement. If the surgeon had skewered a drill bit through his hand or sprayed blood across the ceiling, we might have achieved the dizzy heights of "wicked awesome." Still, this was praise indeed.

I decide to try a different approach.

"What's your name?"

"David."

"Well, David, what makes you want to become a vet?"

For a few seconds the student deliberates, his head weaving side to side as if the weight of his answer keeps rolling from one side of his brain to the other. Then he says, "My mom and dad are MDs. My older brother is just finishing up a fellowship in pediatrics at Children's. My older sister is in her second year of medical school at Johns Hopkins. I guess I wanted to try something different."

I take a step back from the sink, out of range of the winking red eye of the laser that controls the flow of warm water. I keep my hands in front of me, not quite in supplication, water sluicing down my forearms, running into discreet puddles by my sides.

"It sounds like you know what you don't want to be more than what you do," I say.

He shrugs. "I like dogs, if that's what you mean."

I back through a swinging door, find my sterile gown, gloves, and towel and begin the ritual of moving my wet hands from one quadrant of the towel to the next in a carefully choreographed, reproducible sequence intended to drive any residual contamination toward my elbows.

"So why'd you become a vet?" says David.

I shuffle on my paper gown and study him over the nose rim of my paper mask. I could have lied and told him "the calling" germinated in my soul during the transition from breast-fed milk to solid food or that I became infected with the animal doctor virus when I discovered a copy of *All Creatures Great and Small* jammed into the toe end of a Christmas stocking. In fact, I was clueless about my future career until I spent a fateful day with a convicted murderer called Ryan James.

At only fourteen years of age I had secretly entertained a notion of becoming a fighter pilot until a soft haze began to blur all distant objects and an ophthalmologist confidently declared that I was myopic due to oversized eyeballs.

"But I want to fly jet planes," I confided as I tried to remember the sequence of letters in the fourth line down on the eye chart.

Chortling with thigh-slapping amusement, the ophthalmologist made a passing reference to a pair of consolation aviator sunglasses before pitching his new line of expensive contact lenses.

In an attempt to help me see past this crushing, career-breaking handicap, my father informed me that he had organized my spending a day at our local veterinary hospital. I was puzzled. I had grown up with dogs, enjoyed biology at school, and made a point of watching any nature show on television made by Sir David Attenborough, but these were hardly the prerequisites of a budding James Herriot. I remember being annoyed, feeling as though I were being asked to test-drive a career like a new car, only my choice of cars was dictated solely by my father. I would smile and go along for the ride, but in my mind this pushy tactic was already destined to fail.

Lost among the watery details of individual faces and names, the smell of antiseptic in every room, and the reverberating brown tile floors that flowed throughout the hospital, formerly a sprawling Victorian house, I retain a vivid recollection of Ryan James. Before his felonious tendencies came to fruition, James was our family veterinarian, a brawny Welshman, soft-spoken yet syncopated with intense bursts of enthusiasm, and seemingly more at home wrestling hormonal heifers than flirting with fractious felines.

Our morning together would be spent visiting local farms, and as we pulled out of the practice parking lot, James briefed me on his proposed route.

"That's a lot of miles to cover," I said, wishing I had brought my lunch with me.

James said nothing, looking straight ahead, fighting down a smile, and in another thirty seconds I understood why. It was the one and only time that I have been in a vehicle doing 121 miles per hour down a rural highway while grappling for a seat belt that did not exist.

"Hate wasting time," he shouted my way between lighting gear shifts that enabled us to rip past a sports car poking along at eighty-five.

"Worst part of the job. These farms are spread about all over the place. If I don't hurry I'll spend all my day driving."

I nodded my understanding, bracing myself between dashboard and door handle. One might conclude that the man was an irresponsible maniac, yet he was actually an extraordinarily gifted driver, and before long my body learned to relax into the swerves and whiplash as James tap-danced neatly between the brake and the accelerator.

We began to chat.

"Your dad tells me you might be interested in becoming a vet."

I tried not to show anger at my father's assumption and replied, almost as a courtesy, "Well, maybe. I haven't really decided."

He studied me intensely for what seemed like a dangerously long stretch of time given our speed, clearly amused.

"I mean," I felt compelled to add, "I know I don't want to be a human doctor because I cringe every time I see a needle poking into bare skin. Maybe I'd be different with fur."

He checked the road ahead, saw that it was clear, and reached across to the glove compartment, casually perusing its contents, a single finger occasionally twitching at the wheel as he located a map before sitting back in his seat.

"Really," said James, unfolding the map to its maximal size, his view out the windshield all but entirely obstructed. "There's nothing coming, is there?"

I drew in a long slow gasp of air, positive it would be my last and said, "No. You're fine."

"Excellent," he said, handing me the map and an invitation to perform some magical feat of origami. "I wonder how you will get on with needles and eyeballs."

I didn't have time to answer before we pulled into a well-rutted and muddy farmyard cluttered by mountains of straw bales and abandoned tractor tires. Two freckled and fiery-haired men, who I assumed to be father and son, greeted us. Before I knew it, James was introducing me, something he continued to do with everyone we met. To this day I consider this to be one of his most endearing traits. I was a nobody, a kid, an awkward schoolboy, someone he had only just met and someone who didn't even claim to want to be a vet. And yet here he was, without obligation, presenting me to strangers in a way that made me feel as though I were an integral part of his team. It was a completely new experience. It was wonderful.

I can see what he pointed out to be "our" patient even now—a behemoth of an Ayrshire bull trapped inside an enormous metal stanchion, his head sticking out of one end for our inspection. The bull squinted at us in the morning light, copious tears streaming from both eyes, an effect that dampened his intimidating stature even as I noticed the glint of his shiny brass nose ring and the great plumes of dragon breath pouring from each nostril in the cold air.

"Now then, young Mortimer, let the vet here take a look at your eyes," said the oldest of the men.

For a moment I wondered if he was talking to his son, but then James began to wrestle with the bull's head.

"Yep, I think you're right, Ted. Most likely pink eye," said James. "Any others got it?"

"Not so far as I know," said Mr. Senior Redhead. "He's turned out well away from the girls, but I'll keep a watch out."

"Very good," said James, wandering back to his car to get the necessary equipment and returning with three loaded syringes protruding from his breast pocket.

Suddenly I became acutely aware of my proximity to sharp needles and soft eyeballs, a discomfort that must have shown on my face because James took me aside, dipped his knees, slapped a hand on my shoulder, and fixed me with a stare reminiscent of an awkward conversation I once had with my father on the subject of safe sex.

"Just look at him," said James, arching his eyebrows at the great beast. "He's miserable. His eyes must itch something fierce and there's not a damn thing he can do about it." He plucked the largest syringe from his pocket, held it up to the light, and flicked the barrel.

"That's where we come in."

The way James stressed the word *we* did little to thwart my anxiety, and instead of letting me stand back he ordered me closer as he dug his hand into the base of the bull's neck and a thick vascular cord bulged from the muscular flesh.

"I'll just give him a little happy juice, Ted, enough to stop him from jerking his head around." Then, as if confiding in me, added, "drive a train down that," and smiled as he jabbed in his needle, pulling back on the plunger as a blush of dark red blood mixed with the clear liquid in the syringe before he drove the whole concoction back into the animal's jugular vein.

Next he applied a couple of drops of a topical anesthetic to the surface of both eyeballs and instructed the farmers to secure the slumping head as he extracted one of the two smaller syringes from his breast pocket.

"See here," said James, insisting I somehow squeeze between the men and get into prime position to watch the action. James used his chubby fingers to pry open the plump and puffy lids. Mortimer's conjunctiva was angry and engorged with blood vessels, spidery red legs crawling from the margins over the whites of his eyes.

"Watch exactly what I do with this needle," said James, and I did as I was told as he deftly slid the tiniest of needles into the fleshy pink corner of the inner eye and skillfully injected a bleb of white liquid. It was all over in a matter of seconds and Mortimer seemed oblivious to the entire proceedings. I was in a state of shock at how easy James made it look and how the act of taking a small spike of exquisitely sharp metal to the surface of something as delicate as an eyeball had not proven to be as painful for the bull, or as repugnant to me, as I had expected.

Then James jutted his chin in the direction of the opposite eye and surreptitiously mouthed, "Your turn!"

While I stood limp, wide-eyed, and fish-mouthed, he came around the farmers and interposed himself between them and the opposite eyeball. He pulled out a second tiny syringe, uncapped the needle, and handed it to me.

I didn't have time to anticipate or tremble. I looked down at the solitary eyeball staring directly back at me, with the needle hovering millimeters over the sensitive cornea, and I focused on those angry red tissues aching for relief. James physically guided my hands, located the appropriate site, steadied the needle, and drove home the plunger. He did all the work. There was never a question that he was totally in control, and yet the very fact that I was somehow attached to that syringe by the lightest possible touch made it feel as though I had delivered the entire injection. That somehow I had delivered the cure.

When we returned to the practice James went straight into setting a cast on a cat's broken leg closely followed by multiple dental extractions and teeth cleaning on a geriatric Pekingese who would forever change my definition of the phrase *dog breath*. He seemed to glide effortlessly from one task to the next and it all seemed to be this wonderful continuum of diversity. One minute he was an orthopedic surgeon, the next a dentist.

It was not long before we were entrenched in the afternoon's full schedule of appointments, and it was here that I learned his most subtle, seemingly useless but ultimately invaluable and shrewd lesson.

Before the first client entered the room he said, "Watch exactly what I do very carefully."

I nodded that I would and after he had inspected a dog for fleas and given it some vaccine or other, he asked me about my observations. I talked about the way he had handled the dog, the way he had run his hands over the animal's entire, squirmy little body, the way he had looked inside the dog's mouth and listened with a stethoscope to his chest. But I could see by his expression that I had entirely missed his point.

"No. That wasn't it. Let me tell you what that owner will remember more than anything else, more than the way I cooed over his dog, the thoroughness of my exam, the way I made sure all his questions were answered. I guarantee he's going to leave here remembering the way I cleaned my examination table."

My face knitted with confusion and he continued. "Make a show of cleaning your table in front of the client."

At this point he picked up a paper towel and a small bottle of clearly labeled antiseptic solution, and, after squirting some liquid on the surface of the stainless steel table, methodically swept up and down leaving no area untouched.

"If you do this, every time you need to use the table, in front of the owner, there can be no question in his or her mind that you really care for the animal, that their animal is special. Believe me. It's not much, but owners really notice that sort of thing."

I have never forgotten this tip because he was right. They do notice.

At the end of what I will always consider to be the first day of my unexpected adventure, a young man burst into the examination room carrying a large dog in his arms. The man was tall, skinny, with equine features atop a scrawny pipe-cleaner neck, accentuated by his oversized shirt collar. He was breathless as James intervened to help him place the dog on the floor between them.

The large Doberman had an enormous, distended abdomen and given the engorgement of her breasts and nipples, she looked as though labor was imminent.

"She's been like this for nearly a week," said the owner, crouching beside her, stroking the dog's outstretched head as she lay with her eyes closed, weak and oblivious to her new surroundings.

"When is she due?" said James, already moving his hands over her wasted spine and protruding ribs on their way to the pendulous belly.

"No idea," said the owner. "Didn't plan on her getting pregnant. Just never got around to getting her sprayed."

I suppressed a smile at the owner's choice of verb and watched as James donned a rubber glove, applied a lubricant to an index finger, and carefully began a vaginal examination.

"I can make out a puppy's head beyond the cervix, and based on the size of her pelvis I doubt that it's coming out natural."

James stood and flicked the glove into a trash can.

"We'll take an X-ray of her abdomen and see how many she's got inside her," he said, not waiting for a reply and sweeping the animal up and away in both arms.

Minutes later we returned with a grainy image that dripped chemicals across the room. James held it up to the light for the owner to see.

"There's only one puppy. Look," he said pointing, "you can follow her spine all the way to her skull. And she's huge. Only way she's coming out is by Caesarian section."

The owner nodded his understanding and asked, "Can you tell if it's alive?"

"I don't know," said James. "I'm afraid we'll have to wait and see."

The hospital's surgical suite was a compact converted kitchen with a metal table at its core, a small soapstone sink off in one corner, and an assortment of shiny instruments and anesthetic paraphernalia dotted around the gaps in between.

A nurse, who was there to assist with the proceedings, placed me in a corner and inquired as to whether I had watched surgery before.

"No," I confessed, but after surprising myself with Mortimer the bull earlier that day I added that I thought I would be fine.

So I stood and watched in awe. I wore no gown, no cap, no mask, and James himself only donned a plastic apron that made him look more like a butcher than a surgeon.

I became enrapt by the colors: the linen white fat, the red hues of arterial and venous blood, although far less of this than I had imagined, and then, most impressive of all, the great gush of rich, olive green liquid that squirted across the drapes, onto the floor, and made me jump to my right to avoid standing in a steaming verdant puddle.

"It's just the fluid around the fetus," said James, skillfully placing a couple of surgical clamps across the umbilical cord. "Look sharp! Here you go!"

And with that, a warm towel was placed in my hands and a wet slimy creature plopped within.

"If I monitor the anesthesia can you look after the puppy?" asked the nurse.

I had not moved since receiving the offering, holding it up and outstretched before me as if it might be sacrificial.

"I can try," I said, suddenly struck by the weight of my responsibility as she wiped the fluid from the puppy's nostrils and mouth before pulling off the transparent sticky membranes that clung to his lifeless, silent body.

His head appeared inordinately swollen to my untrained eye and I noticed a little tongue protruding between his lips. It was distinctly blue.

"Now wrap the puppy in the towel like this"—the nurse gently swaddled the creature—"and then swing his body down, up, and down between your legs. It'll help get all the fluid out of his little lungs." With this the nurse tightly clasped the newborn animal, raised him to the ceiling and forcibly jerked her arms down toward the ground, as though she were ringing a church bell. She repeated the process half a dozen times and I was incredulous that the puppy did not slip from her grasp and skitter around the tiny room.

"You've also got to rub him, like this, to get him going." She demonstrated a frenzied scouring of his fur with the towel. "Now you try."

I did as I was told, possibly with a little less vigor than my tutor. I was petrified that I would either lose my grip or crush his little body for fear of losing my grip but I kept at it under her watchful eye as James busied himself with closing his surgical incision.

"Now, take a look," the nurse prompted, and I rummaged through the towel. I studied the little black creature, touching the fine wet fur that had clumped into patches. I saw no movement. I heard nothing. His little mouth was open with no discernable change in the color of his tongue.

"Is it dead?" I asked slowly, worried that I had done something wrong. James looked up from his work.

"Not yet," he said. "You just keep at it."

For a full five minutes I rubbed and rubbed, shook, flung, hurled, and launched that tiny projectile in the towel, my impatience gradually infusing me with abandon as I realized I had nothing to lose. And then, lost in a sharp descent, swooping in from the heavens came the wonderful muffled bleating sound of new life.

"That's more like it," said James as he placed his final suture in the bitch's skin. I rifled through the folds of the towel and to my amazement discovered that the sticky dark blob had transformed into a writhing screaming puppy.

Just then a woman poked her head around the door to inform me that my father was waiting for me in the parking lot. For a moment I stood mesmerized, looking down at the angry creature in my hands. There were no bright lights. There was no bolt of lightning. It was simply being there, witnessing this strange intervention, this most, to my way of thinking, unnatural birth. I felt a part of it, not an integral part, just a small part. It left me feeling instantly and profoundly connected.

"You'd best be going," said Ryan James, and his pleasure in my amazement at the proceedings felt palpable. "Come back and see us again."

"Yes," I replied, carefully, almost reluctantly passing the puppy into the basket that was his open hands. "Thank you."

When I got into the car and my dad and I drove off, he got straight to it. "So, how did you get on?"

"It was great," I replied, and began prattling on about the events of the last thirty minutes.

"Do you think this is something you'd like to pursue?" he said.

I'm sure he was holding his breath and with hindsight I should have deliberated longer, if only for effect. But instead, and entirely out of character, I didn't hesitate to say, "You know, Dad, I think it just may be."

And when I next looked over at my father I saw the familiar languid nod of the head begin, his pursed lips failing to hold back a beaming smile of immense satisfaction.

Gowned and gloved, latex hands clasped together in front of me like a pious monk, I walk toward the surgical suite and my anesthetized patient, Tinkerbell, with my novice David, the high school senior, in tow. I gave David the abbreviated version of who inspired me to become a vet, throwing in the convicted murderer part to hold his attention.

"Bear in mind," I say, "English kids leave high school and go straight to veterinary school. The vast majority of students do not have a previous undergraduate degree."

I pretend not to notice the squirmy unease in David's eyes as a technician hands me sterile surgical instruments to unwrap and organize.

"You're telling me that if I lived in England, I'd have to know what I wanted to do for the rest of my life at eighteen years old? I'd have to have decided my entire professional future by . . . now?"

"Actually, more like two years ago, when you were fourteen to sixteen years old," I say. "You have to be taking the right courses at high school in order to be a suitable candidate. Most kids are seventeen when they apply to veterinary school."

I keep my head down, sorting out the forceps, the clamps, the blades, and the assorted scissors into orderly, familiar positions across my sterile table. I am enjoying David's stunned silence. I don't want him wandering into an operating room, playing dress-up, watching some guy "hacking and slashing" away at an anesthetized animal, and thinking cool, this looks like a fun job. To be honest, I'd rather he do what I did, spend time, spend lots of time, hanging out with a vet working in general practice, a vet in the real world, seeing the profession in the raw.

Frankly, despite going through and relishing the English system of veterinary education myself, I believe his concern is well founded. How capable are most teenagers of deciding "what they want to be when they grow up"? When I was lucky enough to come to the States for my surgical residency, being much younger than most of my peers, I was instantly struck by the maturity of the American veterinary students. To my way of thinking, making a decision on whether to devote your life to caring for animals in your twenties appears to be far more measured than during a time of hormonal turmoil before you are even eligible to vote. As a postgraduate, any wannabe vet must also accept the additional, hefty cost of further education, a commitment unlikely to be undertaken by anyone less than totally dedicated to their chosen profession.

Obviously, the UK approach to recruiting veterinarians has been working out just fine. Or has it? In the 2006 Royal College of Veterinary Surgeons' "Survey of the Profession," I discovered an alarming statistic. Bear in mind that nearly half of all the veterinarians in the United Kingdom responded to the survey and, when asked if they would still opt for the veterinary profession if they could start their career again, only fifty-three percent said yes. I should point out that twenty-seven percent were "unsure" and the remaining twenty percent said no, but, even so, I find these figures disturbing. That's an awfully large number of British vets out there disenchanted by the decision they made back in their teens. I'm not suggesting that UK veterinary schools adopt an American approach to recruiting students, but it makes me wonder how American veterinarians would respond to the same question and my suspicion is that the percentage that answers yes would be significantly higher.

"So what happened to your friend the murderer?" asked David.

I pick up a blue sterile towel, take a corner between each thumb and index finger, curl the thick, cottony material around the back of my hands, and approach my patient, an illusionist behind a magic shroud.

"He was *convicted* of murder," I correct. "Ryan James served three and half years in prison for the murder of his wife, a wrongful conviction that was completely overturned. He was exonerated and his license to practice veterinary medicine was restored."

One by one I stalk the unconscious Tinkerbell with three more towels, each placed at ninety degrees to one another, carefully defining the rectangle of my sterile operating field.

"So where is he now?" says David.

At each of the corners where the towels meet, I place a Backhaus towel clamp, securing the interface of material and iodine-stained skin with the bite of steel pincers.

Almost certainly Ryan James has absolutely no recollection of me and no idea about the profound impact he has made on my life. I really don't care about the courtroom drama and the tabloid gossip. To me, he will always be the shy, unassuming Welshman who held my hand so that I could actually feel the rewards of helping sick animals. I know he changed his name. I know where he went when he disappeared off the face of the earth. But what matters most is the meaning in my answer to David's question.

"Don't worry. He's still around."

13

· · · · · · · · · ·

12:54 P.M.

EXTREME MAKEOVER

"So, David, what do you think about a little feline plastic surgery?"

I survey the four pair of breasts belonging to my patient, Tinkerbell Simmons, and notice how my visitor eases back from the table, perhaps out of respect for the sterile field, perhaps out of fear for the extreme makeover he believes I am about to perform.

"Don't be alarmed," I say. "I am not about to transform poor Tinkerbell into a feline version of Pamela Anderson."

I give the fleshy pink three-inch scar over the cat's thigh a squeeze, getting a sense of how much the adjacent skin is loose and mobile. In fact the answer is pretty obvious—not much.

"David, this procedure comes in two parts. In the first part I have to be a cancer surgeon. This scar is all that remains of a tumor. The first vet did a fine job of trying to resect all of the growth, but he didn't succeed. The surgical margins were considered dirty, contaminated with cancer cells, and so everything he did, every place his scalpel blade went, the entire scar and all the surrounding tissue has to go, stopping shy of permanently impairing Tinkerbell's ability to use the leg while doing my utmost to get rid of the local disease once and for all."

My finger traces the cross hatches along the scar where the stitches were placed. It looks like a miniature railway track running down to the back of Tinkerbell's knee.

"Once this part is over, I'll change my gloves and my instruments and do my best to play the part of plastic surgeon. I'm going to make a great big hole in the back of the thigh. Loose skin in this area is at a premium. I can't just leave it like that. So I'm going to give Tinkerbell the ultimate boob job."

David's eyes widen and I hear a giggle from one of the technicians. They know I'm just trying to get a rise out of him.

"Look at all this skin around her belly." I jiggle a little love handle for effect. "It's loose and stretchy and, best of all, abundant. So why not take some of this surplus skin and move it around to an area that could use a little extra coverage."

David remains silent but I notice how his eyes narrow.

"Vets don't do any real plastic surgery, do they?"

I pick up my scalpel, set to work on the scar, and begin to narrate the tale of the time I flew back to my homeland—to England, the great "Nation of Animal Lovers"—to address that very topic.

Birmingham, the second largest city in England, may not be my first European destination of choice, but it does play host to the largest annual gathering of veterinarians and all things veterinary on the far side of the pond. Some eighteen months prior to the meeting, known as the British Small Animal Veterinary Association (BSAVA) Congress, the organizers had invited me to give a series of lectures on a variety of surgical topics. Yet only a few days before hopping on a plane to Heathrow, I received a phone call soliciting my participation in a press conference intended to attract national media attention and kick off the event. I confess that a brooding, conceited alter ego, sadly lurking in an all too shallow recess of my mind, instantly daydreamed a crowded room of journalists buzzing with the anticipation of my arrival. I saw myself stepping up to a podium cluttered with microphones labeled BBC, CNN, ESPN, Al Jazeera, half-blinded by the stroboscopic glare of unrelenting flash photography as I patiently dealt with a deluge of questions from hordes of reporters that I somehow knew on a first-name basis. Needless to say, with such superficial aspirations of fleeting celebrity, I heartily accepted.

During the drive up north in my rental car, finally learning not to smash my right hand into the side of the car door in anticipation of a gear change, I began to question the late hour of this invitation into the media spotlight. I had always found the BSAVA to be extremely well organized. Was I all they could muster at short notice; an eleventh-hour standby? I was not, and am not, by any stretch of my own vivid imagination, an authority on the subject they asked me to address. I merely qualified as a warm, willing, and able body. What happened to the original and, more appropriately, more desirable speaker, for I was sure that there had to be one? Did he or she back out at the last minute? And if so, for what reason?

Swatting away the fly of paranoia with all the contempt it deserved, I found myself one rainy April morning navigating the swish and impressive National Convention Center in search of the Media Suite.

The room was small and already crowded with a turbulent throng of damp and steamy people. There was the steady rumble of polite conversation among tight groups of talking heads, occasionally pierced by harsh female laughter that defied the high ceiling and swooped down to revisit the noisy milieu. It seemed as though everyone sported notepads, Dictaphones, or bulky photographic bags, all intent on blocking my path to a table with help-yourself coffee, tea, and biscuits.

When I finally did make it to my destination and poured myself a cup, an elderly woman with unruly white hair pounced on me. She sported a heavy hand-knitted cardigan and a long gray skirt that failed to conceal a pair of bright yellow Wellington boots, looking as though she had been caught in a storm while attending to her rose garden. I half expected to be attacked with a pair of pruning shears.

"I'm Penelope, but call me Penny," she said, giving my hand the sort of vigorous pumping that made me wonder if I should recognize her as a former Olympic shot-putter. "One of the organizers was kind enough to point you out to me and I thought I might try and catch you before you speak this morning. I thought I might, as our dear colleagues put it over in the colonies, head you off at the pass."

The words spewed from her lips and her voice was so plumy and proper it made the queen's accent sound as though it hailed from some smoggy northern mining community. I looked around for the two men in the white coats from whom she must have escaped, but when they were not forthcoming, she said, "I'm sorry. I can see you're confused. I'm a reporter for the *Times* newspaper."

Her eyes narrowed, and she lowered her voice a few decibels so that it was merely shrill, and added, "I assume you're prepared for this."

"For what?" I tried to ask, but she was already speaking over me.

"Now where exactly will you be during the next week? I'm going to need times, dates, and places where you can be reached for additional comments and interviews. Do you happen to have a mobile phone? Access to e-mail? Undoubtedly this story has plenty of legs, so I'm anticipating an avalanche of commentary, letters, editorials, and so forth. I'm quite sure you'd prefer to be printed up accurately in the broadsheets rather than in one of those trashy tabloids, now wouldn't you?"

She offered me what I'm sure she considered to be her most

charming if somewhat orthodontically challenged smile before taking a gulp of her coffee. She spoke so quickly I wondered if they were serving double espresso spiked with speed. It made me pause midsip and then, over the rim of my cup, I began to notice a number of heads were turned in our direction. People were eavesdropping; eyes were flicking our way and the occasional square chin jutted in the general vicinity of our conversation.

"I'll be visiting my sister and some friends in London," I said. "But I really don't understand what all the fuss is about."

She studied me, an incredulous glare melting into a suspicious smile.

"Your topic, dear boy, your topic. 'Plastic Surgery in Small Animals.' I think you're in for a . . ."—she appeared to be searching for just the right turn of phrase and then added—"a spot of bother."

"A spot of bother," I repeated.

But before the reporter could elucidate her point, she was swept up by a whirling dervish of a diminutive blond woman, who, exuding effervescence to the point of bursting, rifled through a couple of air kisses and, ignoring me completely, informed Penny that she absolutely must come meet some person or other. With little more than a cursory wave and a weak apology, Penny disappeared in the general direction of an unloved table of assorted baked goods.

The vacuum of space left by her hasty exit only enhanced my isolation and I sensed the voyeurs' smiles all around me. I felt like a man who had fallen overboard off the back of a cruise ship and the one person who saw me disappear into the ocean had been easily waylaid en route to the bridge by the prospect of an enormous plate of desiccated Eccles cake, macaroons, and limp chocolate éclairs.

What concerned me was her use of the phrase "a spot of bother." "A spot of bother" is one of many great British understatements. Whereas one might expect it to be utilized in the context of burning the toast or realizing you had run out of milk just as the vicar dropped by for afternoon tea, the phrase is frequently exploited to politely convey somewhat more somber complications. It is almost certain that during the famous Battle of Hastings in 1066 when King Harold took a direct hit from William the Conqueror's forces with an arrow to the eye, he turned to his knights and confessed that he was in "a spot of bother." And I have no doubt that the soporific sailor, realizing that he had been woefully neglectful in his night-watch duties, approached the captain of the *Titanic* using the phrase as part of his opening gambit.

And then, as they say, the penny dropped and I realized why "Penelope, call me Penny" feared for my safety among the middle pages of the British tabloids. The title of my presentation was nothing new for the vets and technicians seated in the dimly lit lecture halls, but for a press conference aimed at journalists hungry for sensation, that which I had been invited to speak on at such short notice must have led her to believe that I was about to embark on a new campaign condoning the use of cosmetic surgical procedures on pets.

Despite having spent the greater part of my professional life working in the United States, I have never lost my British sensitivities when it comes to the practice of cosmetic surgery. The Royal College of Veterinary Surgeons makes it perfectly clear that no such operation can be performed and consequently Britain is replete with Dobermans, schnauzers, boxers, Boston terriers, and Great Danes proudly swishing and twitching long tails and full ears. And Britain is not alone, in fact; most of Europe, Labrador, Newfoundland, New Zealand, and Australia have outlawed ear cropping.

So far, attempts to legislate against the practice of ear cropping in the United States have failed in California, Vermont, and New York, despite an American Veterinary Medical Association recommendation to the American Kennel Club and appropriate breed associations to delete the mention of cropped or trimmed ears from breed standards for dogs. Personally (and at the risk of alienating a great many dog breeders), I would like to see the AVMA take a tougher stance on the subject. In its most recent position statement, the AVMA declared that "ear cropping and tail docking in dogs for cosmetic reasons are not medically indicated nor of benefit to the patient. These procedures cause pain and distress, and . . . are accompanied by inherent risks of anesthesia, blood loss, and infection." But it added, "Veterinarians should counsel dog owners about these matters before agreeing to perform these surgeries." Am I reading this wrong or are we saying it's okay to perform a surgery that's a complete waste of time so long as we let the owner know it's unpleasant for their dog and has no merit?

Please, if necessary, blame my British indoctrination or blame my affiliation to the MSPCA (the Massachusetts Society for the Prevention of Cruelty to Animals refuses to perform ear cropping, tail docking, debarking, or cat declawing), but I have a problem with slicing off a hefty chunk of healthy skin and associated cartilage and then submitting an animal to weeks of ridiculous taping and splinting as you strive to achieve the desirable degree of erectness. I've heard the arguments that ears make for an easy target among breeds of hunting dogs and that cropping reduces injury and even decreases the rate of ear infections, but in the twenty-first century, in my humble opinion, it's cosmetic surgery plain and simple. If pointy ears prevented ear problems, vets would be cropping every cocker spaniel on the planet. What next, ear piercing?

If you argue that Dobermans look more eye-catching, perky, and even more masterful with finely pointed ears, how different is this from some of the goals of breast augmentation? If appearance is what matters, then who's driving the vanity? And consider the story of a pedigree blue Doberman and his gullible owner who had the dog's ears cropped by one veterinarian but was extremely disappointed by the results. My colleague, who saw the case as a second opinion, was left incredulous at the sight of the poor creature by his master's side. The animal was canine, almost certainly pure bred, muscular, Germanic, wearing a short, blue gray coat. But the ears were all wrong, half-cocked and droopy, guaranteed to defy all manner of tape, cardboard tubes, foam inserts, and wire racks that had attempted to keep them upright. How could this second vet make such a bold assertion? Simple. The patient was actually a Weimaraner, a hunting dog blessed with floppy ears that were never meant to be cropped.

My favorite example of gratuitous, anthropomorphic plastic surgery for small animals has to be the use of testicular implants in cats and dogs. There is a certain client, invariably male, aged between eighteen and thirty, for whom the concept of neutering induces an involuntary wince and guarding of their own nether regions. In our narcissistic nip/tuck world of lifts, liposuction,* bypass, and augmentation, prosthetic testicles appeal to this target group.

Testicular implants, patented in the United States and sold as Neuticals, come in a range of desirable sizes and textures that can be slipped inside a vacated sac at the time of castration, affording your male companion the opportunity to still feel himself, so to speak. Neither the owner nor their pet, or both, are left feeling violated by the detachment of testicles from body due to the presence of polyprophylene or silicon balls sitting in their furless scrotum. In this way a dog can retain his essential masculinity by still being able to proudly display his manhood, irrespective of the obvious lack of innervation and lifelong suffering with numb nuts. As many satis-

---

*Recently a scientific article out of Germany promoted the use of liposuction in a dog to produce rapid weight loss (10 percent of the dog's body weight) and thereby reduce lameness due to arthritis.

fied owners report, "He's a guy and I wanted him to remain looking like one."

"Frodo never knew he lost anything."

"Baby Snow has all the benefits of being neutered. Neuticals are just a whole lot nicer."

I imagine that any male dog named Baby Snow needs all the help he can get retaining any vestige of masculinity.

My natural tendency has always been to condemn these implants as mere trifles, an indulgence by the owner. However, for those men whose eyes water at the prospect of their dog's losing his testicles, convinced that his bark will jump two octaves and induce an interest in the music of Barbra Streisand and Cher, perhaps this is a preferable option to avoiding the procedure altogether.

On a Web site touting the merits of Neuticals, I found one rascally pet owner inquiring as to whether anyone had managed to get their dog implanted with oversized testicles in an attempt to boost their manhood. As I mentioned earlier, the Internet is replete with useless veterinary commentary of this nature, and I think it unlikely that some wiry dachshund was fitted for the testicles of a Great Dane just to get a little respect from all the bitches in town.

Of course if it's good enough for a dog, it's good enough for a cat and that's why Neuticals are also available, appropriately sized, for that frisky feline in your life. I'm sorry, but some pet owners must be delusional, because honestly, how many times have you noticed a cat's manhood? Even veterinarians can find it challenging to tell the sex of a cat in some cases.

During the 1970s veterinary plastic surgery was primarily associated with the repair of injuries sustained by vehicular trauma or thermal injury. It wasn't until the 1980s with the advent of aggressive oncological surgical techniques that plastic and reconstructive surgery, as it is more commonly known, developed in response to the need to restore function in a cosmetically acceptable manner. *Acceptable* is a movable feast and a term rarely used in Hollywood celebrity circles. Dogs and cats, for the most part, are not obsessed by their own appearance. Repetitive mirror consultations and bad hair days are the exception.

Oral, nasal, and facial surgeries can generate all manner of owner trepidation and rightly so. The face is the canine or feline personality; the eyes their expressions, what speaks to us, what we come to understand, and therefore any surgery that alters the appearance of the face is viewed with a certain degree of skepticism and fear. Removing a rapidly expanding tumor from an animal's mouth aims to get rid of the aberrant lump in its entirety, to prevent pain, and to allow for normal breathing, eating, and drinking. If these criteria can be met, if the tissue heals and the animal is restored to health, then cosmetics are of secondary importance. When an owner understands this concept, acceptance and satisfaction are possible.

So let us return to that press conference, to the final speaker of the day, the young man about to discuss the merits of plastic surgery in pets. I began by distributing a collection of testicular implants of all shapes, sizes, and textures to the people in the back row and asked them to pass these forward. This opening only appeared to fuel their excitement and I watched as, en mass, the reporters and journalists appeared to lean forward, pens poised, waiting for me to verbally step into something brown and smelly. But of course I didn't. I clarified the disparity, I talked about the good, the bad, and the ugly plastic surgery, but above all I talked about the avoidance of cosmetics in pets purely for the benefit of the owner. And as I spoke—I was slotted for half an hour, but it all seemed to be over in half that time (there really must have been something in the coffee)—I watched as the pens fell, the reporters eased back into their chairs, and the element of mystery and intrigue flitted away.

At the end of the talk I opened it up to questions and noticed

Penny sitting in the front row, smiling as she raised one hand. In the other she held a pair of large, translucent, silicon testicles that she thoroughly kneaded, in rapt silence, before considering the weight of them in her cupped hand.

"These two," she started, holding her hand higher for the rest of the room to see. "They seem to be different. A little larger. Smoother. More natural. Almost . . ."

"That's because they're for humans," I said. "I put them in among the rest for comparison. I'm glad to see you appreciated the distinction."

And with that I turned my head slightly to the left, adding a throaty and exaggerated cough, in the hope that it might help an old lady in her reverie.

14

. . . .

2:47 P.M.

THE CUTTING EDGE

Juggling. We do it all the time. Each and every one of us is a master of the art. For the most part, our three-ball cascade could do with some practice and we might never advance to the fiery torch, unwieldy hatchet, and buzzing chain saw, but we can assimilate, manipulate, and execute a handful of imaginary tasks in the void between our ears with the best of them.

I leave David behind in the operating room. He has drifted into another surgical suite to watch a cat undergoing surgery to remove a brain tumor. Perhaps this procedure will provoke a "wicked" approval rating at the end of his eventful day.

I still have some work to do with Tinkerbell and begin writing her postoperative instructions in her record. She had a lumbar epidural prior to surgery, the liquid opiate guaranteed to linger around her spinal cord for another eighteen hours. Her consumption of inhaled anesthesia during the plastic surgery was a fraction of what it might have been without the injection, optimizing her safety while she was lost in the abyss, assuring a smooth, pain-free transition into consciousness and the beginning of her recovery. Next, I must label the tissue I resected from the back of her thigh, tissue that resembles an ailing jellyfish floating in a private vat of formalin. The jar will be sent off to the pathologists, submitted to histopathological examination, a process necessitating more paperwork in which I document the patient's history, the lesion's anatomical and gross appearance, together with my suspicions for diagnosis. Selfishly, of course, all I really want to know is whether I got it all. Are the surgical margins clean? Is Tinkerbell cured?

I extricate myself from cap, mask, and gown and pass through the swinging double doors of the OR and head for the nearest telephone in the fishbowl, the current version of my to-do list clear and concise in my mind's eye, a row of empty boxes in need of checks. Before I can even pick up a handset, Joe tosses me one more pressing item to juggle.

"Mr. Stark has called three times this afternoon," he says, "demanding Mei-Mei's biopsy results. He's threatening to call every hour until he hears back from you."

Joe hands me both the medical record and an apologetic smile. I remember the case and I certainly remember the owner. Mei-Mei is an older chow chow with a small, solitary, low-grade mast cell tumor studding the cartilage of her right ear. Initially, Mei-Mei's innocuous, almost cute little mole lacked a label, the all-important diagnosis that might guide me as to how I should best proceed. Contrary to the owner's perception that I was only out to satisfy intellectual curiosity or playing academic games, I warned the brusque and bitter Mr. Stark that I would cut wide and deep, that with luck I would deliver the answer and the cure with a relatively minor procedure. I might even have raided my lexicon and exercised the trite analogy "no point in using a nuclear warhead when a bullet will do," hoping to clarify that until we know what it is we seek to cure, lopping off half an ear might prove to be an embarrassing overkill. Needless to say, I imagine the only bullet reference Mr. Stark contemplates is the cap destined for my ass after the report came back that the surgical margins were not clean. The mention of a second surgery was met with hostility, recriminations of incompetence, and a request for full monetary reimbursement since the first procedure was surely botched.

No matter how personable you like to think you are as a veterinarian and in spite of your self-acclaimed, legendary flair as a social chameleon, a failure to connect with certain two- and four-legged clients is inevitable. They think you lack confidence or find you too cocky; you're not affectionate enough or uncomfortably mushy and sentimental. For general health care, pet owners will naturally gravitate toward a compatible veterinarian. Emergency and second-opinion encounters, however, are more like a blind date. Within minutes an owner might realize that the chemistry is all wrong but there's no way out because instead of meeting for coffee they're locked into a candlelit dinner for two and the vet is the one driving them home.

These days I am spared the late-night drunks and stoners that stumble into our emergency room. Instead, with second-opinion cases, I have traded occasional belligerence for occasional high maintenance. Pet owners have high expectations of what I can do for their pet and so they should. Unfortunately, my work doesn't come with a guarantee or a lifetime warranty. Some owners will complain no matter how good a job you do and fortunately most, like Mr. Stark, are easy to spot. Our conversations become more frank, the list of potential complications more extensive, and the documentation of our exchanges more detailed. Most problems occur with the clients you failed to notice, the ones who stewed in silence, waiting to pounce. Sometimes their frustration is perfectly justified. You can spend their money but you can't find a diagnosis. You performed the surgery but you didn't perform the cure. These are tough cases. If I am lucky, a mixture of honesty and resolve might get me through. But if I can no longer win their confidence, I will be sure to offer alternatives, other surgeons, both inside and outside our hospital. If I'm not going to change how they feel about me at least they will know that my reputation takes a backseat to doing right by their animal.

I stick to my original plan, calling Tinkerbell's mom, giving her the details of the surgery, my fingers liberating a hibernating mouse from under a nest of photocopied surgical articles, the creature twitching back to life in my hand as I log on to the nearest computer, find the correct page on the hospital intranet, and scroll down to the section titled "pathology." I shoot a single white arrow into the heart of an empty box before typing in a six-digit number and hit enter, handset sandwiched between shoulder and ear, all the while answering questions and offering assurances that Tinkerbell will be very comfortable and well cared for overnight. Mei-Mei Stark's name appears on the screen as the pager on my hip beckons me to find Dr. Payne as I promise to call first thing in the morning with another update on Tinkerbell's progress. My arrow has transformed into a little white hand flipping me an index finger. I left click. The phone call has ended, the page has ended, and for some reason the hard drive's ability to locate the all-important biopsy results has ended. Seconds shy of slapping the side of the monitor as though I might improve the reception, the screen changes to the final report. I skip the microscopic description, skip the microscopic findings, and head straight for the juicy bits, jumping text, scanning lines, willing the statement to appear as I hunt for the phrase that will make everything all right with the world. And finally, there it is, the bottom line once more proving to be the bottom line.

"Excision appears to be complete."

The English are not renowned for being a particularly tactile nation, but right about now even I could muster an enthusiastic high-five. My smile is far more relief than victory. I locate Mr. Stark's telephone number in the record and dial. Wouldn't you know it, my stalker is not picking up and I get routed to an answering machine. I am all business, rattling off the report's conclusion, hoping that Mei-Mei is doing well, urging him to call back and knowing that I will never hear from him again.

Now, where was I? Ah, yes, paging Dr. Payne.

A minute later and she's calling me back.

"I've got the answers on Barron," she says, "I'm sure the mom thinks I'm a total freak."

"Really?" I say. "She's met you?"

"Very funny," she says. "I meant she must think I'm a weirdo asking all those obscure questions about her dog."

"And . . ."

"And," she pauses before adding, "you were right. The mom believes this back leg problem has been going on for weeks if not months. It was definitely worse after the fall on the ice but it was definitely there before. Believe it or not, Barron is supposed to be pretty quiet at home. She claims he tends to mope around the house."

"What about the good stuff?"

Dr. Payne hesitates as though she might be consulting her notes.

"Well, he eats dry food and it's stored in the basement."

"Moldy, dry, finished?"

"She says the basement is dry and the food is stored in a sealed plastic container. It doesn't sound right for growing a fungal neurotoxin."

"Good thought," I say, genuinely impressed, "but I was ruling out botulism. What else?"

"They have an ant problem around the home, but not until

spring. A pest-control company comes in to spray starting in April. They have no organophosphates on the property. Some kind of poisoning seems unlikely."

I smile. So far she has been following along with my train of thought. Now for the best part.

"And what about the vomiting?" I ask.

"The answer is yes. Occasionally Barron has been throwing up after eating."

"You're sure it's vomiting? Mom's not mistaking this for retching or passive regurgitation?"

There is a silence that tells me she never considered the possibility or she forgot to ask. I help her out.

"No matter. I'd like you to get a set of chest X-rays, place an IV catheter, and then meet me outside J ward."

"What's going on and why the chest X-rays?"

"Don't worry. Just make sure they don't sedate Blitz for the radiograph. With a bit of luck the three of us are about to share a Siegfried and Roy moment."

In my hands I carry three objects: a syringe containing an appropriate dose of atropine, to all intents and purposes the antidote; a syringe containing my mystery solution; and last but not least an endotracheal tube that I can slide into Barron's windpipe in the event of an adverse response to what I am about to try.

Dr. Payne notes the loaded syringes in my breast pocket, but it is the endotracheal tube in my hand that has her worried.

"What is that for?"

She hasn't figured it out. Telling her about the risk is like telling her how to do the trick.

"Just in case," I say with a cryptic flash of my eyebrows.

Her facial expression lies somewhere between agitation and alarm. I press on.

"Did you see his chest films?"

"Not yet," she says.

"Good. Then let's start by walking Olaf up and down the hallway a few times."

She shrugs, gives Barron the word, and those bizarre back legs whisk them away, back and forth. Not until the eighth lap does Barron begin slowing down, seizing up and ultimately coming to a frozen standstill. It is exactly what I observed outside in the parking lot.

"Excellent," I say, finding the hub of the intravenous catheter in his front leg. I inject my potion, withdraw the needle, and offer Barron's butt a slap like a cowboy sending off the last horse in the posse.

To be fair, Barron's performance may not make it all the way to the Bellagio, but watching the response on Dr. Payne's face is magical. In under a minute Barron runs with a fluidity he has all but forgotten, his stride long and even, muscles contracting in harmony. I may not have turned a frog into a prince, but suddenly there's a German shepherd where a kangaroo used to be. With Barron's awakening we finally have our diagnosis. But in another five minutes the effect is starting to wane, the gait more wooden, joints rusting tight until finally, once more, refusing to move at all. The bigger question we should be asking ourselves is "Do we have a cure?"

"A Tensilon test. Edrophonium chloride," she says.

I nod.

"Very good," I say.

"When did you realize he had myasthenia gravis?"

"When I took him out for a walk. I remembered you said that he's lazy at home, doesn't do much. I didn't understand. He seems so wired. He has the peculiar walk but trotting up and down in hallway was not enough to make him slow up completely. To turn him into a classic case of weakness exacerbated by exercise yet attenuated by rest you have to take him farther. Eventually, as you just saw, he turns to stone."

Dr. Payne is already racing ahead, reaching her next "lightbulb moment."

"And that's why you wanted to know about the vomiting. That's why you wanted the chest X-ray. You were worried about mega-esophagus."

Sadly, about 90 percent of dogs with this uncommon neurological disease also have a condition known as megaesophagus, a peculiar dilatation and flaccidity to the muscular tube that conveys food from the back of the throat to the stomach.

"I spoke to his mom myself when I got permission to do the test. From her description Barron doesn't vomit, he regurgitates his food. He lowers his head and a disgusting sausage of masticated food falls out. I've seen the chest films, they confirm the presence of a mega-esophagus. And one more thing. He has aspiration pneumonia."

She glances at the panting dog content and compelled to lie at her feet.

"His outlook isn't great," I say. "Most dogs either succumb to their pneumonia or are put to sleep within a year of diagnosis."

Barron and his doctor say nothing, visibly deflated and confused, as if they both lost something, something they both briefly managed to find.

Before I can offer more, my pager vibrates its warning of another incoming message.

"Call operator 2-5-0, 2-5-0, I have a Dr. Helen Hancock holding for you."

I excuse myself and grab a phone from the corridor wall. I don't believe I know a Dr. Hancock, but I assume it is a referring vet calling about a case. I'll take the call, but I must be brief. Odin, my final case of the day, a two-hundred-pound moose of a black Newfoundland is in the process of being shaved for his surgery.

"Hi, Dr. Hancock?"

"Yes, this is Dr. Hancock, is this the veterinarian looking after my father's dog, Sage?"

I smile. This must be Mr. Hartman's daughter, the doctor, the one who insisted her father call in a staff surgeon in the middle of the night.

"That's right. What can I do for you?"

"Well, to be perfectly honest, I'm rather concerned about what you're doing to my father." Her words uncoil from a tightly wound tongue, catching me off guard.

"I'm afraid I don't understand."

"I had hoped that a surgical specialist might bring a little maturity and wisdom to my father's problem, rather than some scalpel-happy resident looking for more practice. I appear to have been mistaken."

"I'm still not with you, Dr. Hancock."

A forced nasal snort shoots past my left ear.

"I'm just asking for a little honesty, that's all. For goodness' sake the dog's nearly eleven. Isn't that about a normal lifespan for a dog? I can't believe you even took it to surgery, let alone woke it up again. And now my father tells me there are all these postoperative complications. I mean, really, how far are you people prepared to go?"

I bite down hard on my lower lip, feeling the indentation from my teeth, dull pain dampening down a response I might regret as I wait for the pause that tells me it is my turn.

"Dr. Hancock, I can assure you that the medical and surgical care afforded your father's dog has been of the highest possible standards. But you're absolutely right, there have been some difficult judgment calls for Sage, and yes, she is critically ill, but there is still a reasonable chance that with the kind of care we can provide—"

"And exactly how much is all this wonderful care costing? I know it has to be a lot of money because my father won't tell me. Don't you understand that he's a frail and lonely seventy-six-year-old man getting by on a small pension and Social Security? He can't go around spending thousands of dollars on a dog. Surely it would have been better to put the thing out of its misery."

I try to imagine this detractor of all things furry, whimpering in the presence of a boisterous dog, convinced that he or she is rabid, or feigning anaphylactic shock at the slightest whiff of cat dander. I imagine a perfectly appointed house, a place void of muddy paw prints, gnarled and gouged table legs, and the precious gift of disemboweled rodent gracing your welcome mat every morning.

A sharp and clipped exhalation hisses down the line, followed by "What you don't understand is that my late mother got him the dog as a gift, a parting gift because she knew she was going to die."

She is getting to it now.

"Forty-five years of marriage and do you think she could tell him about her heart problem? No way. Not my mother. Protected him to the end. Thought she was protecting him from the grave with a new companion. The dog was still a puppy when she died."

For a second Dr. Hancock pauses, as if she has become the juggler with her thoughts, deciding on which to catch and which to drop.

"Look, I know Sage had the desired effect. She has been a good companion. But at the end of the day she's just a pet that he owns." I feel the chill of her synopsis, degrading the relationship between Sage and her dad to a contractual obligation, to property. She has made her father's best friend sound like his slave. "There's no getting away from the fact that the animal is a constant reminder of my mother's death; to him, to me, to all of us. This whole disaster has got him caring for his dog in a way that he never got to do for his wife."

She sighs and I wonder if she feels like she has said too much. I let the silence hang and then she adds, "I know you probably have no idea where I'm coming from, but I for one care more about children than I do animals. I guess people like you, vets, will never understand that humans must come first. You've lost the ability to draw the line. I mean, how can you justify all the billions people spend every year on animals when there are children in our own country who still cannot receive basic health care?"

I look at my watch and imagine Odin, that enormous black shadow, sailing into the OR on a silver gurney. I swallow the sour sting of her words.

"Look, Dr. Hancock, all I can tell you is this: For some people animals become as important as, and sometimes much more important than, their own children. It is not for me to judge the merits of this bond. I respect its strength and my ability to influence it. Be assured that I will do my utmost to preserve the bond but not beyond the realms of reason and what is best for both the animal and the owner."

A nasal huff simmers through the airways after a minimum of consideration.

"I must apologize," I say. "I have a patient going into the operating room. I have to go, but I'll keep your comments in mind when next speaking to your father."

"Please do," she says, and hangs up.

Odin Phillips was dropped off yesterday as part of our routine preoperative protocol for exactly the kind of surgical procedure that would have infuriated Dr. Helen Hancock. Odin suffers from congenital hip dysplasia, that inability of a young dog's hips to form a decent ball-and-socket joint, and in his case, the disease has progressed into a state of severe and debilitating arthritis making it virtually impossible for him to get to his feet, let alone do stairs or go for a walk. Mr. Phillips, his owner, is a firefighter; six foot five, with a neck the size of my waist and the ability to get this dog up and off the ground like he was four pounds of Yorkshire terrier. Believe me, the next time you find yourself trapped in a burning building, Mr. Phillips is the guy you want with the ax and the respirator to get you out alive.

Despite the assistance of an oversized log carrier as a sling, Odin is barely able to get around, and at four years of age his quality of life is suffering. He has grazed his way through the nutritional supplements, through the anti-inflammatory painkillers and the weight-loss programs, and they helped for a while. But the soreness in his hips never fades from Odin's big brown eyes, however much he tries to smile and please.

This is why total hip replacement is an excellent option for Odin. He was dropped off at Angell the day before surgery for a series of chest X-rays, blood work, and urinalysis to confirm that, as far as we can tell, he is in perfect health. From an orthopedic perspective, his knees, his ankles, his spine, his front legs, everything is fine aside from the bright balls of arthritic bone residing where healthy cartilage used to live in his hips. So why not replace the old hip with a brand-new artificial one? Why not give this gentle giant the best opportunity to get as close to normal on his back legs as possible?

When I put this option to Mr. Phillips, there was nothing to discuss—the new roof on his house, the down payment on a car, a much needed vacation in the Caribbean—they never got to the negotiating room, let alone the table. Odin was getting a new hip because family comes first. It was that simple.

Canine hip replacement has actually been around since the 1970s, but its widespread acceptance by the veterinary and pet-owning community as the ultimate technology for salvaging a painful, arthritic hip joint only dates back to the 1990s. So what has transpired over the last decade that has altered the importance of the animals in our lives and our belief that they should get the best that modern medicine has to offer?

For a better understanding of this transformation, look no further than the most recent national survey of pet owners by the American Animal Hospital Association. It provides wonderful insight, like a State of the Psychosis address. Be advised that the results are not, as some may think, the opinion of a few obsessive cat ladies, insecure nut jobs, or breeders on the fringe. The fact is that the survey polled regular dog- and cat-loving members of the public across thirty-seven states, offering a fascinating perspective on the real world of animal-human relationships and animal health care.

Clearly, large numbers of you, nearly two-thirds, believe that in the face of danger your pet would actually go out of their way to perform some type of rescue. Maybe I might feel differently if I owned a Newfoundland or a Saint Bernard, but I can guarantee that if I were drowning in a body of open water my Labrador would lose all interest in my gurgling and flailing as soon as she spotted a swan or something remotely edible like a tree stump or old car tire. Conversely some 93 percent of owners thought it likely that they would risk their own life for their pet. This statistic I can believe having met a stoic Samoyed rescued after falling through the ice on a frozen pond. The dog was saved. His master was not so lucky. The man drowned, eventually pulled from the water still clutching his dog's leash.

When asked if the pet has humanlike personality traits I was not surprised to find a resounding 94 percent said yes. Respondents selected "emotional/sensitive" and "outgoing" as the two most popular traits. Sounds to me like some people spend too much time filling out pet surveys and applications to dating agencies. In fact, only 7 percent confessed to using their pet "to attract a new friend or potential mate." Potential mate! How wonderfully primordial! Perhaps the pollsters thought your average pet owner might see through "did you buy your dog to improve your chances of having sex" as brash and insensitive?

Once your pet is embraced by the family unit, it seems clear that household hierarchy and dynamics will inexorably and irrevocably change. Nearly 50 percent of owners thought their pet listened better than their spouse. Over two-thirds of owners let their pet break household rules when the spouse was not present, and if stranded on a desert island and forced to choose only one companion, more people would pick a pet than a human. No wonder the divorce rate is so high.

That being said, certain canine virtues may prove particularly popular to the male members of the household. Over a third of owners said their pets enjoy watching television with an overwhelming majority labeled as avid fans of Animal Planet. Coming in third, behind cartoons, 13 percent said sports constitute their pet's viewing pleasure of choice. How very convenient. I can just see all those devoted husbands, leash in one hand, remote control in the other, selflessly fixed on the game insisting that they are merely keeping their dog company.

When I read all this data, that one in five pet owners has attended a pet birthday party, that in another survey 100 percent of owners said they talk to their pets, 97 percent felt they knew what their pet was saying, and, best of all, 78 percent said they speak *for* their pets, speculating on what they would say if they could talk, one truth cuts through all the numbers and thumbs its nose at the likes of Dr. Helen Hancock. Companion animals have moved from the periphery of the American family to its center in a love affair that has shifted the paradigm from accessory to necessity, from mere propriety pet to the status of an adopted child. No wonder more American households have dogs than children.

Pet owners are now pet parents, their biological children reduced to pet siblings, forced to accept the fact that their furry little brother or sister never has to leave the security of Mom and Dad's bed. These days the majority of my clients implore me to understand that their pet *is* their child. One woman even spawned a disturbing image by insisting that I consider both her Labradors as physically coming from her womb!

With this level of passion and commitment to the animals that share our lives is it any wonder that Americans are spending nearly forty billion dollars a year caring for their adopted sons and daughters? It has been reported that owners visit a veterinarian twice as often as they would their own doctor and as a result of all this enhanced pet care our companions are living longer, healthier lives.

But longevity comes at a price. Regular tune-ups may help ensure that you put more miles on the clock, but eventually things will start going wrong, seize up, break down, or drop off, and it's back to the shop for a major overhaul. There was a time when either fixing the problem was not an option or a decision was made to call it a day, to write it off, save the cash and trade in for something new. Not anymore. Staggering progress has been made in all facets of veterinary medicine over the last three decades, driven in part by owners demanding that the advances in their own health care be made available to their animals. The exact same procedures being performed in pets come at a fraction of the human cost even if you go bargain-basement shopping in India or Thailand. Cataract phacoemulsification, artificial hip and elbow replacement, chemotherapy and radiation therapy, open heart surgery, renal transplants, and prosthetic limbs are just a tiny sampling of what is available to twenty-first-century pets, and don't be thinking this trend is closing in on an end point. Whether it's a dog or a child, owners and parents of the sick want cures. The genie is out of the bottle and they are not just popping the cork, they're cracking the glass and clambering to get at what's inside.

With all this new technology and equipment, diagnostic tools, and requisite skills, there was clearly a need for specialization beyond a general veterinary degree. Think about it, how many of you would contemplate taking your child to the family practitioner for an appendectomy or correction of a hideously disfiguring overbite (with the exception of my mum)? Is it any wonder that in the past decade the number of board-certified veterinary specialists in the United

States has grown 76 percent, and now stands at over eight thousand individuals tending to narrow fields of expertise.

Yet there are detractors that suggest this growth in specialization may be driven by a motive altogether more sinister. An April 2006 *Wall Street Journal* article raised awareness of the most common cause of canine lameness, a torn cruciate ligament (or torn ACL), with over a million dogs going under the knife annually. It quoted from a paper published in the *Journal of the American Veterinary Medical Association* that estimated U.S. pet owners spent $1.32 billion to treat ACL problems alone in 2003. And with this little factoid, we start getting to the crux of the sentiment.

"Such treatments have helped fuel a doubling of the number of veterinary surgeons in the U.S. in the last decade. . . ."

Maybe I'm wrong but the story left me feeling like I spend my days drifting from one dog park to the next, throwing Frisbees and tennis balls, attempting to induce knee injuries while doling out my business card for all the inevitable surgery that would surely come my way.

If you think I'm being overly sensitive, consider the July 2003 *Consumer Reports* article entitled "Veterinary Care Without the Bite." The piece hemorrhaged with concerns that pet owners felt their animal's health care cost too much and left them feeling manipulated and breathless with sticker shock. The article suggested shopping around for the best prices, like getting a mortgage or car insurance, and they offered helpful advice on ways to fight back.

"Vet charges can be influenced by how much in college loans a newly minted vet has to pay off, how new or fancy the vet's office is, and whether the office, which vets often call an animal hospital, is located in a high rent part of town."

Ouch! It didn't read like fair and balanced reporting to me and the bias continued with lines like, "*Veterinary Economics* magazine has prodded vets to outfox shoppers. . . ."

What has been happening to my profession's time-honored reputation for ethics and honesty? Why am I being made to feel like an ambulance-chasing lawyer? Veterinarians have been consistently lauded as members of one of the most respected vocations, typically ranking third or fourth. We are sworn by oath to provide relief of animal suffering. Last time I looked they still haven't added the addendum "so long as the client forks out the big bucks!" This means, as our hospital dictates, "all animals with life-threatening conditions will receive immediate and comforting stabilizing care." At a time of crisis it doesn't matter if you're Bill Gates or a homeless person, because our focus is on the pet. If payment is simply not an option, our mission remains the same. Relief may come in the form of emergency surgery, it may come in the form of euthanasia, but the cost for this lifelong commitment to animal welfare comes directly out of our pocket. We do not build this loss into our prices or into our budget. There is no special fund to draw upon. It is a fee we quietly and graciously accept as part of our promise.

It saddens me when pet owners feel swindled or exploited. The notion that we are in the business solely for the money is ridiculous. When the *Consumer Reports* article was published, after four years of undergraduate education and four years of veterinary school, mean educational debt for new veterinary graduates was nearly $73,000. The average starting salary for these "newly minted" doctors was a little over $43,000. Does easy money sound like the driving force behind a life devoted to working with and caring for animals?

Perhaps some of the alleged distress of pet owners stems from a sense of disappointment and sadness, that everything their veterinarian represents derives from a cleaner, simpler, bygone era that no longer exists. These days the image is fuzzy, more and more difficult to evoke, but it clings to the psyche and no one wants to see it fade because it feels like the last holdout of something honest and meaningful. For nearly half a century, veterinarians have engendered and basked in a public image based on the writings of Alf Wight and his wonderful tales of James Herriot. The allure, the romance, the challenge, the satisfaction, it still holds true today, but placing a cardiac pacemaker in a dog's heart in exchange for a cup of tea, a slice of Bundt cake, or a plateful of black pudding is no longer going to cut it. What's not to respect in a profession that works solely for the love of helping animals? *All Creatures Great and Small* was set in the Yorkshire Dales of the 1930s, before the advent of antibiotics, where diseases acquired evocative labels like strawberry foot rot, kinkyback, louping ill, and greasy pig, and ailments were rectified with a tincture of *nux vomica*, oil of juniper, infusion of rhubarb, and spirit of camphor. Given the choice between a modern approach to the treatment of a penile tumor and a vintage technique of bathing the culprit with cocaine solution, a snip of the scissors, and a soothing application of carbolic acid applied with a camel's hair brush, which option do you think your pet would choose?

Sometimes progress in veterinary medicine has not always percolated down from a complementary human equivalent. Consider the innovations of a colleague, a hugely successful veterinary entrepreneur named Jack. I was asking Jack to try to define some of the greatest secrets of his success and, as I was reaching for notepad and pencil, he instantly came back at me with, "Closed-circuit television."

I considered his handsome face and a tan that smacked of a lifestyle and not a recent vacation.

"Not exactly what I was expecting you to say," I replied.

"Best thing I did in all four of my practices. Put cameras throughout the hospitals."

"You mean hidden cameras, surveillance cameras?"

"Not hidden. Everyone knows they're there. In the treatment area, the kennels, the intensive-care unit, anesthesia induction, recovery, even in surgery."

"My God," I said, "and where does one view this reality TV pleasure?"

"From the waiting room. You should see it. Sometimes it's like Super Bowl Sunday in there. Some clients bring in their friends, just to check it out. It's fantastic."

"But don't they get to see what really goes on, behind closed doors? I mean, what if FiFi turns into a land shark, decides to lunge at a technician, and has to be appropriately restrained."

"Then the owner sees it all."

"But what if you're in the middle of surgery and you hit some big important vessel and the blood starts flying."

"Not a problem. The owners appreciate that this is real. They're not watching an episode of *ER*."

My mind started racing with all manner of possible flaws in his premise.

"But what about a cardiac arrest? What if little Muffin is about to have a routine dental cleanup and Mom and Dad are all cozy in their molded plastic chairs enjoying the spectacle and wondering if they might purchase a copy of the videotape to show their friends at their next cocktail party when bam, the dog starts to flatline on the monitor and every face looks flustered and panic-stricken."

He waved me off with an open palm and a knowing smile. "Believe me, we've done it all. Look, animals die, problems happen, but it's all about how you tried, what you did for the patient, your compassion, your determination to do what's best, and when the owner sees how valiantly you've given your best, even if you're not successful, they appreciate it all the more. They've told me so. Over and over."

I was amazed. "Wow!" was all I could offer, somewhat pathetically. And then I noticed him hesitate.

"There's only ever been one problem," he said.

I managed to suppress my smile. I knew it. The owner who fought his way back into the operating room, believing he knew how to save his dog from certain surgical disaster because he saw it once on Animal Planet.

"I had a technician, Becky. Best technician I'd ever worked with in over thirty years of practice. Truly fantastic. Great with the animals. Adored by the clients. Just one problem. Absolutely hated the cameras."

"Really," I said, "why?"

"Because they were a constant reminder of the enormity of her nose." He brought his forefinger and thumb together and held them off the tip of his own nose, pulling an imaginary Pinocchio proboscis out and far away from his body. He went on, "The camera only seemed to accentuate its immensity. It cast an evil shadow across every room she entered. No backstroke in open water for her, no sir. Anyway, we'd had the cameras in place for a couple of months, the feedback from the clients was fantastic, and then Becky came to me and said she was quitting. I asked her why and she told me she couldn't stand the perpetual sight of her ugly profile on the monitors."

"So you lost her?"

"God, no. I paid for her to get a nose job. Good technicians are hard enough to find, let alone great ones. She got the plastic surgery and we've never looked back. Now she loves the camera and the camera loves her. She looks great and you can imagine her loyalty. Best five grand I've ever spent."

6:35 P.M.

FOREIGN BODY

With Odin's surgery complete, orders written, and his dad, Mr. Phillips, up to speed, I breeze into CCU expecting to catch Mr. Hartman during the evening visiting hour, only to find myself walking into a war zone. A trail of blood, spatter, and clots leads the eye to the central work station and a swarm of gray, green, and plum uniforms moving like a precisely choreographed marching band. It hits me like the unexpected chill of an air-conditioned room, a frisson of heightened tension and concentration, and I feel assaulted by information as I take in three animals on three separate examination tables. I see a cat, a Himalayan, either asleep, heavily sedated, anesthetized, or dead, lying on a white towel. Next to the cat is a dog, a Staffordshire bull terrier, the source of my Hansel and Gretel trail, blood pouring from his mouth, his lower jaw dangling off his face, a technician sucking free air from his chest via a butterfly catheter, three-way stop-cock, and 35 ml syringe.

But in a split second of agony, an obscured glimpse of a canine paw melting into the blackness of a distended, oversized plastic bag has me rushing forward on a panicky jolt of adrenaline. It is a moment that stretches in painful, muted increments, giving slowly like pulled sugar because in my racing heart I know who it is and who is responsible.

"It's not Sage."

I hear the words before I reach table three, wondering if it is simply the will of my inner monologue.

"She's fine."

I turn to see that it is Dr. Maganiello, head down, fiddling with an intravenous catheter in the terrier's back leg.

"It's Chipper," she says, "the Rhodesian ridgeback with the broken back. The owner finally allowed us to put him to sleep."

Inexplicably I take a peek inside the bag, making sure there hasn't been some sort of a mistake. I even read the identifying tag attached to the dog's rear paw.

"I found out why Chipper's dad was having such a hard time."

Now I can turn to see the doctor peering over the lenses of her tortoiseshell glasses, wiggling the thin plastic tubing of a catheter that has kinked in the Staffie's saphenous vein. She adjusts the alignment with a strip of surgical tape, tests the patency with a smooth flush from a syringe of heparnized saline, and the flow of intravenous fluids is restored.

Straightening up to face me, Dr. Maganiello says, "Sorry about that. It's been a little crazy here for the last ten minutes."

"I can tell. What were you saying about Chipper's dad?"

She's already changing the drip rate, reaching for a cuff to set up the blood pressure monitor.

"It turns out his mother was in the hospital last month for a biopsy of a suspicious shadow in her lung. Something went wrong and what should have been a routine procedure ended with her being fitted for a body bag. And here's the kicker, the lesion in her lung was perfectly ordinary and benign."

I'm speechless. No wonder the poor guy was having such a hard time. No wonder he was hesitant and skeptical.

"That's awful," I say. And then, as if to ease my own conscience, "When you write a condolence card, would you run it by me, before you send it off? I'd like to sign my name on it."

I catch her cursory nod, but I can tell she has moved on. Chipper's outcome may not have been pleasant, but given his situation she knows it was for the best. There is nothing more she can do. Her focus has shifted to where she can still make a difference, eyes gesturing to her latest patient.

"If I can get him stable overnight, do you have time to squeeze in a jaw fracture tomorrow?"

The Staffie is like a little canine Greco-Roman wrestler, stocky and buff with a muscular head and neck that might intimidate the unacquainted even though they are as friendly as they are fearless, content to be patted despite the prickle of a needle sticking into his chest and a lower jaw swinging like a hammock in a summer breeze.

"Car chaser?" I ask.

"You got it," she says. "And Dad was at the wheel."

For some reason, certain dogs—often young, intact males—develop a fascination with spinning rubber tires. They become both hypnotized and incensed by the site of a moving vehicle, compelled to pursue and restrain. Most of the time they are simply that crazy neighborhood dog, snapping at every passing vehicle, but occasionally they manage to catch up to their prey and when a jaw capable of generating a force of up to 450 pounds per square inch bites down hard on a fast-moving radial, the consequences can be disastrous.

The mention of the dog's owner being the driver of the vehicle is Dr. Maganiello's way of saying, "Don't worry about the bill." Like I've said before, nothing motivates like a heavy dose of guilt.

"Sure," I say. "Add him to the schedule."

But my mind is elsewhere.

"Hey, did you happen to see Sage's dad? Old guy? Hard time getting around?"

This time she stops what she is doing and looks straight at me. I feel as though I am being scrutinized, read, like she is trying to understand the reason for my interest. Her head tilts ever so slightly to one side and I think I can see the barest hint of a smile creeping into the corners of her lips.

"He was here but we kicked everybody out early when Loki began to seizure in her cage," she points to the Himalayan starting to stir after her shot of valium, "and Spike rolled in on a gurney spraying blood everywhere."

She anticipates my next question.

"I got him a chair. Sage was able to stand. They both seemed to be doing pretty well."

I imagine Sage's wet nose on Mr. Hartman's dry lips, their eyes inches apart, the connection complete.

"Thanks," I say, moving on, as though our encounter broke my rhythm. "Let me know about the jaw."

Standing in front of Sage I get the same flutter of panic every new parent gets when they struggle to see the subtle rise and fall of their baby's chest by nightlight. She is lying perfectly still and anxious seconds pass. Her breaths are so shallow, almost imperceptible. I try to count them as the minute hand on my wristwatch swings through fifteen seconds. I multiply the number by four. Despite the hubbub around her, at eight breaths per minute, Sage has managed to fall asleep.

I don't pat her head. I don't enter her run. I want her to rest. She's been through so much she must be exhausted. I simply check that her fluids are running on schedule and flick through her chart. I need to find that rectal temperature one more time. And there it is—

a fabulously boring 101.9°F. She is comfortable enough to sleep and her temperature is normal. There is only one more thing for me to do before I head home—one last call to Mr. Hartman.

On a nearby computer I pull up Sage's record and check out the list of contact numbers. Mr. Hartman's home number on the Cape is listed, as is his daughter's, but I am loath to call Dr. Hancock after our earlier encounter. Then I notice that a third number is listed for a cellular telephone. This surprises and amuses me, the notion of Mr. Hartman whipping out a black Motorazr in public. I wonder if his grandchildren, if he has any, have customized the ring tone with a catchy jingle, something uncharacteristic like the opening bars to the latest from Eminem. Then I realize that the phone is probably a baby monitor, for keeping in touch and keeping tabs, another demonstration of a daughter's love and concern for her father.

I place the call, disappointed that Mr. Hartman doesn't pick up with a flippant "Whasup!" and at the same time relieved that I am instantly patched through to voice mail. I assume the phone is not turned on. I would hate to have the old man distracted as he negotiates some busy Boston intersection. I apologize for missing him during the visiting hour, reassure him with a "so far so good," and all the while wonder if he even knows how to retrieve his messages.

I head back to my office. I'm out of my scrubs and into my regular clothes, pausing for a ritualistic moment of hesitation. Did I forget anything before I leave? Are my patients all set for the evening? Have I spoken to all their owners? No, yes, and yes. Finally, after a long day, I am all done and I can't wait to get home.

Passing through the waiting room en route to my car I catch sight of a coordinator pointing me out to a woman clutching a cat, making me freeze like a bad boy on one of those reality TV cop shows. The woman and the white longhaired cat clinging precariously to her shoulder are joined by a man with a little girl in tow, a little girl I recognize as one of my daughter's friends from school.

"Thank goodness we caught you before you left for the day. I'm Tony Duggan," a nod and a handshake are exchanged, "and this is my . . ."

"Dianna," his wife interjects, flashing a smile.

"And of course you know our daughter, Kerry." A chubby little girl with blond pigtails rolls her eyes in my direction before nuzzling for the security of her mother's hip.

"Yes, of course, hi, Kerry."

"And last, but not least, this is Snowball, Kerry's cat."

Tony seems to be making a point that this is his daughter's cat, and taking her cue, Kerry grapples for Snowball, fearless little fingers ripping the creature from the cat's sanctuary as a fur boa.

"Snowball's been feeling awful all day," says Dianna, sweeping white detritus from her shoulder. "She must have thrown up a dozen times and when we took her to see our local vet he said she might be obstructed and might need surgery. We thought of you and rushed straight down here."

Mrs. Duggan does not hide her embarrassment at taking liberties with the tenuous connection between us, but it is Kerry's sad blue eyes that seal my fate.

In an examination room Snowball stands perfectly still on the table, her abdominal muscles relaxing just enough for me to appreciate the abnormal wad of small intestines bunched up inside her little belly like a tiny concertina. I place one of my fingers on her lower incisor teeth, push down, open her mouth, and inspect under the base of her tongue.

"What do you think?" asks Dianna.

"Does Snowball like to play with string?" I ask.

Head nodding all around.

"Could she have gotten into a sewing kit or the inner workings of a cassette tape?"

The parents frown as if the suggestion is absurd. Then Kerry begins to tug on her mother's arm. A whisper passes behind a cupped hand.

"Kerry thinks Snowball might have been locked in the bathroom for part of the day. Would that make a difference?"

I smile.

"Possibly. Could she have gotten into dental floss?"

Dianna gasps as though she has caught a glimpse of the estimate I am beginning to work on.

"That's it!" she says. "I found an empty dental floss container on the floor this afternoon and I only opened it a few days ago. I couldn't understand how we went through it so fast."

"Well, whatever it is, it's acting as what we call a linear foreign body. The material gets lodged or hooked up somewhere within the alimentary canal, allowing the guts to crawl and concertina their way toward the anchored obstruction. Cats frequently get the foreign material caught up under the base of their tongue, but I've checked and Snowball's tongue looks fine."

"So where else can it get stuck?" asks Tony.

"The next stop is the stomach, typically getting knotted up in the pylorus, or outflow portion, just before heading into the small intestine. This would be my guess with Snowball. If it's okay with you, let me see if we can get an abdominal X-ray and confirm my suspicions with a radiologist."

"And if you're right?"

"Then we're probably looking at surgery," I say.

Foreign bodies combine mystery, intrigue, incredulity, and guilt to make for a fascinating and fickle assortment of surgical diseases. Over the years, one specific foreign body story more than any other has been recounted to me by numerous veterinary students, interns, and residents. I too have encountered subtle variations on the same theme, and so, trusting authenticity more than urban legend, I will attempt to convey its message.

A vet is examining a chocolate Labrador puppy that will not stop vomiting. He is palpating the dog's abdomen, appreciating the muscle and bowel wincing in his hand as the pet audibly grunts, when he glances over at the owners. Richard and Denise are immaculately dressed, business suits all round, and he cannot fail to notice the enormous sparkling rock weighing down the fourth finger of her left hand, its brilliance searing his retina. Richard begins to ask a question but Denise shushes him, insisting he let the doctor concentrate on little Hershey (alternatively insert the name Cocoa or Mocha). As the vet allows the tension between them to flourish in the silence, he discerns two distinct and separate emotions on their faces: concern on hers, guilt on his.

"I think I'm feeling an obstruction in Hershey's small intestine," the vet tells them. "Any chance that he got into something he shouldn't have?"

Denise looks appalled at his suggestion, as though he has accused her of animal cruelty. She turns to Richard, who, after a moment's hesitation, vehemently denies the charge. Perhaps a little too vehemently.

"Not a problem. We'll take an X-ray and see what's going on inside his belly."

Half an hour later the vet returns with a black-and-white image that confirms the presence of a foreign body trapped inside a loop of bowel.

"Given the progression of clinical signs and the degree of abdominal discomfort, I think we should take Hershey to surgery," the vet says.

The owners agree, settle into the waiting room, Richard nibbling a cuticle, Denise buried in the latest issue of *Bridal Magazine*, while the vet drags a number ten scalpel blade down and through Hershey's midline to discover the cause of the obstruction. After careful manipulation of a corrugated and inflamed portion of Hershey's small intestine, he is able to "milk" the culprit back into the stomach from where it can be easily removed.

"There was an obstruction fixed in his stomach, extending into his small intestine," he tells them.

"What kind of an obstruction?" asks Denise, intrigued.

"Well, it turned out to be a stocking," he says. "Not an uncommon foreign body for puppies, especially Labradors."

Denise looks confused. Richard looks like the proverbial deer in the headlights.

"Not pantyhose?" says Denise.

"No. It was definitely a stocking."

Given that she is pursuing this line of questioning, the vet flashes his eyebrows and offers Richard a saucy grin adding, "A black fishnet stocking to be absolutely precise."

Richard's facial expression suggests he just won a date with Lorena Bobbit, a set of Sabatier carving knives, and a roll of duct tape.

Still wearing his lascivious smirk, the vet turns back to Denise in time to see her initial shock replaced by a tsunami of pure anger.

The vet stood back as dreams of a Vera Wang wedding dress disappeared before his eyes—wrung with the rest of her magazine into an improvised billy-club that landed with swift and deft precision on the bridge of Richard's nose.

There seems to be no limit to what our pets will try to cram into their mouths—size, shape, texture, and taste often playing little or no part in an oral obsession that for many owners can become a difficult and costly vice to curb. So why do our dogs, cats, and even ferrets crave foreign bodies and why are so many of these pets repeat offenders?

Young animals of two years of age or less are most commonly afflicted, and so, like inquisitive toddlers intent on putting everything into their mouths, simple curiosity plays a part. It has been suggested that in dogs it reflects the need to hunt, that it is instinctive and a throwback to a time when their prey was eaten in its entirety.

Some animals appear to enjoy the act of chewing, experimenting with the feel of an object in their mouths. My favorite theory, and one I believe I can safely share with the majority of Labrador owners, is that "it was there, so I ate it."

Undergarments—socks, stockings, pantyhose, panties—often prove to be popular offending items. Here, perhaps, another etiology applies. In much the same way that bear attacks on people may occur more frequently among menstruating females, the olfactory stimulation of ripe underwear of either sex might prove too tempting for your curious pet. One cat owner took this hypothesis a step further by making her cat a homemade toy from fresh catnip stuffed inside an old nylon stocking, a dangerous cocktail that induced one game of playful ecstasy and a visit to the operating room.

Foreign bodies related to food make perfect sense. Peach pits, corn on the cob, and all manner of bones can prove irresistible to the scavenging instinct of a dog. Those little plastic pop-up timers that tell you when your chicken or turkey breast is perfectly cooked are drizzled in tasty fat and despite being made of tasteless plastic, slip down nice and easy until they reach a cat's small intestine. The teriyaki stick laden with succulent meaty pieces may not go down with quite the same ease, but who cares until the sharp wooden skewer begins piercing its way through a variety of abdominal organs on its errant journey through the abdomen?

For some pets, the object is simply a curiosity. Ferrets have an affinity for rubber bands and pencil erasers. Cats have a penchant for Christmas tinsel. How else can we explain the allure of a diamond ring, a needle and thread, a fishhook and nylon leader, a backpack, bottle caps, coins, golf balls, a leather leash that remains attached at the collar, string still tethered to a helium-filled balloon? The list of irrational objects is endless and limited only by one's imagination. Occasionally the problem can become an addiction. Maisie was a two-year-old Weimaraner with a penchant for stones.

Her tastes went beyond the occasional pebble, brick end, or fragment of rock because Maisie's drug of choice was the gravel driveway of her home. We're not talking about one or two rocks, here. Sometimes Maisie might binge on fifty to a hundred large pieces of coarse rock that would either accumulate in her stomach or obstruct her small intestine. After her third surgical procedure, the owners realized it was far cheaper to put asphalt on the driveway than to continue to pay her medical bills.

Excessive grooming and the formation of fur balls can result in an intestinal obstruction. As owners we learn to reduce this risk by grooming our pet more frequently or adding a laxative to their diet. But sometimes we choose to ignore what our pet's behavior is telling us. Consider the case of one golden retriever who underwent gastric surgery twice after swallowing a tennis ball whole. The catch here is that the dog had two quite separate surgeries to remove the exact same ball. That's right, the owners wanted her favorite ball returned to them after the surgery and gave it back to the dog to play with once again.

It would be remiss of me to neglect the respiratory system when it comes to foreign bodies. Notwithstanding a cunning anatomical design and the expulsive power of a cough reflex, bizarre objects still manage to go down the wrong way. As a resident I recall being badgered by a breathless intern in desperate need of a surgeon.

"I've got a ten-year-old cat with a foreign body in his trachea and I think he needs emergency surgery right away," she said, waving a radiograph in my face and clutching a ginger tom that looked as if he couldn't care less.

I made a brief, visual note of the cat's breathing and lifted a lip to look at the color of his gums. His respiratory rate was slightly elevated, but he breathed through his nose and he was nice and pink aside from the fur of pale yellow plaque that coated his teeth like the inside of an old kettle. Holding the radiograph up to the light, I could clearly see a bright white object smaller than a dime lodged all the way down his windpipe where it splits into the smaller airways.

"Any idea what it can be?" she asked.

I nodded. "Have you looked in the back of your cat's mouth?"

The intern appeared puzzled.

"Take another look," I said. "I think you might find your answer."

I watched as she placed the cat on a table, opened his mouth wide, and peered at the back of his throat. It took a while but eventually I was rewarded with wide eyes and a big grin.

"How did you know he inhaled one of his own teeth?"

I could have told her it was a lucky guess. I could have casually shrugged and left her incredulous at my clinical acumen. Instead I confessed to seeing an identical case just one week earlier. Despite the rarity of this event, lightning had struck twice. On the first occasion I found the freshly vacated socket only after surgically extracting the wayward molar. With hindsight, where else would it have come from?

Inside Snowball's abdomen I find things much as I expect; loose, lazy switchbacks of pink bowel replaced by a lumpy knot of bruised intestines. Carefully I inspect the surfaces of the duodenum and jejunum, looking for purple areas of perforation where the foreign body might have piano-wired its way through the entire wall, allowing digesting food to leak into the abdomen. Most of her guts might look like twisted phone cord, but the tissues appear to be healthy aside from the presence of a thin linear material trapped inside the intestinal lumen.

I was always trained to start at the point of fixation, in this case Snowball's stomach. The luxury of pulling a linear foreign body out of a single incision is unusual, especially for an object as intent on getting out the other end as this one, so opening the stomach affords the surgeon his or her first glimpse of the culprit as well as an opportunity to cut the anchor, breaking the drawstring effect and releasing the tension on the bowel. Fishing in the stomach yielded the offending item and it was most certainly not a length of dental floss.

It takes two more small incisions in the intestine to remove the entire problem and after everything is sutured up and Snowball is resting comfortably in recovery, I head to the waiting room, apprehensive about what I am going to say.

The Duggan family sits watching the television but they are up on their feet as soon as they see me approach. I smile. As I cover the distance between myself and an anxious family, before any of us can speak, I use my face to reassure them that all went well.

"Snowball's doing great," I say. "I had to open the stomach and make two small incisions in the jejunum to get it all out but the bowel looks great and there was no evidence of perforation. We'll start offering her food in the morning and she might even be able to go home tomorrow."

Now everyone is smiling and Tony wants to shake my hand.

"So it was the dental floss?" asks Dianna.

I try not to dither and say, "No. It was definitely not dental floss."

Kerry tugs on her mother's sleeve, whispering about some candy she needs from the vending machines as both Tony and Dianna look bemused.

"I'm not sure exactly what it was. It was like string, but thicker, sort of like a cord, but it was difficult to tell, what with all the fur and poop and all. Difficult to say really. I can show it to you if you like."

Dianna's face winces, my description having had the desired effect.

"Thanks, but no thanks," she says.

"The main thing is it's gone. You just need to watch her more closely. Make sure there's no string left lying around. Things like that."

I proffer more smiles and nods and Mr. and Mrs. Duggan seem content.

"Well, if you'll excuse me, I'm going to set up Snowball's orders for the night and then I'm going to head home."

They thank me and encourage Kerry to say thank you as well.

I bow my head to acknowledge her praise and in doing so see exactly what I was looking for.

I smile one last time and head back to the recovery room.

The answer to this mysterious foreign body had been in front of my eyes the whole time. Mrs. Duggan was wearing pumps. Mr. Duggan, a pair of well-worn work boots. Kerry Duggan sported a pair of old sneakers made unusual by one feature common to both feet—crisp, white, brand-new shoelaces.

Guess what happened to the old ones?

16

. . . .

10:02 P.M.

REASONABLE DOUBT

I hear the zombie before I see her, the rhythmic squeak of compacted snow underfoot making me look up from my car door handle to glimpse the white-washed head floating in my direction. The body of the walking dead finally emerges from behind a row of parked cars and I can tell Dr. Payne is lost in thought.

"How did it go?"

Instantly, she comes back, my question gauged to pierce her reverie.

"Not good," she says. "They're going to take him to their vet this weekend and have him put to sleep. As soon as I told the dad that most dogs don't last much more than a year, he made up his mind like there was nothing more to discuss. He said he couldn't let his kids watch their dog slowly dying in front of their eyes."

She is defeated, beaten by a disease and an argument she knows she cannot win. Some interns would be undeterred, digging out a black turtleneck and a ski mask and threatening to kidnap the dog and nurse him themselves. But not Dr. Payne. She is learning to accept and respect the loss. She is learning there will be plenty more where that came from.

"Don't upset yourself," I say. "It was a great case and you did everything you could for that dog."

She's unconvinced.

"Yeah, but what good is that if he ends up dying all the same?"

We are standing by my car, talking like cartoon characters, our words trapped inside frosty speech bubbles, and I would dearly love to turn the engine over and warm up my car but I don't want to lose the moment.

"Look at it this way. You took a dog with a mysterious set of clinical signs and achieved the Holy Grail of any medical investigation, not just a diagnosis, but the definitive diagnosis. It's not your fault that a bunch of nerdy guys in lab coats staring down microscopes have failed to come up with a cure for your discovery!"

She says nothing and I begin to climb into my car.

"You know these are the kinds of cases you really remember, not the ones that come with a bouquet of flowers. These are the cases that stay with you your entire career. They are the real challenges, the tough ones, the ones that carve deep through the bark and leave their mark in the trunk."

There is the beginning of a smile, the possibility of capitulation. She says, "Yep, you're right. I guess I'll remember the name Barron."

I roll down the window as I'm pulling away, hunting for a puzzled expression and say, "Who's Barron?"

By the time I get home, everyone, the wife, the kids, even the dogs, are asleep. This has not been another typical, boring day at the office, but then they never are. Unpredictability is one of the many perks of the job. It can also be one of the many flaws. How many family dinners have I missed? How many piano recitals, doctor's appointments, Lacrosse matches, and swim meets have passed me by, reduced to a verbal synopsis, a photograph, or a video clip? Veterinary medicine is a kind of one-man show where the performer in the spotlight gets to play all the characters in a complicated play. Like me, this actor might have been drawn to the part by an opportunity to show off his range, to become a Jack of All Trades, versatile and equally at ease as the dentist or the brain surgeon. As it turned out I naively aspired to become a Master of One. What was I thinking? For all the years of training, the obsession with a singular performance, I try my best to be a social worker, a psychologist, a grief counselor, mentor, carpenter, plumber, cosmetologist, athletic coach, magician, grim reaper, and, occasionally, guardian angel. Sometimes I worry that I am going to run out of hats.

Believe me, I know I am lucky to be in this profession. How many people get to wander around all day in a pair of blue pajamas? How many careers not only excuse illegible handwriting but accept my chicken-scratch scrawl as mundane? How many jobs afford the opportunity to burst into crowded rooms, dramatically tearing off surgical cap and paper mask, blowing out a deep breath before delivering the somber line, "Everything is going to be fine," even if I was just clipping a toenail. And as for staying in shape, I never have to use the phrase "Let's do lunch." Long hours and an endless stress diet will keep your friends jealous and convinced that you secretly harbor a prodigious intestinal parasite. My office is a hospital OR, a space where warm and cozy has been traded for simplicity and efficiency, medical function over feng shui. It may offer no room with a view, but I breathe filtered and purified air, absorb age-defying artificial light, and have a healthy obsession for clean hands.

At the end of the day, some surgeons might take their manual dexterity home with them, able to whittle a couple of old wooden boards into a handsome reproduction Louis XVI armoire, to fix a leaky hymen valve on a '56 Chevy, and convert their house from forced hot-air heating to forced hot water, all in a single afternoon. Unfortunately, as my wife will attest, I am not one of them. In my defense, I routinely return home with gifts the whole family can enjoy. To my dogs I offer up the magic of chinos impregnated with the odor of strange animals like some canine aphrodisiac guaranteed to drive them into a sniffing frenzy. To my daughters I offer up the lingering indentation across my forehead from the elastic border of my disposable bouffant cap. It looks like a frontal lobotomy scar, a useful accessory for any protective father determined to thwart the advances of their young male suitors. And to my wife I occasionally offer up a frightening stain on my boxer shorts where blood has seeped through my scrubs.

I have learned so much and I still have so much more to learn. I have learned not to be afraid of the sight of blood but to be afraid of the sound of blood. I have learned that I miss the cows, the horses, the sheep, and the pigs, but I'm sure they are better off without me. I have learned to appreciate the fact that although I don't work on people, my impact on people through their sick animals can be no less daunting and no less rewarding. I have learned that all my training is worthless if I fail to listen to what the interns, the externs, the residents, the referring vets, my colleagues, the owners, and, not least, the patients have to teach me. I have learned that mistakes are inevitable, but what is not, and what will set us apart, is our ability to learn from them.

One of the most important lessons I have learned has been to quietly and privately savor every small victory, every subtle moment of success, every surgical decision that went my way, every animal that leaves the hospital feeling better, to wallow in it and to file it away on a dusty, neglected shelf in a tiny library in your mind. It is not about being self-absorbed, it is about learning to absorb the professional and emotional bumps and bruises that fill our working days because for every impossible fracture that comes back together, every cancer in remission, every paralyzed dachshund that scampers out of your office, you are only seconds away from a dozen anxious phone calls, oozing incisions, dirty margins, and bones that prefer not to heal. These are not disastrous, they are not failures, they are a normal consequence of what we do, but somehow their impact has more weight and longevity, like a loudmouth or a bully shouting over the fading whisper of success and lingering like an echo.

More than anything, I have learned to embrace this struggle. It is the first sunny day after a month of rain (who said there was nothing to be gained from a British summer). It is the fizz in the champagne. Without it the drink wouldn't taste nearly so good.

To those intransigents with a hankering for a bygone veterinary era, consider this thought: I may not wear green Wellington boots to work or peel off my shirt to perform rectal examinations. The scenery may have changed since James Herriot's day, and we certainly have a lot more special effects, but the flavor of the script and the nature of the essential characters persist. Romance, pathos, eccentricity, and humor are inherent to the profession, with or without a backdrop of open fields and obstreperous farmers. Herriot's legacy of compassion and humanity is assured. For all the silly little letters after my name, I am just another regular vet spending his working days with the animals in our lives.

I find dinner, spin it in the microwave for a full minute, and eat alone, sipping on a cold beer as I scan the *Globe*. I have that second-wind thing going—the one that leaves you tossing and turning in your bed if you try to beat it too soon, the one where you're wired from replaying your entire day like one of those stock market ticker tapes looping around and around on the inside of your brain. The caffeine buzz I craved all day has finally arrived too late.

Part of the reason is the inevitable second-guessing. Surgeons do a lot of this, particularly during the early part of their learning curve.

Did I overtighten that bottom screw? Did that vessel really stop bleeding or will it continue to ooze all night? Did someone forget to count the sponges? Eventually, after you do a dozen replicas of a procedure, hands and instruments performing the same moves, and each time the animal wakes up, goes home, and turns out fine, you begin to relax. Repetition builds security, not complacency.

I think some people assume that surgeons have a God complex, the surgical ego, that they relish the power to choose between life and death, and wield it through their eyes, their hands, and their scalpel blade with everything they see and touch. To me, nothing could be further from the truth. Surgeons are not God. God doesn't have to worry. God doesn't feel guilty. God doesn't make mistakes. And we most certainly do.

A little less than twenty-four hours ago it would have been so easy to step back from Sage's open belly and decide to call it a day. I could have saved my anguish for a different time and a different animal, moved on, and let exhaustion take me back to that world of dreamless sleep.

Then again, what would my resident have thought? Would she have learned to be a quitter? That it was easier to reach for the blue juice of a euthanasia solution than to take a chance? Given the same situation with the next dog, what would she do? Opt for the conservative approach, play it safe, condemning marginal cases as hopeless and inoperable because she was taught that "this will not survive"?

And what of Mr. Hartman? Right now he has uncertainty and fear, but he still has hope. I could have delivered finality, loss, and sent him on a quest for that elusive commodity some call "closure." I could have gone back to my dream world, while Mr. Hartman spent the wee hours of the morning dwelling on a burial versus cremation, a communal or private burning, a plastic or a bronze urn. And then there would be the guilt; that he had somehow let down his wife, that it had been his fault that the dog overate and got into the full bag of kibble. After all, who else was to blame?

Then I thought about the single most important component of this complicated equation—the patient herself, Sage. When I focused on this animal, the way her eyes had locked on mine, the warm greeting from her tail despite the agony, if ever a dog deserved a chance, this dog did, because, bottom line, here was a bitch with balls. You and I would be ripping the arm off every passing nurse or doctor and screaming for morphine, and yet this selfless creature placed more importance on the simplicity of a human connection than on the unrelenting pain she was more than prepared to endure. Faced with gray I had trusted to white over black, a glass that remained half full and not half empty. I firmly believed it had been the right thing to do. Now, all I could do was pray that I had done the right thing for Sage.

Inky black print covers my fingers and thumbs. Somehow the words have been bypassing my eyes and I realize I have been looking but not reading. It is time to call it a night.

Consigning the dirty plate to the dishwasher I stretch my back, arms, and shoulders and wonder whether chiropractors make house calls at eleven o'clock at night. Alternatively I could take a bath, but it is quite possible that I might fall asleep, and the image of one of my daughters discovering my naked hypothermic body in the morning makes me decide against it.

And so, resigned to the simplicity of bed, I make for the stairs, when the phone rings.

Even before the second ring, before I snatch it from the cradle, my mind is reaching for the keys, heading to my car, and speeding back to work, back into surgery and the decision that must have gone wrong.

There are times, and this is one of them, when I yearn for one of those magnetic flashing lights favored by 1970s TV cop shows like

Starsky and Hutch or *Kojak*. You know, the ones that you slap on the roof of your car, justifying high speeds, hairpin turns, and a tendency to weave and lose wheel rims around sharp corners. In order to be easily recognizable to the fine male and female troopers of the commonwealth, I would recommend a unique, professionally apropos color, perhaps a Hunter or British Racing green light, something that might become synonymous with another brave veterinarian hurrying to an animal emergency. Instead, when pulled over for speeding, my tactics are limited to accentuating my British accent, appearing perplexed to be driving on the wrong side of the road, or inquiring as to how one might procure a fine pair of those masterful Mussolini jodhpurs. In fact, an apology and an honest confession that I was racing to the hospital in order to try and save the life of a dying pet sometimes goes a long way. In my experience most Stateys have pets, some of them working dogs, and, after verifying that I really am who I claim to be, they have let me off with a warning. A police escort might have been better, but still, adopting the little green light idea might save them considerable trouble.

When I took the call detailing Sage's rapid decline, I was asked if they wanted me to page Dr. Keene. After all, she was the original resident on the case. I said no, it would not be necessary, a reply met with a momentary pause of understated surprise. It's not that I don't want Dr. Keene to be there, it is simply that I don't want to waste her time. I fear there may be little that any of us can do for this poor dog. As a resident in our program, Dr. Keene is on call for emergencies every other night. If she doesn't get some sleep tonight, her night off, how incisive will she be for the emergency she faces tomorrow? As a staff surgeon, I am on backup to the residents one week in four. I'm never called in more than a handful of times a year at most. I'm going to hate tomorrow's peach fuzz congesting my brain and the concrete blocks resting on my eyelids, but at least, over the next few days, I stand a far better chance than Dr. Keene of catching up on sleep.

Of course there is more to this than professional bonhomie. Something intrinsic is drawing me toward Sage and Mr. Hartman, my two familiar strangers, like the migratory promise of warmth in winter. It occurs in the silence between the words and the barks, distilling in their eyes, a mutual friendship and love that is so understated and simple, it makes you want to pull over and fill up with more so you never come close to running empty. With most of my patients and owners I try to resist the tug, not least for my own well-being, but there is something about them beyond the obvious similarities to my father's relationship with Patch. It makes you want to share their presence, to learn their secret, to feel their silent collective wisdom. Maybe neither one of them would have quite the same effect when taken individually or if each were with someone else, but entangled in each other they are irresistible.

And let's not forget the uncompromising Dr. Helen Hancock. I take her earlier dissatisfaction and terse comments as a warning of pending complaint letters to the hospital, the State Veterinary Board, the Better Business Bureau, and the State Attorney General. I am determined to make sure that her list of grievances does not include a lack of commitment to patient and owner.

They are waiting for me when I arrive, standing in the waiting room, Mr. Hartman forcing an appreciative smile, and a woman I take to be his daughter, the good doctor, mouthing, "Is that him?" as I approach. She is probably in her late forties, her hair short, dark, and damp from the quick shower she probably insisted on taking before setting out, determined to be awake, sharp, and ready for a fight. She has striking cheekbones and a high forehead. By forsaking eyeliner and trading lipstick for lip balm, her features have been flattened, but she still retains an attractive Eastern European look that I could have pegged as belonging to the USSR or Yugoslavia in the days when schoolboy geography was so much simpler. She is a little taller than her father, thin despite a bulky winter coat, and she stands to his side and slightly in front of him. *Bristling* is too strong a word, but I am meant to see the thunderheads roiling behind her eyes. She is making it quite clear that she has come to do a job.

I introduce myself, she takes my hand with a curt, snappy grip, and we lock eyes. She ensures I read her intent before I turn to Mr. Hartman, who offers a nod and a "Thank you for coming out." He might want to say more, to tell me he is resigned to losing Sage, to apologize for his daughter's air of hostility, to convince her that Sage still might have a chance, but his plea will have to wait.

"Can someone tell us exactly what is going on with my father's dog?"

I turn to Dr. Hancock.

"I've spoken with the emergency doctor. For the last two hours Sage has had a rectal temperature of 104°F to 104.2°F. High normal would be around 103 but it could go up with pain and inflammation. The doctor reviewed her pain medications and checked her surgical incision and everything appeared to be in order. That was when she decided to perform an abdominal tap."

Dr. Hancock, who has been twitching like a rookie defense lawyer eager to object, jumps in.

"What's an abdominal tap?"

My surprise at her question stalls on my face before I can plow ahead. Surely a first- or second-year medical student would understand the term? Then again, they might use different terminology?

"Using a long needle and syringe, she suctioned up a little fluid from inside the belly, squirted it on a slide, and looked at it under a microscope. It proved that there are free bacteria inside the abdominal cavity."

I half-expected this medical revelation would be the catalyst that launched an attack, but nothing followed.

"The presence of free bacteria most likely means that there is a leak, most likely from the stomach."

"You keep saying 'most likely,' 'most likely.' To me it seems most likely that you really don't know what you are talking about."

Her outburst feels tempered with disconcerting control, but I try to ignore the insult, brushing it off, a weak blow that I should have seen coming from the moment we met. I convince myself that it is nothing more than a release, a pop-off valve, borne of frustration, sadness, and love for her father.

"I'm sorry, but this is not an exact science. Some fluid could have been left over from the original surgery, although that seems un- likely. Bacteria could have resulted from the needle inadvertently puncturing the intestinal tract when the doctor performed the proce- dure, but in those cases I might expect to see particulate food matter as well. This leaves us with the very real possibility that an area of the stomach wall has died, allowing the fluid inside to leak and spill bacteria into the belly. The doctor was not able to obtain much fluid, which is good. Most like—" I catch myself, before adding, "The leak is thought to be small."

Mr. Hartman turns from me to his daughter, but she chooses to ignore him.

"Whichever way you spin it," she says, "the outlook seems grim," and without further consultation, without releasing me from her laser stare, she says, "I'm sure my father is grateful for your efforts, but it sounds like we have finally come to the end of the road."

Pain vibrates in the old man's hands and eyes, his pale lips part, breaths coming quickly as he fumbles to find words before tears.

"Is there nothing more to be done for her?"

"Dad, come on now. You have to let it go. You're being cruel and selfish. Sage has suffered enough as it is. At least put it out of its misery."

It.

Once again, Dr. Hancock has degraded the relationship between dog and man. She thinks of Sage as an "it," as a belonging, an inert consumable, exchanged for money, disposable, with all the emotional attachments of a car or a flat-screen TV. Part of me thinks I should just shut up, back down, and side with her logic, help her father through the euthanasia. But her disregard for the weight of Sage's significance has a SWAT team of words poised to barge through my lips.

"I think there's one more thing we can try."

The very next moment, standing there, she and I face-to-face, is like that moment in a gunfight when the two cowboys draw for their guns in the final showdown, and, fortunately, it is my open palm "hear me out" gesture that comes out cocked, loaded, and much faster than her affronted glare.

"I'd like to take her back into surgery, to open her up and find where the leak is coming from." I turn to Mr. Hartman. "If part of her stomach is dead, then I think we should put Sage to sleep while she remains under anesthesia."

"And if it's not?" asks his daughter, making each word come out slow and prickly. I would hate to be the poor kid who enters her house wearing muddy boots.

"If it's not, I'll see if I can fix her problem."

Her head rolls back, keeping up with her eyeballs and an exasperated sigh. I dive in before the assault.

"Believe me, Dr. Hancock, I understand your concern, but I will not let this dog suffer. You don't know me or what kind of a vet I am—and why should you?—but I promise you that I am blind to the surgical tunnel vision you fear. I try my best to anticipate and to know when it is time to give up, and in my opinion, before taking one last look, this is not the time."

Anger sparks in her eyes, but it fails to ignite, smothered by the old man as he moves forward, tentative, as if bracing for an awkward reunion with a long-lost brother, like he has been waiting his whole life to meet me, before letting himself go, abandoning his reserve, daring not to hope but thanking me for this glimmer with a solid hug. I watch the fight ebbing from her body, weakened not only by her proximity to his pain, but by his absolute lack of hesitation to take a chance. She looks at him as one might the parent of a sick child—remote, sympathetic, unable to relate, and grateful not to have to. When she turns back to me, the silent message she conveys is an unequivocal "I hope you know what you are doing!"

"I'm going to change into scrubs and we'll get started as soon as possible," I say, noticing that Mr. Hartman is rummaging for something deep in his overcoat pocket.

Dr. Hancock concedes a reluctant weak handshake in contrast to her father, who is suddenly the consummate politician, opting for a double hander. But instead of hand-to-hand and hand-to-elbow combat, he sandwiches my right hand between both of his, squeezing tight, jabbing something that feels hard and plastic into my palm.

"Do your best; I know you will," he says, but all the while he is shielding our contact from his daughter, his desire for secrecy clumsy, almost childish.

I comply, my sleight of hand not exactly David Copperfield, but I manage to secrete the mysterious object into the pocket of my pants.

I don't think Dr. Hancock noticed.

I don't think Dr. Hancock cares.

Without direct instructions from Mr. Hartman, I put the object in the breast pocket of my scrubs (consigning it to the trash might have appeared a tad insensitive), assuming that its physical presence in the operating room is what Mr. Hartman has in mind. I quickly regret this decision when a spiny unforgiving prominence begins chaffing at my left nipple as soon as my sterile surgical gown is secured around my body. Too late to do anything about it now, I think, as I begin to take out the staples and stitches from Sage's fresh incision.

I hate going back into a belly. Aside from the glaring proof of failure, it is invariably a slow and untidy process. Sharp, clean lines of white and red are traded for jagged edges of lavender and crimson where virginal tissue has been crushed and bruised by the preceding scalpel, scissor, needle, and forceps. They are the ugly, earliest phases of healing and they are unflattering reminders of the trauma in what we do, unnoticed because ordinarily we never have to look. The coarse seamstress in me ignores the inferior fabric, patiently plucks out all the threads, draws back the heavy pink curtains of the abdominal wall, and stares down at the scene within.

At first all I do is look, and it is not what I see but what I don't see that counts. I don't see black, I don't see gray, and I don't see green. I don't see ingested food splattered on the surface of abdominal organs like an exploded paint bomb in a bag of stolen money. I don't see a stomach that has decided to die or an infection that is out of control. I don't see disaster and I don't see despair. Within seconds of looking the most important thing I don't see is a reason to put this dog to sleep.

The area of the stomach that Dr. Keene and I stapled off is bruised and inflamed, but it glows with the vibrant pulse of tissue that will survive. I feed the entire small and large intestine through my fingers, pale and endless kielbasa, looking for a perforation, a defect, something that we overlooked the first time, something to account for the free bacteria in the aspirated fluid, but there is nothing to be found. This leaves only one possible explanation—the site where Dr. Keene inadvertently punctured the stomach when she was trying to secure it to the abdominal wall.

From the outside, there is nothing unusual to be seen, and so I carefully cut out a number of her superficial sutures to visualize the more delicate tissue below. The small defect she made in the stomach wall is bruised and swollen, punched rosebud lips split by the indentations of the stitches sealing them shut. But when I milk and compress a pocket of stomach gas into this area, I notice how the tiniest blob of yellow green liquid bubbles and bursts at the cut surface. I repeat the process to convince myself that this is truly the source of the free bacteria and, like trying to extract the last dreg of toothpaste from the tube, squeeze out a single drop of the lethal liquid contaminant.

It is not what I expected. I had imagined a raw gaping mouth dribbling pea soup baby food and what I find seems subtle and insignificant. I wonder if I am missing something: after all, it is not exactly a natural bodily function to take two free hands, manipulate a pocket of gas, and try to make fart noises through a rent in a distended stomach like it was a whoopee cushion. But what else can there be? I revisit the stomach staple line, run the intestines one more time, and once more come up empty. I have been logical, methodical, and conscientious. There can be no other explanation. The leak, if it can be labeled as such, may be minor, tenuous, and of equivocal significance, but this has to be the cause.

As I carefully place additional stitches to reinforce the original repair, I realize I was wrong, almost selfish, not to call in Dr. Keene. She will want to know what I found and what to learn. Finger-pointing at rounds will be replaced with a quiet word, in private, a suggestion and, most of all, reassurance.

For the last time I test for bubbles, restore the sutures I removed, and reward Sage's poor stomach wall with a revitalizing and cleansing bath in ten liters of warm, sterile saline.

Mr. Hartman is sitting in his favorite corner of the waiting room, still dressed like a skinny snowman, head slightly bowed with one liver-spotted hand tightly clasped in the other. I pat my breast pocket as I walk toward him.

"Your friend did the trick," I say, smiling. "Sage is going to be just fine."

I study his response as I sit down next to him, the pain of relief no less than the pain of loss. It takes him a moment to contain the tremble in his lips, the long fingers of his left hand shielding his eyes from mine. My turn to pat a bony shoulder.

"Sage is awake and back in the Critical Care Unit. The leak was tiny and easily fixed. Best of all, the part of the stomach I was worried about pretty much told me it has no intention of quitting on your kibble anytime soon. It looks good. It should continue to heal fine."

He leans forward, left elbow on knee, hand clamped across his mouth. Is he unable to find the words, or afraid to let them out? All he gives me is his eyes and that is all I need. They are a billboard that says thank you.

"You'd best have this back," I say, reaching into my pocket to pull out the object. "Sage may need him for another fight."

It is about three inches long, boasts that it is made in China, "pings" as though it must be hollow, and is one of the tackiest religious figurines I have ever seen. It appears to be a Benedictine monk, and therefore I assume that it must be Saint Francis, the patron saint of animals. It is male, although the rouge cheeks and the red lipstick give me pause, has a neatly trimmed beard sans mustache, shaved bald dome with residual halo of brown hair, dressed in a robe, with a pair of twittering gray birds, one in his left hand and one pecking at his feet. His right hand is outstretched with an open palm, the fingers and thumb inordinately sharp and dangerous as I had discovered. He stands on a small pedestal and on the base in French, Spanish, and English, I am warned, "When applied on non-magnetic surface, please remove this protective label."

"My wife gave it to me," he says, his voice small and worn out. "It's not Saint Francis, it's Saint Sergius, the patron saint of Russia.

It's silly, but it makes me feel better having him around, and I was in such a rush to get here the other night I forgot to bring him."

I nod, not entirely sold on the identity of the statuette but recognizing that this was where Dr. Hancock acquired her characteristic genes. She must look like her late Russian mother. And where is Dr. Hancock? I was almost looking forward to a second inquisition.

"Your daughter didn't stay?"

"She had to leave. We came in separate cars. She has to work in the morning. She's an engineer."

That would explain it. The doctor is a PhD not an MD. That's why she was confused by the medical language. Perhaps she uses the title to get bumped up from coach to business, to impress a busy maître d' at a fancy restaurant, to intimidate and bully her way into our phone system. To be honest, I don't blame her. I'm sure she has earned her credentials. She's only using them for the benefit of her dad.

"She . . ." He searches for the words. "She doesn't mean to be rude."

I smile and shake away any need for an excuse.

"You should be getting home yourself," I say. "It's late and I'm sure a certain young lady is going to want a visitor come eleven-thirty tomorrow morning."

He nods, gets to his feet mechanically, and points to the figure asleep in my palm.

"Keep him," he says. "You never know, he might be able to help out some other sick animal."

I'm surprised and in an embarrassing, absurd way, honored. "Are you sure?"

"Positive," he says, adjusting his cap as he eases toward the automatic doors. "I know you'll put him to good use."

And he was absolutely right. I have.

ACKNOWLEDGMENTS

· ·

An acceptance of my own fallibility is a central theme throughout this book, and therefore, despite reviewing hundreds of textbooks, scientific articles, and Web sites in the course of my research, any mistakes in content or their interpretation are mine alone.

If you are perusing this page expecting to find your name, then you probably deserve to be here. Please accept my apology and know that I would not have a story to tell, a profession to laud, without an exhaustive list of unsung colleagues, friends, clients, and animals who continue to educate me to this day. However, certain individuals need to be mentioned here, including my father, Duncan, for instilling in me his spirit of determination; my mother, Pauline, for teaching me the art of patience; and my sister, Fiona, for her tolerance of a nerdy big brother; Lisa Allen; John Berg; Faith Hamlin; Donna Hartman; Jeni, Jon, and "Wilkey" Howe; Ted Leclair; Anastasia O'Melveny; Mike Pavletic; David, Ann, and Nicole Petrucci; Harry Smith; Brynne Anne Wegener; Dick White; and Nigel and Helenka Wood.

ACKNOWLEDGMENTS

Many thanks to my agent, Kristin Lindstrom, for her enthusiasm, guidance, and love of hedgehogs, and to all the fabulous folks at Broadway, including Ellen Folan, Anne Watters, and, of course, my editor, Christine Pride. Christine saw the potential in my proposal, saw the book in my manuscript, and, with a deft touch, she worked her magic. She gave me a chance I thought I would never get, and for that I will be eternally grateful.

Finally, none of this would have been possible without the love and support of my wife, Kathy. It goes well beyond her prescient editorial advice and ability to curb my English idiosyncrasies. Like so many mothers of children with chronic disease, she has quietly sacrificed her life for the greater good of our family. All too often her selfless dedication goes unnoticed. But not here, not by me, not this time.

ABOUT THE AUTHOR

Nick Trout graduated from veterinary school at the University of Cambridge, England, in 1989. He is a Diplomate of the American and European Colleges of Veterinary Surgeons and a staff surgeon at the Angell Animal Medical Center in Boston. He lives in Massachusetts with his wife, daughters, and two dogs, Meg, their yellow Labrador, and Sophie, a Jack Russell terrier.